N

wick

Holtye

LEY • EAST GRINSTEAD

Worth

Forest Row • Withyham

• Hartfield • Bayham

West Hoathly • Coleman's Hatch • Lamberhurst

alcombe • Wych Cross • Wadhurst

• Ardingly • Crowborough H I G H • Ticehurst R Rother

Lindfield Horsted Nutley Duddleswell • Rotherfield Hurst

Keynes Green

Birch Sheffield Fairwarp • Mayfield Bodiam

ckfield Grove Green Maresfield • Burwash Northiam

• HAYWARDS Fletching • Buxted Robertsbridge

HEATH • Uckfield Cross-In-Hand Burwash

• Wivelsfield • Framfield Heathfield Common

URGESS HILL • Chailey Waldron Old Heathfield • Brightling W E A L D

rpoint Halland East Warbleton Rushlake Dallington

eymer Hoathly Green Penhurst Winchelsea

Ditchling Streat Barcombe Chiddingly Battle Icklesham

yton Plumpton Hamsey Laughton Hellingly Ashburnham

be combe S Molling Ringmer Ripe Lower Dicker Herstmonceux

• Stanmer LEWES Glynde • Chalvington HAILSHAM Ninfield

• Falmer Kingston Beddingham Michelham • Hooe

reston Rodmell W Firle Arlington Barnhorne HASTINGS

de Woodingdean Southease Alciston Pevensey BEXHILL

RIGHTON Piddinghoe Berwick Wilmington

Rottingdean Newhaven Alfriston

• Saltdean Bishopstone • Willingdon

Peacehaven E. Blatchington West Dean

SEAFORD Jevington EASTBOURNE

R Cuckmere

ENGLISH

CHANNEL

R Rother

Rye

Winchelsea Camber

Icklesham Old Winchelsea

THE MAKING OF THE ENGLISH LANDSCAPE

THE SUSSEX LANDSCAPE

THE MAKING OF THE ENGLISH LANDSCAPE
Edited by W. G. Hoskins and R. Millward

The Sussex Landscape

by

PETER BRANDON

HODDER AND STOUGHTON
LONDON SYDNEY AUCKLAND TORONTO

To my mother and late father

Preface

"You must be so good as to tell me my road and if there is anything in my way worth stopping to see—I mean literally to *see* for I do not love guessing whether a bump in the ground is Danish, British or Saxon."
Horace Walpole, *Letter to the Rev. William Mason,* 1772

" . . . whoever was up-rooting a thistle, or bramble, or draining out a bog, or building himself a house, that man was writing the history of England . . ."
Thomas Carlyle, *Lectures on the History of Literature,* 1830

Those who share a historical curiosity in the appearance of the land may find that this book goes some way towards answering their questions. This account, however, cannot be more than interim and outline, for too much of the Sussex past still remains to be recovered from the surface of the land itself. In the course of writing it I have pointed to some gaps in our knowledge. Some of these will be filled by research being currently undertaken. Such studies may ultimately demolish some of my arguments and correct me on fact. Meanwhile, I hope this will prove to be an acceptable introduction.

Walking the ground, photographing it from the air, digging over it and combining these techniques with the examination of documents, maps and surveys are necessarily slow tasks, ideally needing many minds and hands. The preliminary investigation of the ground itself, the basis of all further study, is very much in the hands of nature. In woodland much of the detailed work must be concentrated into the winter months when sites are less obscured and entwined by briars and bramble. Even then the good depth of leaf mould that lightens a walker's step impedes the close study of the surface. On bracken-covered ground the field season is a matter of the few weeks between the flattening of fern in spring by frost and wind and the rapid growth of new fronds in May. Fortunately, just when the heaths are again becoming a closed book, the marshes and saltings are drying out, so becoming available for an annual inspection. Careful planning, season by season, enables the field-worker to cover a great variety of ground but in order to accumulate sufficient clues he needs to repeat observations at promising sites in all conditions of light, weather, soil moisture and land use. It is only in the course of writing this book that I have come to appreciate how long it takes to become familiar with even a small part of the county. A more comprehensive study than this would have had more to say about the interesting towns in the north of Sussex, such as Horsham and East Grinstead, or about the landscape of the Kentish and Hampshire borders. There is, indeed, ample scope for further observation all over the county and one hopes to see field-work being increasingly organised on the basis of team-work rather than on the uncoordinated efforts of individuals.

The study of local history, archaeology, and kindred subjects has flourished in Sussex for decades and I have utilised much published material which has a bearing on the evolving Sussex landscape. As it is impossible for me to cite all my sources in a book of this kind, I am glad of this opportunity of acknowledging my great indebtedness to a host of writers, both living and dead.

Throughout, I have written this book in the hope that readers will take to the by-roads, footpaths, bridleways, coastal creeks and waterways, and so savour the real essence of the Sussex scene. For this reason I have assumed that readers will use the relevant sheets of the Ordnance Survey One Inch maps.

It is a great pleasure to say 'thank you' to many people who have given me help: Mrs C. Brent and her colleagues at the East Sussex Record Office; Mrs P. Gill and her staff at the West Sussex Record Office; K. W. Dickins, W. K. Ford, E. W. Holden, Mrs V. B. Lamb, G. A. Holleyman, J. Pettit, B. Short, F. W. Steer, C. F. Tebbutt, A. E. Wilson and the late L. F. Salzman. I have mentioned the receipt of other help in the text. To Monica Coode, who drew the maps, and Eileen Booth who typed and re-typed my untidy manuscript, I owe especial thanks. From Ann Winser I had invaluable improving comments on the manuscript. I further record my sincere gratitude to the general editors of this series, Professor W. G. Hoskins and Dr R. Millward, for their friendly help, advice and encouragement at all stages in the preparation of this book.

PETER BRANDON
Kingston Buci,
Shoreham-by-Sea, Sussex

Contents

List of plates

ACKNOWLEDGMENTS

The author wishes to thank the following for permission to use their photographs:

Edward Reeves, Castle Studio, Lewes: Plates 1, 15, 18, 23, 36, 37

The Committee for Aerial Photography, Cambridge: Plates 7, 8 (photographs by J. K. St Joseph, Cambridge University Collection, copyright reserved)

Meridian Airmaps Limited, Lancing: Plates 9, 12

Charles Cattell: Plate 26

Country Life: Plates 19, 20, 21, 31, 35

The Trustees of the British Museum: Plates 32, 43

The News Centre, Portsmouth: Plate 38

Aerofilms Limited: Plate 46

List of maps and plans

ABBREVIATIONS USED IN THE NOTES

B.M.	British Museum
E.S.R.O.	East Sussex Record Office
P.R.O.	Public Record Office
S.A.T.	Sussex Archaeological Trust
Suss. Arch. Colls.	Sussex Archaeological Collections
W.S.R.O.	West Sussex Record Office

Editor's Introduction

SOME SIXTEEN YEARS ago I wrote: "Despite the multitude of books about English landscape and scenery, and the flood of topographical books in general, there is not one book which deals with the historical evolution of the landscape as we know it. At the most we may be told that the English landscape is the man-made creation of the seventeenth and eighteenth centuries, which is not even a quarter-truth, for it refers only to country houses and their parks and to the parliamentary enclosure that gave us a good deal of our modern pattern of fields, hedges, and by-roads. It ignores the fact that more than a half of England never underwent this kind of enclosure, but evolved in an entirely different way, and that in some regions the landscape had been virtually completed by the eve of the Black Death. No book exists to describe the manner in which the various landscapes of this country came to assume the shape and appearance they now have, why the hedgebanks and lanes of Devon should be so totally different from those of the Midlands, why there are so many ruined churches in Norfolk or so many lost villages in Lincolnshire, or what history lies behind the winding ditches of the Somerset marshlands, the remote granite farmsteads of Cornwall, and the lonely pastures of upland Northamptonshire.

"There are indeed some good books on the geology that lies behind the English landscape, and these represent perhaps the best kind of writing on the subject we have yet had, for they deal with facts and are not given to the sentimental and formless slush which afflicts so many books concerned only with superficial appearances. But the geologist, good though he may be, is concerned with only one aspect of the subject, and beyond a certain point he is obliged to leave the historian and geographer to continue and complete it. He explains to us the bones of the landscape, the fundamental structure that gives form and colour to the scene and produces a certain kind of topography and natural vegetation. But the flesh that covers the bones, and the details of the features, are the concern of the historical geographer, whose task it is to show how man has clothed the geological skeleton during the comparatively past—mostly within the last fifteen centuries, though in some regions much longer than this."

In 1955 I published *The Making of the English Landscape*. There I claimed that it was a pioneer study, and if only for that reason it could not supply the answer to every question. Four books, in a series published between 1954 and 1957, filled in more detail for the counties of Cornwall, Lancashire, Gloucestershire, and Leicestershire.

Much has been achieved since I wrote the words I have quoted. Landscape-history is now taught in some universities, and has been studied for many parts of England and Wales in university theses. Numerous articles have been written and a few books published, such as Alan Harris's *The Rural Landscape of the East Riding 1700–1850* (1961) and more recently Dorothy Sylvester's *The Rural Landscape of the Welsh Borderland* (1969).

Special mention should perhaps be made of a number of landscape-studies in the series of Occasional Papers published by the Department of English Local History at the University of Leicester. Above all in this series one might draw attention to Laughton: *A Study in the Evolution of the Wealden Landscape* (1965) as a good example of a microscopic scrutiny of a single parish, and Margaret Spufford's *A Cambridgeshire Community* (*Chippenham*) published in the same year. Another masterly study of a single parish which should be cited particularly is Harry Thorpe's monograph entitled *The Lord and the Landscape*, dealing with the Warwickshire Parish of Wormleighton, which also appeared in 1965.[1]

[1] *Transactions of the Birmingham Archaeological Society,* Vol. 80, 1965.

Geographers were quicker off the mark than historians in this new field, for it lies on the frontiers of both disciplines. And now botany has been recruited into the field, with the recent development of theories about the dating of hedges from an analysis of their vegetation.

But a vast amount still remains to be discovered about the man-made landscape. Some questions are answered, but new questions continually arise which can only be answered by a microscopic examination of small areas even within a county. My own perspective has enlarged greatly since I published my first book on the subject. I now believe that some features in our landscape today owe their origin to a much more distant past than I had formerly thought possible. I think it highly likely that in some favoured parts of England farming has gone on in an unbroken continuity since the Iron Age, perhaps even since the Bronze Age; and that many of our villages were first settled at the same time. In other words, that underneath our old villages, and underneath the older parts of these villages, there may well be evidence of habitation going back for some two or three thousand years. Conquests only meant in most places a change of landlord for better or for worse, but the farming life went on unbroken, for even conquerors would have starved without its continuous activity. We have so far failed to find this continuity of habitation because sites have been built upon over and over again and have never been wholly cleared and examined by trained archaeologists.

At the other end of the time-scale the field of industrial archaeology has come into being in the last few years, though I touched upon it years ago under the heading of Industrial Landscapes. Still, a vast amount more could now be said about this kind of landscape.

Purists might say that the county is not the proper unit for the study of landscape-history. They would say perhaps that we ought to choose individual and unified regions for such an exercise; but since all counties, however small, contain a wonderful diversity of landscape, each with its own special history, we get, I am sure, a far more appealing book than if we adopted the geographical region as our basis.

The authors of these books are concerned with the ways in which men have cleared the natural woodlands, reclaimed marshland, fen, and moor, created fields out of a wilderness, made lanes, roads, and footpaths, laid out towns, built villages, hamlets, farmhouses and cottages, created country houses and their parks, dug mines and made canals and railways, in short with everything that has altered the natural landscape. One cannot understand the English landscape and enjoy it to the full, apprehend all its wonderful variety from region to region (often within the space of a few miles), without going back to the history that lies behind it. A commonplace ditch may be the thousand-year-old boundary of a royal manor; a certain hedge-bank may be even more ancient, the boundary of a Celtic estate; a certain deep and winding lane may be the work of twelfth-century peasants, some of whose names may be made known to us if we search diligently enough. To discover these things, we have to go to the documents that are the historians' raw material, and find out what happened to produce these results and when, and precisely how they came about.

But it is not only the documents that are the historian's guide. One cannot write books like these by reading someone else's books, or even by studying records in a muniment room. The English landscape itself, to those who know how to read it aright, is the richest historical record we possess. There are discoveries to be made in it for which no written documents exist, or have ever existed. To write the history of the English landscape requires a combination of documentary research and of fieldwork, of laborious scrambling on foot wherever the trail may lead. The result is a new kind of history which it is hoped will appeal to all those who like to travel intelligently, to get away from the guide-book show-pieces now and then, and to know the reasons behind what they are looking at. There is no part of England, however unpromising it may appear at first sight, that is not full of questions for those who have a sense of the past. So much of England is still unknown and unexplored. Fuller enjoined us nearly three centuries ago

"Know most of the rooms of thy native country
before thou goest over the threshold thereof.
Especially seeing England presents thee with
so many observables."

These books on the Making of the English Landscape are concerned with the observables of England, and the secret history that lies behind them.

Exeter, 1970   W. G. HOSKINS

1. The natural setting

The face of Sussex. Local building materials

SUSSEX TO MOST people means 'good old Sussex by the sea'; the salt tang of tingling sea air; crowded, sunny esplanades and dignified terraces; incredibly good shops and restaurants in Brighton; yacht marinas, discotheques, skittle alleys, tea gardens and antique shops; the endless sprawl of coastal bungalows owned by retired people; and railway stations massed twice daily with London commuters. This is the Sussex devoted to leisure, health and pleasure which has only developed since the eighteenth-century discovery of the recreational value of the seaside.

Happily, much of the traditional pattern of town and countryside in Sussex still holds out against this modern residential development. Even within walking distance of the coast, sheltering in little folds of the South Downs from November gales and bitter winter winds, are remarkably unspoiled villages shaded by towering elms breaking the monotony of treeless surroundings. Here man has been shaping the scenery, not for a single lifetime or even less, as along much of the coastal strip, but for several thousands of years, and the ground itself bears many marks of this long occupation. The huge cornfields envelop grass-grown tumuli, the circular burial mounds of Bronze Age settlers, leaving them as little green islands, and cut into, but rarely destroy, the buttresses of Iron Age hillforts. Downland trackways, probably the oldest human feature of all, lead to little flint-built churches with squat tower and spirelet, or 'Sussex cap'. Age-old manor houses lie adjacent to great, rambling barns, ancient dovecotes, a cottage or two (and because these downland settlements have been long half-deserted) signs of vanished homesteads under the grass of grey-walled enclosures. These little pockets of unspoiled England are rich records of country life stretching back over many generations (Plate 1).

One's imagination is also stirred by many tranquil scenes in the Sussex Weald, for long a wide-ranging forest and marsh bordering the productive coastal plain and downland. The pioneer farmers who laid the axe to the roots of primeval trees and raised up the earthen banks which still exist round their first fields died out before the close of the fifteenth century, and many scenes have since come and gone unwritten. Nevertheless, reading the land like a document, we shall find that the Wealden landscape preserves some record of generations of labour expended in the gigantic task of creating a civilisation out of a wilderness. The imprint on the ground of countless marl pits (dug in the constant search for manures to revive the quickly-failing fertility of the land); innumerable minepits peppering the fields; impoverished vegetation on the high heaths, partly induced by the long-standing custom of burning heather or cutting bracken to apply to the meadows; and peasant homesteads, marking a family's victory over the unkind clay soils; these, and many other features, in the present landscape constitute visual evidence of what have been appropriately called the 'grass-roots' of history.

As for the older towns, with which Sussex is well endowed, their present streets and buildings provide the best existing record of the people who built them and the motives underlying their making. Even the changing width of a single street is an important clue to the site of old cattle markets not held within living memory, as in the middle of Lindfield, or the little triangular space in the centre of Storrington. The open space still existing between Seaford's southern edge and the esplanade marks the site of its old harbour, abandoned when engineers in Henry VIII's reign diverted the river Ouse to a new outfall at Newhaven. The present street pattern of New Shoreham, as we shall see, confirms that half of the town was destroyed in fourteenth-century storms. It is unnecessary to question that early Petworth lived as much by agriculture as by trade when its undulating fields still bear the extensive impress of medieval lyncheting. The name of Rye, which in Old English means an island, is no longer puzzling when we see the low ground surrounding its hill-top site, once formerly overflowed by every high tide.

The face of Sussex

The best way of acquiring some familiarity with this historic Sussex landscape is to view the face of the county spread before the observer on one of the many vantage points ranged around the Weald. The northern ramparts on the Surrey-Sussex border open up memorable panoramas which have passed into literature. The view of Sussex from Leith Hill in 1717 thrilled John Dennis to the point of ecstasy. "I saw a sight', he wrote (regarding it as surpassing anything he had seen in Italy),"that would transport a stoic . . . Beneath us lay open to our view all the wilds of Surrey and Sussex, and a great part of Kent, admirably diversified in every part with woods, and fields of corn, and pastures, being everywhere adorned with stately rows of trees . . ."[1] His eulogy of "the most delicious rural prospect in the world" is one of the first signs of a conscious appreciation of the man-made beauty of the English lowland. This particular scene, generally reputed one of the most beautiful in England, also cast its spell over Tennyson who from his Sussex home on the summit of Blackdown Hill penned his appreciation in simple but deeply expressive lines:

[1] John Dennis, *Original Letters* (1721), p. 32.

> You came, and looked, and loved the view
> Long known and loved by me
> Green Sussex fading into blue.
> With a grey glimpse of sea.

Protected by successive generations, this view has not yet been spoiled, despite the destruction of so much of the 'green' countryside near London. Its future preservation, however, now hangs in the balance because of the proposed expansion of Billingshurst and other towns to meet the needs of the sharply rising population of south-east England.

From the crest of the South Downs, recalling the poetry of Hilaire Belloc and Kipling, the views over Sussex are as beautiful and instructive. The eye then ranges over small-scale country in which an uninterrupted succession of quickly changing landscapes compose a mosaic of great richness. The seaward view takes in gleaming dykes entwining wild marshes and shingle flats, the haunts of myriads of wildfowl. Slow-moving streams cutting through the Downs are bordered by wide watermeadows which until recently were transformed into great lakes each winter. Close at hand are numberless folds and ridges of the South Downs themselves, terminating abruptly in a steep northern escarpment, stark and bare, a perfect foil for the wooded country beyond.

Framing the panorama on the north is the Sussex Weald —the heathy and wooded country of an entirely different character. The blue haze which dims its outlines when viewed from afar renders it somewhat mysterious, as is fitting, for it remains the least known part of Sussex. The Sussex Weald has never been the subject of a regional portraiture of the insight and charm of W. H. Hudson's *Nature in Downland* and although Kipling awakened interest in its delightful folklore and legend, it has never received as much attention from naturalists, archaeologists and historians as the South Downs. What explains this neglect of the Wealden landscape? Its concealment behind abundant trees and steeply-banked lanes is perhaps a partial answer. The main obstacle to the study of the remoter parts of the Weald, however, was the inaccessibility of its wet, miry country before roads were metalled early in this century. Even now, to make an intimate acquaintance with the Sussex Weald one has to travel on foot by reedy ponds, across damp, rushy fields, fern-covered slopes, extensive woods and along unused footpaths. Such journeys will reveal timber-framed manor houses with half-hipped gables and encircling moats; weather-boarded or tile-hung cottages with external chimneys built wide to serve wood-burning hearths; disused oast-houses and shingled spires, and the many relics of old mine-workings such as pen-stocked streams, abandoned mills, forges and mounds of bloomery wastes. All these survivals are set amidst small, tree-bordered fields which frequently give way to free-standing oaks and elms, imparting a parkland appearance to the ground. Undoubtedly, the Weald is not the kind of landscape that instantly impresses itself on the mind, but once it casts its spell, it awakens a lifelong curiosity.

Unusually diverse rocks and soils bordering the sea underlie the exceptionally varied Sussex landscape. This physical build has been consciously altered and moulded by man according to changing human needs. Such are the rapid alterations in the geological canvas that even a short journey introduces the traveller to a number of individual scenes each with a different human imprint. These extend even to the finer details of domestic architecture or hedge-row patterns so that the study of the evolving Sussex landscape is like tracing every thread of a complicated tapestry. As S. W. Wooldridge lucidly demonstrated in *The Weald*, the geological map is "*par excellence* our guide and key" to the differing historical development of the traditional Sussex landscape. This shows Sussex to be divided into belts of country extending from west to east in a simple scheme (Fig. 1). First comes the coastal plain, a wedge-shaped district which has been the chief cornland of Sussex throughout history. Its flat seaward margins support stoneless loamy soils which hold the warmth of a generous sun and are easy and rewarding to work. Where farmland is not obliterated by modern housing or glasshouses this double blessing makes for a trim, efficiently run countryside, all under corn or rich grass.

The back slopes of the eastern Downs, carved into rounded spurs and dry valleys, support both fine red loams and the thin, flinty white soils at higher elevations, the 'dry and stony' soils of medieval surveys. These, together with the strip of fertile marls beneath the scarp edge, were readily improvable by sheep-folding, the chief means of soil amendment until recent times. West of the Adur the downland changes in physical appearance. It becomes broader and higher and is amply clothed with groves of magnificent beeches and carefully preserved yew woods. On the flatter surfaces the soils are unpleasantly sticky in wet weather. These are derived from Clay-with-Flints, an infertile heavy soil, less easily improved than other downland soils and less suitable for sheep-rearing. This helps to explain the presence of parkland and pheasantries on the western Downs, land used more for amenity purposes than for economic gain.

Continuing to trace the geological strips further northwards, and passing beyond the ribbon of fertility provided by the marls beneath the Chalk scarp, the soils instantly fall to the level of mediocrity and, with steepening ground to the north-east, decline still further to reach sterility on the highest ground towards the county's northern edge. The Gault Clay is so stubborn to cultivate that the expression 'as hard to dig as gault' was already current in Elizabethan times. This outcrop in turn is followed by the Lower Greensand formation, which in north-west Sussex forms pleasant vistas of heaths and woods. Its coarse sands

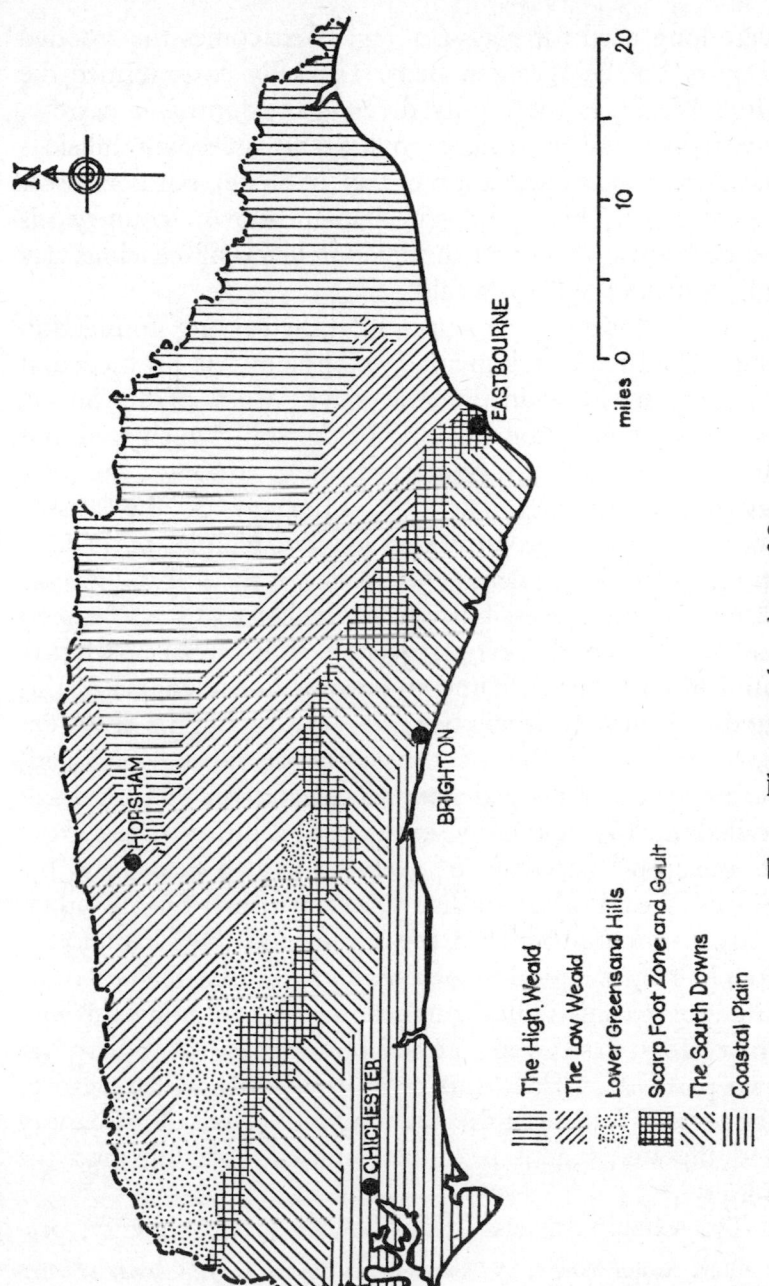

Fig. 1. The natural regions of Sussex.

The High Weald
The Low Weald
Lower Greensand Hills
Scarp Foot Zone and Gault
The South Downs
Coastal Plain

were long used for glass-making. Next comes the wooded country on the Wealden Beds. The hilly core, termed the High Weald, is the highly diversified country of narrow, ravine-like valleys (called ghylls) and sweeping hillsides developed on an alternation of clay (or shale), sands and soft sandstones. This delightful 'up-and-down country' is bordered by broad gently undulating levels of tenacious clay which make the Low Weald.

The historical occupation of this varying foundation and its subsequent human development has proceeded at different rates and in different ways. Much of the Sussex past is steeped in the working of the soils which were not uniformly suitable for pioneer farming. Amongst the basic factors influencing man's modification of the Sussex countryside have been the varying potentialities of the land itself, shown in the depth and quality of the soil and its ease of cultivation. Accessibility to navigable water has been an essential pre-condition of large-scale commercial agriculture until modern times. Time and again, in the course of this landscape history, it will be necessary to recall the divergent development of the two instantly distinguishable landscapes: the coastal plain and downland on the one hand (called the 'Champion' by seventeenth-century writers, from its once open stretches of great undivided fields) and the Sussex Weald (Old English *Wald*, a forest) on the other. This distinction between the Weald and the Champion is rooted in geological structure. Perhaps the first to draw attention to this radical physical division running through the county was Arthur Young junior who wrote that "no two parts of England can be more distinct with regard to the general feature of the country, the system of husbandry and the soil, than this of the South Down hills and the Weald".[2]

The Champion has always been a land of plenty, pre-

[2] Rev. Arthur Young, 'A Tour through Sussex' (1793), *Annals of Agriculture* [edited by his son, Arthur Young], Vol. 22 (1794), p. 616.

cociously developed by man at every point in past time, and for many centuries the only relatively densely populated part of Sussex, its roads, walls and settlement sites having their origin in England's remote past. As early as 1086, when the Domesday Survey gives us the first view of the economy and settlement of Sussex, it figures as an 'old land' where the landscape had already been fashioned into a complex palimpsest by successive stages of human occupation extending over fifty centuries. The general aspect of the human landscape is that typical of an old English countryside where the feudal magnates superintended cultivation. From the Downs the medieval knight or peasant would have looked down upon an abundance of ancient, tightly-clustered villages, as many as two to a mile, at places where spring water gushes out in fountains from the Chalk. Each of these villages was formerly furnished with a large manor house, great barns, fish ponds and open fields worked under a system of communal rotation. These agricultural settlements were interspersed with many quays kept busy with the shipment of corn, wool, wood, wine and fish.

Until this century the most resistant part of the Champion to change was the downland where the sheep-and-corn husbandry was the basis of the oldest civilisation in Sussex. As recently as 1900, W. H. Hudson asked, "Which common sight takes us further back in time?"—the cluster of cottages making a downland village, the cloaked shepherd, his rough-haired dog, the plough team of coal-black or red Sussex oxen, or the sickles still occasionally in use for reaping.[3] He might also have added the turn-wrest plough (in almost universal use until early in this century), wattled folds, the dewponds (formerly indispensable for watering the downland flocks) and the close-cropped turf, rendered fragrant by the scent of wild thyme which Dudeney, the famous schoolmaster-shepherd, told his pupils made "our

[3] W. H. Hudson, *Nature in Downland* (1951 edn.), p. 30.

own Southdown mutton beyond compare".[4] In little more than half a century since Hudson's essay was written the old downland men, their flocks and implements have died out and with them have gone into oblivion the wild birds formerly sharing their solitudes—the buzzard, the stone curlew and others—and attempts have been made to erase even the landscape itself with the utmost finality bulldozers can accomplish.

By contrast, the forest barrier and miry roads long left the Sussex Weald in a state of cultural seclusion from the rest of England and indeed, in some respects, from the remainder of Sussex. Accordingly, individual landscape features mark the Weald, even in these fast-changing times, as one of the most distinctive of the English landscapes. Doubtless, because of its inaccessibility and more difficult environment, it lay unredeemed from nature for many centuries after the taming of the coastal fringes, and much still wears the aspects of a wilder landscape little removed from its primeval look. To this day a distant view across the Weald conveys the impression that almost all the Sussex Weald is still unbroken woodland as was the Saxon *Andredesweald* (Plate 2). A closer acquaintance confirms this to be an illusion and that man, in his full and undisputed possession, has transformed most of the primitive waste into what may be likened to a large and majestic garden. In truth man's imprint in the Weald is almost as great as anywhere else in Sussex, and the false impression of an uncleared waste is conveyed by the commingling at a distance of the wide strips of residual wood (called shaws) bordering the relatively small fields, and the copses of broad-shouldered trees which fill every dell and hollow. The Wealden landscape thus furnishes a classic illustration of the truth that a marked attribute of man is to become habituated to his surroundings, and although the axe has

[4] R. W. Blencowe, 'Southdown Shepherds', *Suss. Arch. Colls.*, Vol. 2 (1849), pp. 252-6.

been laid down generally in the Weald for more than five hundred years the former forest, as will be seen, has left a lasting impression on the face of Sussex.

In sharp distinction to the inherent fertility of the forwarder land of the Champion, the Sussex Weald has responded more slowly to progressive amelioration by man and was for many generations a pioneering region of mere openings between woods and wastes. This has been a hard-won battle with several setbacks. The clearest outward signs of its fluctuating fortunes have been the advance and retreat of cultivation and settlement according to the pressure of population and economic conditions. As late as the thirteenth century the Sussex Weald still held large wastes, forlorn and sinister. To this day large parts of the High Weald have never been turned to full account. The heavy, moisture-retentive soils of the Weald are most apt for the growth of trees and shrubs. Anyone who has observed the splendid oak and elm in hedgerow and woodland, fine specimens of exotic trees and shrubs recently planted in gardens such as Wakehurst Place, and the high quality of fruit on the fringes of Ashdown Forest or in Kirdford will concur with Repton's view that "every berry soon becomes a bush and every bush a tree". Such is this extraordinary tree-growing power of its clays that ever since the Weald became the home of man, the life of Wealdsmen has been bound up with trees. Successive generations expended much of their energy battling with the primeval forest. By the early fourteenth century pioneering had waned and woodland was being grown as a crop. The rural ornamentation of the landscape with trees began in the mid-seventeenth century and during the past fifty years commercial fruit-growing has extended across the face of the county. The ancient lore of tree craft involved in the maintenance and renewal of woodland, it can be said, has burned itself into the very mind of Sussex, and fostered a love of trees verging on idolatry.

From a farming point of view, however, the Weald has always tested the skill and patience of its husbandmen, and has broken many hearts and stout backs. Much Wealden soil is cold and wet and hence tricky to plough, sow and harvest in adverse weather. Medieval society was freer in the Weald than in the Champion but this was a dear-bought advantage because the land kept people poor and life generally had the uncouthness associated with pioneering frontiers for many generations. Although far from being completely poverty-stricken, much of the Sussex Weald has been a country of hardship rather than of increment for most of past time and the greater frequency of crop failure because of harsher natural elements must have exacted a severe toll of human life. The rhythm of life in forest villages was demanding and special effort was required of individuals who wanted to enjoy a good standard of living. The inscription cut into an old ridge tile before baked and used at Chiddingly Place bears this advice:

> Plough deep
> While others sleep
> Then you will have corn to sell
> And corn to keep.[5]

Unfortunately, so appalling were the roads for much of the year until turnpiking brought some improvement in the eighteenth century, that it was difficult to transport surplus food out of the Weald, except for live animals, which went to market on the hoof. For generations farmers grew only sufficient corn for local markets to absorb and with the approach of winter, when by-ways were passable only by saddle horses, they reconciled themselves to a long spell of tedious isolation. This existence bred sturdy, independent, resourceful peasants who developed many crafts, to offset the poor livelihood from the land, in particular textiles and

5 Quoted in Countess Wolseley, *Some of the Smaller Manor Houses of Sussex* (1952), p. 174.

iron-making. These have left their own individual marks on the Wealden landscape.

Although the two principal landscapes of Sussex developed so divergently and at different times and rates, they should nevertheless be regarded as a single unit, the one complementing the other, because ties between them were formerly closer than now. On the ground the most conspicuous of these many links are the wide-bordered, high-banked, drovers' roads linking the Sussex Weald to the coastal borders. Down them, cattle were driven from their rearing grounds in the forest to fattening pastures on the better lands beyond the Weald, from whence they came back to market in London, or elsewhere. Autumn would see sheep driven to the shelter of secluded uplands for 'winter keep'. Swine were also herded to mast in the Weald and driven back to the coastal villages before Christmas. This seasonal rhythm, affecting the lives of people until modern times, indicates the age-old importance of the woodland in Sussex as a natural boundary of human existence.

The zone of contact between the two major landscapes in Sussex constitutes a physical and human divide which is one of the most interesting parts of the Sussex countryside. Lying as it does under the downland edge at the foot of the steep escarpment it may be termed the scarp-foot zone. Along this line the austere beauty of the downland merges with the more elusive qualities of the Weald and for generations the varied soils have offered unmatched farming and sporting possibilities. The string of great houses and parks, the wealth of manor houses and yeomen's farms which lie interspersed between a chain of market towns along this thoroughfare bear ample witness to its everlasting appeal.

Local building materials

Quite apart from its influence on the general landscape appearance, the varied geological foundation of Sussex is stamped architecturally on the older buildings by the usage of local building materials. The warm-coloured sandstones dug from the Tunbridge Wells and Ashdown Sands of the High Weald in the vicinity of East Grinstead, Crawley and Crowborough are generally accounted the loveliest building stone in the Weald. Of these the Tilgate Stone, being massive and little jointed and easily sawn into suitably shaped blocks, was the most durable sandstone and has distinctively reddish or rusty-brown hues imparted to it by its ferruginous nature. Slaugham, just off the Brighton road, and West Hoathly are but two of many villages where one can admire the beautiful weathered appearance of this stone. Many church towers, including those of Brightling, Fletching, Lindfield and Penhurst, are built of this material, which, mellowed by age and sun, greatly enhances the visual character of the landscape.

Little less attractive than Wealden sandstone, and of equal fitness for building, is the coarse grey Bargate Stone, a sandy limestone, quarried at several places below the west Sussex Downs. The Hythe Beds also yielded relatively good building sandstone of a buff tone and for this reason the villages along the Western Rother valley such as Trotton or Woolbeeding, or in the Petworth area, as at West Burton, Byworth or Upperton have outstanding examples of cottages built of agreeable local materials. This stone was also conveyed northwards some distance into the Low Weald and used in attractive farmsteads in Kirdford, Plaistow, Lurgashall and Loxwood.

Of all local building materials used in Sussex nothing adds so much to the charm of old buildings and passes so naturally into the landscape as the flaggy varieties of Horsham Stone used for roofing purposes throughout central Sussex from early medieval times (Plate 5). These heavy slabs, delightfully mellowed by weathering and moss, are so durable that many existing buildings still retain their original covering, as is indicated by a liberal amount of soot derived from the hall fire of a farmstead before the 'lofting-over' of a hall during the Great Rebuilding of the sixteenth and seventeenth centuries. The immense weight of such a roof required it to be low-pitched, typically at an angle of forty-five degrees, but even so it bore heavily on a strengthened timber frame, and a sagging ridge on buildings roofed with this stone is a common feature.

Brick-making materials were plentiful both in the Weald and on the coastal plain. As brick-making was done by hand it was formerly a highly localised activity. Each site tended to produce bricks under different technical conditions causing a pleasing variation in texture, size and colour, depending upon the nature of the clay, the process of firing and the type of fuel used. From Keymer, for example, came the famous 'Sussex Red', from a unique local vein of red clay, whilst at Worthing the earliest buildings are recognisable by cream-coloured bricks made from a local clay dug from the foreshore. At Kirdford, on the Low Weald, the well-made, locally produced, cherry-red brickwork of the early nineteenth century adds grace to a distinguished group of village houses.

The Chalk country worked in quite different material. The harder varieties of chalk stone, called 'clunch', were used for infilling between timber frames, as in the villages below Bury Hill. Also characteristic was the use of flint which was sometimes quarried but more often merely gathered from fields or beach and dressed by local craftsmen according to the prevailing fashion of the times. It is possible that the ubiquity of flint and the absence of ashlar stone accounts for the singular round church towers in the Ouse valley at Piddinghoe, Southease (Plate 3) and St Michael's, Lewes. By the thirteenth century the fracturing of flint into rectangular blocks with a flat face ('flint-knapping') had been perfected, as in Norfolk. This highly skilled treatment of flint, giving the appearance of well bonded stone- or brick-work often took the form of 'flush-work', squared blocks of flint alternating with masonry. The ancient custom house called Marlipins in Shoreham and the fine church tower of Burpham in the Arun valley are built in this attractive style.

A development which became popular in the seventeenth and eighteenth centuries along the coast was the use of flint cobbles set in neatly bonded courses of even size as a facing material on house façades and garden walls. Good examples of this can be seen in the houses of Church Street, New Shoreham (Plate 4), Church Lane, Ferring, and indeed throughout the old coastal villages, while at Brighton it was the characteristic style in the 'Old Town' and many of the earliest lodging houses are similarly faced. Few people today are prepared to work in flint and consequently the repair of walling or restoration of houses in this fashion is becoming increasingly difficult. Nevertheless, the old skills have not entirely died out in Sussex despite the almost universal use of new building materials such as concrete, plate glass and steel, and the new impetus for conserving the large heritage of buildings in the county will preserve historic craftsmanship for several more generations to come (Plate 6).

SELECT BIBLIOGRAPHY

Hall, A. D. and Russell, E. J. *Agriculture and Soils of Kent, Surrey and Sussex* (1911).

Hodgson, J. M. *Soils of the West Sussex Coastal Plain* (Harpenden, 1967).

Venables, E. M. and Outen, A. F. *The Building Stones of Old Bognor* (Bognor Regis Natural Science Society Publication, 1969)

Wooldridge, S. A. and Goldring, F. *The Weald* (1953).

Yates, E. M. *A history of the Landscape of the Parishes of South Harting and Rogate* (1972).

Plate 1 Little more than tiny church, a large farm and house or two remain at the shrunken settlement of Tarring Neville in the Ouse valley, its "straggling sparseness of tenements almost fatal to its title of village", as A. F. Cocke remarks in his *Off the Beaten Track in Sussex*. Note the ruined site opposite the church. A similar scene is reproduced all over the Sussex downland. See p. 26.

Plate 2 From the High Weald at West Hoathly an illusion of a continuous forest is created by thickly timbered hedgerows and closely spread copses. "There is no good land to be seen from (East) Grinstead steeple" is an old local saying. See p. 34.

Plate 3 One of the many unspoiled and simple downland churches is that of Southease in the Ouse valley. Recently discovered medieval frescoes adorn the interior. See p. 39.

Plate 4 Rounded flint cobbles were a characteristic building style in the coastal towns, as in Church Street, New Shoreham. See p. 40.

Plate 5 A combination of Horsham Stone roofing, locally quarried building stone and tile-clad fronts impart a charming distinction to West Hoathly and other High Weald villages. See p. 38.

Plate 6 Flint, weather-boarded and tile-hung walls give a neat, spruce appearance to Glynde, a Chalk settlement, for long an 'estate' village of the Morleys and Trevors of Glynde Place. See p. 40.

2. Earliest man-made landscapes

The prehistoric legacy.   Roman Sussex

The prehistoric legacy

IT IS STILL arguable when man in Sussex began to modify his habitat to any significant degree and what is the extent of the prehistoric legacy in the present scene. Until lately it was conjectured that the influence of prehistoric man on his natural environment was a comparatively slight one. Modern thought on this matter now tends to draw a directly opposite conclusion. In particular, more stress is laid on man as an agent of ecological change. The evidence for this is mainly derived from the analysis of fossil pollen grains and spores and the more exact chronology of change provided by radio-carbon dating. This gives greater recognition to the influence of prehistoric man on the primeval forest which covered most of western Europe from the Boreal climatic period (*c.* 7000–5000 B.C.). Unfortunately, the ecological history of Sussex has been much less fully investigated than areas with wider spreads of stratified lake sediments and peat, wherein the fossil pollen remains are preserved. The evolutionary sequence of Chalk vegetation is still particularly obscure owing to the lack of plant-preserving deposits.

For this reason we must take into account the implications of conclusions drawn by palaeo-botanists from other sites in lowland England. These pose questions, for example, as to the age and origin of the treeless downland of east Sussex, and of the many heaths developed on the Lower Greensands in the north-west of the county and on the sandier formations of the Hastings Beds.[1] The older view was that much of the present-day open county was 'natural' and indeed that it had attracted early settlement partly on that account. This belief is being revised as a result of recent work. There is growing evidence that the numerous sandy heaths were in antiquity covered with deciduous forest, doubtless lighter and drier (and hence more susceptible to fire) than on the impervious soils of the Weald. In some instances the removal of this woodland seems to have been completed by the Iron Age. The association of charcoal with the artefacts of Mesolithic hunters at Iping Common near Midhurst, one of the many Mesolithic settlement sites in the western Weald, suggests that even the pre-farming cultures in Sussex cleared woodland by means of fire, probably accidentally but also perhaps sometimes deliberately, to increase the amount of pasture supporting their prey. On richer soil this destruction of the forest did not prevent its regeneration, nor did the subsequent effects of long-continued shifting agriculture and grazing by Neolithic and Bronze Age farmers impair its fertility. By contrast, the poorer soils, such as the sands, degenerated under this human interference and their low recuperative power was still further reduced by the lack of humus formerly derived from the woodland cover. On these soils heath probably replaced forest during prehistory.

As for the Downs, despite large-scale destruction of the evidence by recent ploughing, they still bear many vestiges of intense and prolonged prehistoric and Romano-British settlement. The ecological changes brought about by early human interference are only now becoming appreciated. The spontaneous growth of woodland in fenced-off areas suggests that without the modifying hand of man forest would have been the climax vegetation of the Chalk in

[1] G. W. Dimbleby, *The Development of British Heathlands and their Soils* (1962).

prehistoric times and the examination of mollusca at archaeological sites is beginning to confirm this conclusion. This view is in conflict with that expressed by archaeologists as late as the 1950s, but the opinion of botanists such as A. G. Tansley[2] that the Downs have never been climatically or edaphically unsuited to tree growth from Boreal times has now come to be accepted. As on the sands, the freely-drained Chalk soils were doubtless less wooded than the heavy clays of the Weald but the forest was probably dense enough to require much human effort in its clearance. On parts of the Downs plastered with Clay-with-Flints the woodland cover was probably thicker. We must therefore envisage the eastern part of the South Downs as wearing quite a different aspect from that which it has assumed throughout the historic period.

The probability is that when man in Sussex began to grow crops and keep domestic animals, developments originating in Neolithic times, he could only have found room for them by clearing woodland. The former doubts about man's ability to alter significantly his surroundings with stone axes have been overcome by controlled experiments; and it is now possible to assess the likely effects on vegetation of shifting agriculture on a 'slash and burn' basis (though direct proof of this practice in Britain has yet to be established). It seems, therefore, that almost all the open country in Sussex has been created by man in the process of the progressive disforestation which in England ultimately led to the virtual destruction of deciduous woodland. This forest clearance in Sussex has thus had an immensely long history stretching over more than five millennia. It began even before man learned to grow his food and was accelerated under the impact of shifting agriculture and gained still more impetus when settled agriculture was established in Sussex at least from the middle Bronze Age (*c.* 1000 B.C.).

[2] Sir A. G. Tansley, *The British Isles and their Vegetation* (1949 edn.), pp. 164–5.

It is now almost, but not entirely, complete. This shrinkage of the forest will be one of the main themes in the story of the changing landscape for the swing of the Sussex axe has formed the ground base of all the county's history. The role of prehistoric man in this connection is an important one because two of the most distinctive landscapes of Sussex, the beautiful bare uplands of the Downs and the wild heathlands of the Weald, are a scenic inheritance which probably owes as much to early man as to nature itself.

Our main task, however, is to examine the traces of man's handiwork on this land won from the forest. The strongest and most enduring signs of human interference are preserved on the steeper slopes of the northern escarpment of the Downs, or the spurs separating the branching valleys, where the action of ploughs, the wheels of carts, the trampling of feet, and the deliberate construction of various earthworks have involved the greatest displacement of the soil. On such steep slopes massive banks and ditches have formed. The most ubiquitous of these remains are the lynchets, the cultivation banks caused by the gradual downslope movement of soil from the upper part of a field to the lower at each ploughing, so forming an eroded steep-sided bank up to ten feet high or more on the upper side (called a negative lynchet) and a bank of accumulated soil (a positive lynchet) on the lower. The survival of such evidence can mislead us. It was for long a firmly held and strongly expressed opinion, apparently supported by the distribution of the surviving evidence, that prehistoric man was a hill-dweller by predilection. It is now recognised that the visible evidence is susceptible of quite a different explanation. The existing traces of early man are seen now as the chance survivals of a much wider settlement of which the evidence has been virtually erased by the all-pervasiveness of later ploughing, as on the crest of the Downs, or by the long-standing occupation of the lower ground throughout the historic period. One development which has invalidated the older belief is that of aerial photography which has recovered widespread ancient field patterns on the coastal plain of Sussex and in the river valleys cutting through the Chalk. Another is the more systematic investigation of the neglected Weald, which is revealing a widely-ranging settlement pattern. In the light of this new knowledge about the distribution of prehistoric man we may even come to regard the existing remains of upland corn-growing in the present landscape as marginal in the economic sense, even in antiquity, as Clark suggested.[3] Certainly we must constantly bear in mind the increasing evidence that the richer soils of the county were exploited earlier than was formerly considered probable.

After this preliminary discussion of the nature of man's impact on his physical background during antiquity, the sequence of changes in the Sussex landscape which falls within the prehistoric and Romano-British period will be considered in rather more detail. Man's record in Sussex extends over more than 400,000 years but not until about 3000 B.C., when agriculture was introduced, did he leave any recognisable earthworks in the present scene. We are not, therefore, concerned with the immense span of time when man struggled for survival between successive glaciations, and when climatic changes were the chief agents of landscape change. Nor need we devote much attention to the Mesolithic nomads who wandered westwards across Europe in the wake of the final retreat of the ice sheets into the new territories being opened up for habitation by increasing warmth. These people dwelt typically beside the streams which interrupted the prevailing deciduous forest, subsisting on deer, birds and fish. Their numbers were very few but as agents of vegetation change, as already noted, they may have had an importance out of all proportion to their population. In other respects their place in the human record of landscape change is a small

[3] J. G. D. Clark, *Prehistoric Europe: the Economic Basis* (1952), p. 99.

one. Their winter quarters were simple pit dwellings, roofed over with hazel boughs and heather and, lacking digging implements except of the most primitive kind, they preferred to scoop out their homes from sands or other soft rocks. Sites of this kind have been identified at several places in such sandier parts of the Sussex Weald as High Rocks, near Tunbridge Wells, and Balcome and Stone Farms, East Grinstead. Another group of settlements lay in the Horsham district, both on sands and on the Weald Clay, where a special type of microlith was fashioned. This is the first of many instances of distinctive societies harboured by the isolation of the Wealden forest.

A new era in Sussex began with the arrival from the continent of the Neolithic peoples who brought the invention of agriculture and the arts of pottery, flint-mining and trade.[4] The record of their occupation of the South Downs is well authenticated, mainly through the solid substance given it by the persistent researches of the Curwens. The Neolithic peoples were probably semi-nomads who practised some form of shifting agriculture based on the hoe or spade without fixed fields. It is surmised that they grew corn after first clearing woodland by burning and with the aid of polished stone axes. Then they merely harrowed seeds in amongst the wood ashes in the manner of all primitive peoples and reclaimed fresh ground frequently to replace that abandoned as it became spent. We ought probably to envisage the gradual replacement of the primeval wood with clearings and in turn scrubland. The intensity of this cycle is far from clear but the advance of agriculture at the expense of Chalk woodland is likely to have been considerable. Stray finds of Neolithic axes in the Weald suggest that the numerous flint mines in the Chalk were sunk to produce axes for clearing forest not only locally but perhaps further afield. Yet the prevalence at their settlements of large

[4] Summarised in E. C. Curwen, *The Archaeology of Sussex* (1954 edn.), Chapters 5 and 6.

quantities of cattle and swine remains, in comparison with those of sheep and goats, has been taken as a sign that the environment was still well wooded. The simple Neolithic husbandry techniques here described may be more representative of earlier rather than later stages in cultural development since radio-carbon analysis now puts back the advent of the Neolithic peoples to well before 3000 B.C., thus allowing more than 1000 years of agricultural improvement. It is not surprising that there is growing evidence of a variety of land use in other areas of Neolithic settlement, and proof of cross-ploughing, as distinct from digging with simple hand instruments, in either late Neolithic or early Bronze Age times has been obtained from Cornwall. Similar evidence from Sussex is wanting at present but it may eventually be found beneath a Bronze Age barrow.

The outstanding memorials of the Neolithic Age in the Sussex landscape are the causewayed enclosures, the long barrows in which the dead were buried, and the flint mines. Each block of downland appears to have possessed an assemblage of these features. Four 'causewayed camps' are known—Coombe Hill (Jevington), Whitehawk (Brighton), Barkhale (Bignor Hill) and the Trundle near Chichester, where the Neolithic enclosure is surrounded by the more massive ramparts of an Iron Age hillfort. Whitehawk is an oval enclosure with four concentric ditches interrupted by causeways of solid chalk. The other enclosures are similar, but the pottery at the Coombe Hill site is of local origin, unlike that of the others, which have well-known western England affinities. No fully acceptable explanation has yet been vouchsafed for the peculiarity of their construction. Possibly they were used for tribal gatherings, fairs and the like, or for coralling animals for slaughter. The long barrows are earthen mounds up to 200 feet long and easily distinguishable from the round barrows of the succeeding Bronze Age. About a dozen remain on the Downs, one group lying between the Adur and Beachy Head and the other near the Trundle.

Flint-mining has left its mark on the countryside in the grass-grown pits and spoil heaps that break the surface of the Chalk at no less than four sites near Worthing; Blackpatch, Cissbury, Church Hill and Findon, as well as in the Chichester district, Windover Hill near Wilmington and several other places. The localisation of the axe industry was mainly in the mid-Downs along the so-called 'secondary escarpment' (the line of steeply rising ground parallel to the main escarpment) where good quality flints in the Upper Chalk formation are brought close to the surface by folding. Not content with surface flints, the miners dug out shafts more than fifty feet deep and followed the seams of unweathered flint nodules by means of horizontal galleries, using as tools only picks made from deer antlers and shoulderblade shovels. The flint mines at Cissbury, four miles north of Worthing, occupy a hummocky area consisting of more than 200 pits, making this, next to Grimes Graves in Norfolk, the most famous site of its kind in Britain. The pottery found in the shafts and tips indicates that although mining began in the Neolithic phase it continued into the early and middle Bronze Age. The radio-carbon dates indicate early working (between 3390 and 2700 B.C.).

The Bronze Age in Sussex was one of fundamental change in the organisation of farming and settlement and the basic patterns which evolved on the South Downs persisted into the Pre-Roman and Roman Iron Age. These changes are unlikely to be attributable to the Beaker people, whose arrival in Sussex about 2000 B.C. traditionally marks the end of the Neolithic period, for these appear to have practised semi-nomadic shifting agriculture in the manner of the natives. The Beaker folk are represented in the present landscape by little more than the round barrows they raised to their dead. Nearly all these are shaped like an inverted bowl with a circular ditch. More than 400 such barrows, not all datable to the early Bronze Age, however, are on the high ground lining the South Downs ridgeway (now called the South Downs Way) between Harting and Eastbourne, where they still show against the skyline. This was clearly a major route in the Bronze Age along an obvious line of open country.

The stages by which the simple economy of Beakerfolk was replaced by settled agriculture on the basis of farmsteads with round buildings integrated within small squarish fields are still very obscure. Thanks to the remarkable activity of Sussex archaeologists we at least know that this more advanced civilisation was well established by about the eleventh century B.C. The evidence comes from the downland where a large number of sites have been excavated. The wind blows with unhindered vigour on this high part of the Downs and the first need of the settlers was shelter. They erected their thirteen round huts within a palisade in the lee of Itford Hill round about 1000 B.C., a date obtained from the radio-carbon analysis of carbonised grain found at the site. Only two of the huts appear to have been used for sleeping. On this evidence G. P. Burstow and G. A. Holleyman consider that the downland farms of the period were occupied only for relatively short periods and the small, irregular fields nearby are the work of later Celtic farmers.[5]

All these developments were on the light soil of the South Downs but the distribution of Bronze Age antiquities also reveals the extension of cereal-growing on the loams and, locally, on the heavier soils. The construction of a suitable plough to take advantage of heavier and more fertile soils is one of the most critical events which have modelled the face of the Sussex countryside. As far as the loams are concerned, clearly by the late Bronze Age human interference was actively spreading from the Chalk on to wastes

[5] G. P. Burstow and G. A. Holleyman, 'Late Bronze Age Settlement on Itford Hill, Sussex', *Proceedings of the Prehistoric Society*, Vol. 18 (1957), pp. 167–212.

formerly used only for hunting and grazing, thus anticipating by many centuries the better known assault on the heavier soils associated with the Belgae migrating from the continent. The belief, not finally exterminated, that prehistoric man was held a prisoner on the light soils by his inability to make more than a primitive scratch plough, technically called a 'beam' or 'crook-ard', which could not work the richer soils, cannot be sustained for Sussex. On the loams Bronze Age farmers did not have to sacrifice soil fertility to ease of working, as they did on the Downs, but how effectively they cultivated the loam terrains in Sussex is unfortunately incapable of proof. We may well discover that their technical accomplishments were greater than expected. It is reasonable to assume that their plough was more efficient than the simple ard for it must have had some means of turning a heavy furrow slice to draw off rainwater.

The Bronze Age economy was based on mixed farming, and we must now consider the effects of pastoral activities on the landscape. These include much-debated earthworks, such as the ditches between two banks which have been variously called 'covered-ways', 'cross-ridge dykes' or simply 'cross-dykes'. Numerous examples exist on the South Downs, typically running across spurs thus linking heads of valleys. They have been regarded as sunken droveways between wooded cover at either end. Some 'cross-dykes' possibly functioned in this way but R. Bradley has recently argued that others were almost certainly farm or ranch boundaries. The larger enclosures on the Downs, such as at Butser Hill, Belle Tout near Eastbourne and Ramscombe near Lewes, which have weak defences, possibly bounded grazing land and several hillforts of the Iron Age may have originated in the Bronze Age as stock enclosures.[6]

[6] R. Bradley, 'Stock Raising and the Origin of the Hill Forts on the South Downs', *The Antiquaries' Journal*, Vol. 51 (1971), pp. 8–29.

The iron-using communities in Sussex, at least down to the Belgic invasions on the eve of recorded history, perpetuated a rural economy rooted in the previous Bronze Age (Fig. 2). Round houses with storage pits for grain were still characteristic and the basic agricultural pattern based on woodland and pasture on the downland crest, and arable farming on the lower slopes, persisted. The unit of settlement remained small but its precise nature is often difficult to establish. Many appear to have been farmsteads, like the Itford site established much earlier, but the possibility that some were small hamlets ('clachans') associated with a patch of arable communally tilled and grazed, cannot be ruled out. It is a great misfortune that nothing positive can yet be expressed about this critical point. New factors significant in terms of landscape evolution are the more substantial nature of buildings and the evidence of permanently occupied sites. Moreover, it is clear that the population was becoming increasingly numerous. Park Brow, a settlement on the dip-slope of the Downs near Worthing, appears to have been in continuous occupation for at least 150 years and, although farm buildings were then rebuilt on lower ground, the fields continued under cultivation for a further five centuries.[7] This quasi-permanence implies that some form of crop rotation and amendment of land by sheep-folding, and possibly by marling, had been evolved. The prolonged occupation of the site explains the massive lynchets still observable in the neighbourhood. Several score more Iron Age farmsteads are known in Sussex and this intensity of occupation, together with the mastery over woodland conferred by iron tools, led to the further retreat of the Chalk woodland.

The most characteristic monuments of the Iron Age are the 'camps'. Some of these have feeble ramparts and were doubtless stock compounds. More spectacular are the 'hill

[7] G. R. Wolseley, 'Prehistoric and Roman Settlement at Park Brow', *Archaeologia*, Vol. 26 (1927), pp. 1–40.

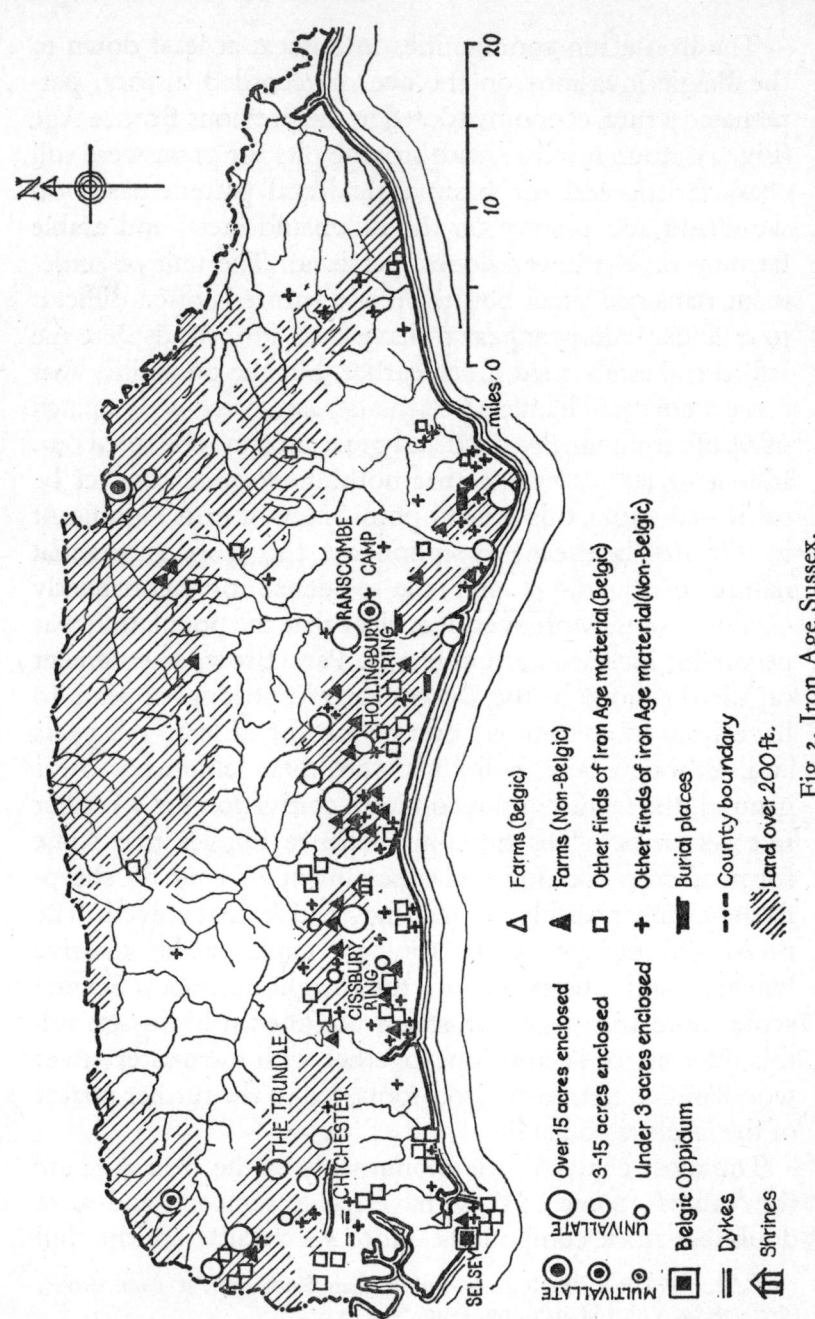

Fig 2. Iron Age Sussex.

Over 15 acres enclosed

3-15 acres enclosed

Under 3 acres enclosed

UNIVALLATE

MULTIVALLATE

Belgic Oppidum

Dykes

Shrines

△ Farms (Belgic)

▲ Farms (Non-Belgic)

□ Other finds of Iron Age material (Belgic)

+ Other finds of iron Age material (Non-Belgic)

▬ Burial places

—·— County boundary

Land over 200 ft.

THE TRUNDLE

CHICHESTER

SELSEY

CISSBURY RING

HOLLINGBURY RING

RANSCOMBE CAMP

miles 0   10   20

52

forts', mostly attributable to about the third century B.C. Once regarded as defences raised against enemies from overseas or the work of martial overlords in their newly conquered lands, the presumption now is that they were the product of the fierce local rivalries which were such a peculiarity of the native peoples of the Iron Age. The defences of the larger forts are truly prodigious, yet in their present degraded form and without timber revetments, they can convey little of the impregnability of their prime.

The most impressive of the Sussex hillforts is Cissbury where sixty acres are enclosed within a massive ditch and rampart with a counterscarp bank (Plate 7). When approached from the north or west the natural strength of the defensive site on a steep promontory is very noticeable. To the south and east, where the ground slopes more gently, the ramparts are stronger and up to forty feet higher than the bottom of the related ditch. The hummocky area in the western part of the enclosure marks flint-workings older than the great ramparts described earlier and also detectable both on an aerial photograph and on the ground are plough lynchets made when the hillfort was cultivated from Roman to at least medieval times. Another impressive hillfort is the Trundle, which was constructed in the same manner as Cissbury, as was Torberry near Harting, the other fort west of the Adur. East of this river the hillforts are small and have a different history. The fortification at the Caburn (Plate 9) probably enclosed no more than one farm, possibly the rural seat of a member of the nobility who practised an economy similar to that at the famous type-site of Little Woodbury in Wiltshire. None of the larger hillforts has been completely investigated, and their precise function still remains debatable. Some may have given protection to men and herds when danger threatened but the Cissbury and Trundle forts appear to have been occupied for a lengthy period and can perhaps be regarded as embryonic market towns providing services for small blocks of downland.

Important innovations in the landscape of a more civilised kind are associated with the advent of the Belgae from northern Gaul before the end of the second century B.C. The Belgae were a technically advanced people who made lavish use of iron for heavy axes and iron-shod spades, so facilitating the clearance and drainage of the heavier soils. They continued to inhabit the light soil areas but coin and other evidence suggests that they also colonised the richer soils, especially the loams. Their activity appears to have been chiefly in the Manhood peninsula south of Chichester which has yielded many finds and now emerges with a clear cultural identity. The principal settlement was probably in the Selsey district at a site now under the sea but the striking linear earthworks some ten miles in length on the gravels north of Chichester are plausibly regarded as marking the bounds of the countryside within its *territorium*. The abandonment of the west Sussex hillforts in the first century B.C. suggests that this lowland Belgic site, Chichester, had assumed the functions of the hill towns.

Roman Sussex

Sussex has a number of impressive monuments of the Roman practical genius which draw attention, in different ways, to its military and commercial importance as part of a remote province of the Roman empire (Fig 3). The southwest of the county was of pivotal importance to the Romans in their initial advance across southern Britain. Its people were staunchly pro-Roman and depended on the Romans for support against the Catuvellaunian aggression from the north. The Romans for their part wanted the district as a base against the tribes in Dorset and Wiltshire. The landscape still bears the marks of this conjunction of imperial with native needs. The magnificent palace at Fishbourne, where presumably resided the client-king Cogidubnus, uniquely styled 'king and legate to the emperor in Britain', is its most outstanding relic. The new town of Chichester called *Noviomagus Regnensium* ('the new market of the people of the kingdom'), the Stane Street thrown across the Weald to London and the thickly scattered romanised farmhouses also attest to a turning point in development when this district was advancing by leaps and bounds. Following upon the Belgic colonisation a marked imbalance in economic development in Sussex became apparent which persisted into medieval times, for the Weald was merely a mining preserve throughout the Roman occupation. Yet this also bears a framework of new trunk roads linking the iron districts to London and the coast running across the formidable miry clays which so bogged down later transport.

East of Stane Street, two other roads led southwards to the Downs near Brighton and Lewes. These intersected an east-west road along the Lower Greensand outcrop below the Downs. I. D. Margary's discovery of the central Wealden roads serving the iron district demolished the old idea of a 'trackless wilderness'. With the aid of air-photography and detailed field-work he traced long stretches of abandoned Roman roads in the northern forested area of Sussex. Where these disused roads cross public open spaces they are still easily traceable. The London–Lewes Way, for example, is seen at its best in Ashdown Forest between Camp Hill and Five Hundred Acres Wood where it runs on a distinct, if narrow, embankment (*agger*) and can again be followed without difficulty across the heath at Fairwarp. A short length further north at Holtye has been stripped of its overlying soil to expose the rutted iron slag surface. Several miles of the disused section of Stane Street traverse the downland above Bignor villa in a fine *agger*. From these trunk roads many 'feeder' roads diverged, especially in the iron-producing districts and some of the many artificially terraced ways which cross the South Downs escarpment are possibly also Roman.

Domestic bloomeries had been created in the Weald long

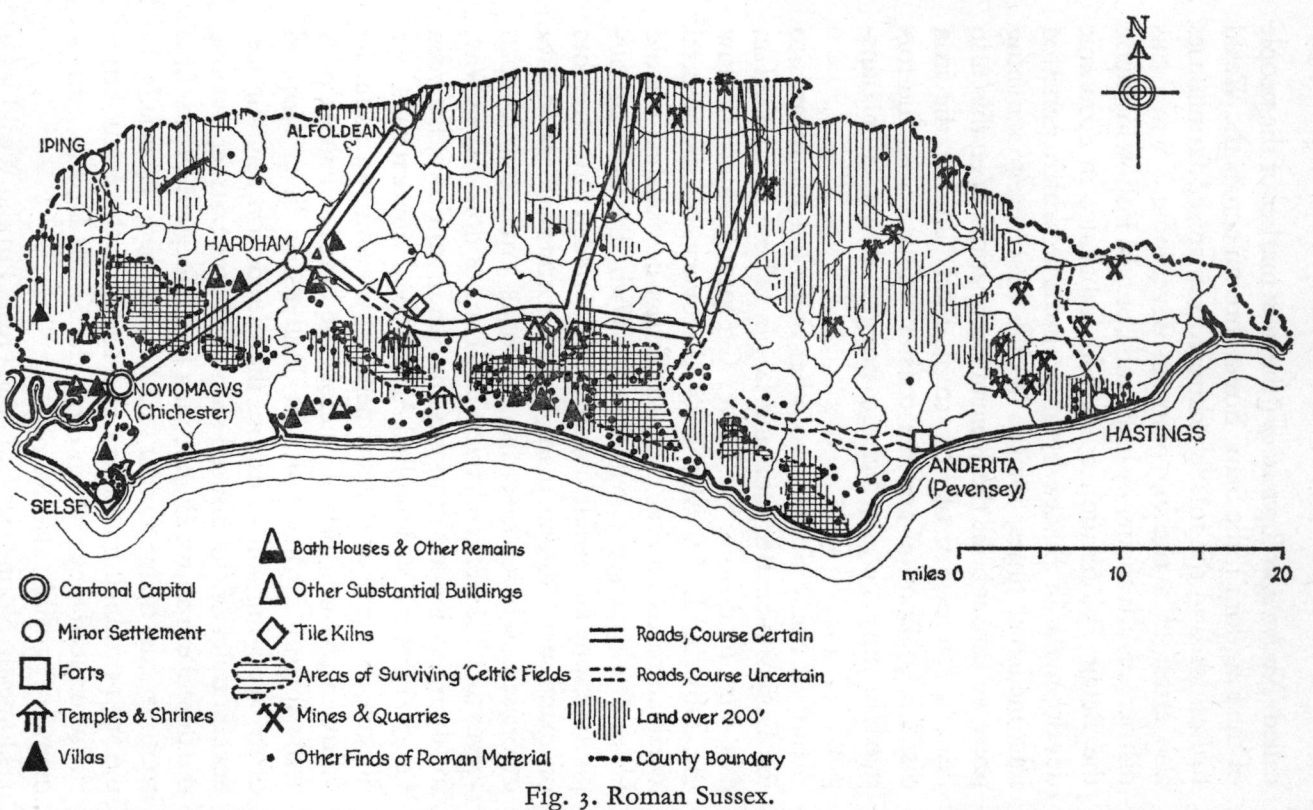

N

IPING

ALFOLDEAN

HARDHAM

NOVIOMAGVS
(Chichester)

SELSEY

ANDERITA
(Pevensey)

HASTINGS

miles 0   10   20

◎ Cantonal Capital

○ Minor Settlement

□ Forts

⛩ Temples & Shrines

▲ Villas

◮ Bath Houses & Other Remains

△ Other Substantial Buildings

◇ Tile Kilns

▨ Areas of Surviving 'Celtic' Fields

✕ Mines & Quarries

• Other Finds of Roman Material

▬ Roads, Course Certain

╍ Roads, Course Uncertain

▥ Land over 200'

•—•—• County Boundary

Fig. 3. Roman Sussex.

before the Roman invasion, but in Caesar's day the volume of Wealden iron production still remained small. Radiocarbon dating is enabling these early bloomeries to be identified. C. Cattell's discovery at Sandyden Gill in Mayfield has charcoal in closely packed slag and burnt clay dated to *c.* 220 B.C. Commercial workings were probably first established under Belgic influence and the great amounts of slag available for early Roman road-making show that iron output had greatly increased. The slag heaps of the Iron Age and Roman period are distinguishable from medieval and later workings by the higher metal content resulting from more primitive methods of iron-making. This material was again highly prized for turnpike road construction and the destruction of Romano-British iron-working sites was severe. Some of the huge mounds of waste such as those at Beauport Park and Oaklands Park, both near Hastings, and the banks at Oldlands in Maresfield have been quarried to virtual extinction, but extensive slag heaps still exist in Crowhurst Park, near Battle, Bardown in Ticehurst and Crawley Down. Smaller bloomery sites are very numerous and many still await discovery. The larger sites are stratified into alternate layers of charcoal, roasted ore and burnt clay, evidence of repeated and prolonged working. The presence at these larger sites of roofing tiles stamped CL BR, the mark of the Roman Fleet in Britain, supports the idea that the larger workings supplied metal to the army guarding the north and west of Britain. It is hoped that the excavations at Bardown Hill will produce further information about the economic basis of the main producing centre. Coin evidence suggests that the principal period of iron-making in the Sussex Weald was in the first and second centuries A.D. after which it was overtaken by the Forest of Dean.[8]

During the Romano-British period the reclamation of

[8] H. Cleere, 'The Romano-British Industrial Site at Bardown, Wadhurst', *Sussex Archaeological Society, Occasional Paper No. 1* (undated). Interim report on excavations 1960–8.

virgin land continued on the richer soils. The newly won agricultural areas were mainly loams; the heavier soils of the Weald with their dense forests still proved an intractable problem. The coastal plain early attracted capital investment on a large scale. This is confirmed by the existence of the big villas of Southwick and Angmering and the many other romanised farms studding the district, most of which were flourishing by the first and second centuries A.D. In particular, Romano-British sites on the plain near Chichester are abundant and fresh sites are constantly coming to light with the current spate of road construction and new building. Another strip of forest which was actively retreating in the Roman period lay on the stiff loams at the foot of the Chalk escarpment where the magnificent villa of Bignor and a string of lesser country houses and romanised farms reflect a high level of material culture. In these newly colonised districts there are possible traces of the Roman method of systematic land division based on *centuria* or squares of 776 English yards (20 Roman *actus*). The evidence of this ground plan is not beyond dispute but Margary has suggested that the pattern of roads and other boundaries in the Ripe and Chalvington area near Lewes indicates centuriation.[9] Slighter impressions of precise rectangularity are conveyed by field patterns at Hurstpierpoint, also associated with Roman pottery and other finds, and in the Littlehampton district. All these sites warrant detailed field-work in conjunction with early manuscript maps and documentary evidence.

Sussex is exceptionally well endowed with the remains of Roman villas. Unsurpassed in size and opulence by any building so far discovered in the Empire outside Italy itself is the Roman palace of Fishbourne, which was constructed towards the end of the first century A.D. This comprised unusually long ranges of stone-built rooms on one level around a garden courtyard and fronting another large

9 I. D. Margary, *Roman Ways in the Weald* (1949), pp. 204–7.

garden extending down to the sea. Its spacious layout, exquisite mosaics, moulded stucco and inlaid marbles still convey something of its former grandeur as the supreme showpiece of Roman imperial policy in Britain. Its fine suites of administrative and audience rooms are almost outrivalled in interest by the large central formal garden also disinterred by Professor Cunliffe. This was embellished with basins and fountains and bordered by a private colonnade. The edges of paths, the lines of hedges and even the very holes containing the fine loam in which grew plants and shrubs have been revealed by the archaeologists' spades. These discoveries have made possible the reconstruction of the garden with living plants and trees. This garden at Fishbourne throws valuable new light on Romano-British life in Sussex at the highest level, and as the earliest known in the country it has its unique place in the history of English gardening.

Of mansions below the regal scale, Bignor was the largest and most sumptuous (Fig. 4). Whoever owned it in the fourth century enjoyed the life of a fine country gentleman. This courtyard house was built on a shelf of land facing the downland escarpment and surrounded, as at present, by fields of early corn, must have long been a familiar landmark to travellers making for London by way of Stane Street. Its fourth-century mosaics, of exceptional beauty and quality, were discovered in 1811. Yet it is only lately that its origin has been established as an unpretentious timber building which, with several elaborations, finally attained its splendour in the late Roman period. The main suite of rooms lay in the north wing at the top of a gentle slope. This section had a floor level higher than the rest of the villa and so lay open to the sun and the picturesque scenery of the Downs and the Arun valley. The main bathrooms were richly ornamented with marble and black floor tiles made from Kimmeridge Clay from Dorset. The west wing was mainly occupied by domestic servants and

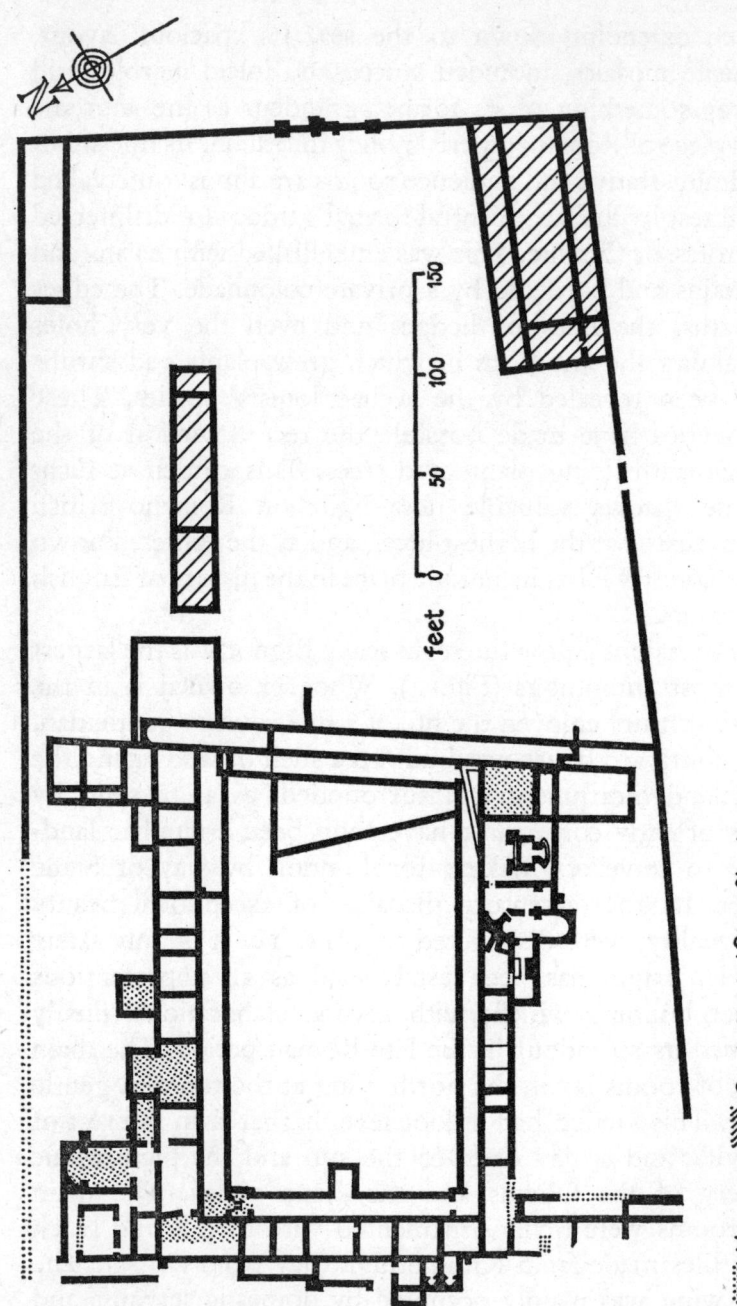

Fig. 4. Bignor villa.

Mosaics ▦ Cattle Sheds/Store Sheds

feet
0 50 100 150

slaves and the east wing, in the lee, was devoted to agricultural purposes.

It is only recently that the field pattern and economy of the villa estates has come to be considered in relation to towns and the co-existing native farms and villages. S. Applebaum has shown the surprising amount of information on these aspects that can be inferred from a detailed study of the size and proportions of barns and stock compounds. At Bignor he estimates that twenty-four plough oxen (twelve plough-teams), fifty-five other cattle and about 200 sheep were kept and that some 800 acres were annually cultivated.[10] He also considers that enough manure would have been produced to grow root crops. The larger villas were, therefore, important elements in the basic framework of rural life. The shape and size of their fields is still unresolved but at West Blatchington, near Brighton, evidence of systematically planned fields has come to light through aerial photography.

Even more fundamental is the controversy surrounding their relationship to the visible pattern of contemporary settlement and cultivation. Briefly summarised, it is the opinion of G. R. G. Jones and S. Applebaum that the larger villas in Sussex are so closely associated with peripheral Romano-British settlements as to suggest that the latter were in subordinate relationship to them.[11] Cited as examples are the five or six small Romano-British sites close to Bignor and the similar pattern about the villa of Wiggonholt which is interpreted, with some plausibility, as part of a discrete estate which also embraces the single farms in the neighbourhood where the *coloni* who worked the villa resided. L. Alcock's denial that in the Brighton area there is a demonstrable relationship between villas and native

[10] S. Applebaum in H. P. R. Finberg (ed.), *The Agrarian History of England and Wales*, Vol.1, Part II (1972), pp. 182–4, 212.

[11] G. R. G. Jones, 'Settlement Patterns in Anglo-Saxon England', *Antiquity*, Vol. 35 (1961), pp. 221–32.

farms and Applebaum's rebuttal cannot be discussed here for lack of space but they indicate the lively debate which has ensued on this matter, and the need for local studies.[12] Whoever seeks to trace the development of the Sussex landscape will never cease to wrestle with the evidence on the ground which helps us to construe this difficult question. Really detailed and systematic research on the relationship between villas and other contemporary settlements still remains to be done. There is a need for further search for sites, at present possibly represented by little more than a scatter of potsherds and tiles. The importance of this extends far beyond the chronological limits of the Roman occupation because it is G. R. G. Jones' working hypothesis that the threads of the present rural ground plan of village, hamlet and farm lead back to developments even further in antiquity. This aspect of the changing face of Sussex will be discussed later.

For all the changes wrought by Roman efficiency and enterprise the life of most inhabitants of Roman Sussex probably continued much as before. This appears to be particularly true of the downland communities. Most of the settlements in the Brighton and Worthing districts reveal little sophistication but notable exceptions are the rectangular houses at Park Brow which had wooden frames and tiled roofs and contained traces of coloured plaster, window glass and a door key. Romanisation here falls short of that at the larger villas but it is an interesting instance of a veneer of civilisation being adopted by the peasantry. More significant are the indications that the downland peoples were tending to congregate into hamlets. Whether this is attributable to Belgic influence is not clear at present but a number of settlements of the hamlet type appear to date from the end of the pre-Roman Iron Age.

There is unfortunately much room for different interpretations concerning the status of Romano-British and

[12] L. Alcock, *Antiquity*, Vol. 36 (1962), pp. 51–4; Applebaum, *op. cit.*

earlier settlements. Before 1940 the profusion of pits at these sites was taken to signify a group settlement but it is now accepted that many pits were for grain storage and that groups of these are frequently found in association with a single farm. Since most of the Sussex 'villages' were excavated before 1940 some conclusions must be regarded with dubiety, but two in particular were carefully excavated and the published records inspire confidence. One of these hamlets was Park Brow where five adjacent platform houses co-existed in the Romano-British period.[13] Another site, which appears to have been larger, developed outside the Thundersbarrow Camp near New Shoreham in the first century B.C. and was occupied almost until the end of Roman times. It may have been a 'street village' because a group of round houses lined a ridgeway where it widened out to form a kind of 'village green'. Both these sites are associated with a wide area of lynchets[14] (Plate 9). Applebaum is undoubtedly correct in suggesting that local investigation will reveal others. There seems no reason to assume that such 'clachans' did not also exist on the coastal plain and along the foot of the Chalk escarpment. It has long been the view of local antiquaries that some of these are still represented in the present landscape by living villages and hamlets. Now that Romano-British 'villages' are again finding their way back into history in certain regions based on new ideas and methods of analysis, the large number of Sussex settlements of this period would repay fresh study.

Of all the more conspicuous of the older works of man none equals the importance and interest of the so-called 'Celtic' fields. Before food shortages induced the ploughing-up of downland, ancient field remains occupied as much as one quarter of the Downs in the Brighton district and

[13] G. R. Wolseley, 'Prehistoric and Roman Settlement at Park Brow', *Archaeologia*, Vol. 26 (1927), pp. 1–40.

[14] E. C. Curwen, 'Excavations at Thundersbarrow Hill, Sussex', *The Antiquaries' Journal*, Vol. 13 (1933), pp.109–51.

similar blocks of downland elsewhere abounded in them. Well-preserved specimens of 'Celtic' fields are now rare. The finest surviving examples include those on the flanks of Coombe Hill in Jevington and on Windover Hill, Wilmington. Most of the feebler cultivation banks of other systems have recently been ploughed out and even the more massive lynchets are being progressively degraded. From the air much of the former pattern is still recoverable because even levelled banks leave bands of different colouring in the soil according to whether they were 'negative' or 'positive' lynchets. Typically, 'Celtic' fields are arranged in blocks on a south-facing slope and bounded by lynchets up to ten feet high or more and are distinguished by their small size (one to two acres) and their sub-rectangular appearance. On sloping ground they can still be discerned as a staircase of 'risers' and 'treads'. Curwen considered that some of the surviving vestiges existed coevally with dwelling sites of about 1000 B.C., such as those on New Barn Down near Worthing and on Plumpton Plain, but as a rule the residue of ancient fields belong to the pre-Roman and Roman Iron Ages and so it is appropriate to consider them here.

Remarkably little information has been abstracted from Sussex prehistoric fields since Cecil Curwen concluded his pioneer researches more than thirty years ago[15] and the broader socio-economic issues raised by this particular type of peasant agriculture still remain a challenge. The 'Celtic' fields of Sussex have not been submitted to the kind of detailed land-use interpretation that Applebaum has made for the system of Figheldean Down in Hampshire nor have any been scientifically excavated as have those on Overton Down in Wiltshire. We know nothing at present about the crop rotations and grazing exercised over them and since the status of their associated settlements is often still in

---

[15] These are summarised in E. C. Curwen, *Plough and Pasture* (1946), pp. 48–77. See also *idem, Air Photography and Economic History: the Evolution of the Cornfield* (Economic History Society, 2nd edn., 1938).

doubt it is uncertain whether any systems were cultivated by bondmen settled in hamlets. Their ultimate oblivion in the near future makes a renewed study of ancient Sussex fields a matter of extreme urgency.

SELECT BIBLIOGRAPHY

Bowen, H. C. *Ancient Fields* (1961).
Cunliffe, B. *Fishbourne: A Roman Palace and its Garden* (1971).
Curwen, E. Cecil. *The Archaeology of Sussex* (1954).
Jessup, R. *South-east England* (Ancient Peoples and Places Series) (1970).
Margary, Ivan D. *Roman Ways in the Weald* (1949).
Smith, A. G. 'The Influence of Neolithic Man on British Vegetation' in D. Walker and R. G. West (eds.), *Studies in the Vegetational History of the British Isles* (1970), pp. 81–93; J. Turner, 'Post-Neolithic Disturbance of British Vegetation', *ibid.*, pp. 97–115.
West, R. G. *Studying the Past by Pollen Analysis* (1971).

3. The age of English settlement

The coming of the English. The infiltration into the Weald. Early English settlement patterns and the question of continuity. Saxon churches

SUSSEX WAS ONE of the seaboard cantons of Roman Britain that bore the brunt of the Early English invasions. The coastal area was subjected to a swift and thorough settlement of dramatic intensity from which emerged the South Saxon kingdom of Sussex. Culturally, this amounted to a retrogression. Sussex was wrested from its close links with the remainder of Britain and the Roman Empire, ties fostered by its wealth of corn and iron, and turned into a petty fastness, secure but isolated, between the great forest of the Weald and the sea. At no other period do the limits of the geographical county of Sussex more closely coincide with the natural frontiers within which the Sussex landscape evolved. The long period of cultural seclusion has left a marked influence on its church architecture, which is distinctive in several respects from the rest of England. Another legacy of this remoteness is the great number of archaic elements in Sussex place-names which, as will be seen, are an invaluable clue to changing conditions in the countryside.

During the six centuries from the coming of the Saxons to the making of Domesday Book in 1086 (in effect a record of the transformation undergone by the countryside between these events) were more than twenty generations of unceasing, though obscure, endeavour at the expense of woodland, heath and marsh. This fundamentally altered the relationship between man and the natural setting. At the beginning of the period man was still dominated by wild nature over most of Sussex and continued to select land for occupation which was naturally cultivable and relatively free from forest. Ecologically speaking, therefore, the English invasions did not constitute a break with the past. By the end of the period Sussex was involved in an agrarian revolution greatly extending the boundary of settlement as a fast-moving frontier across the face of the Wealden forest. This start on the physical conquest of the wilderness, apparently beginning from the eighth century as a result of population pressure, is as significant, if not more so, in terms of landscape history, as the military conquest by the English three or more centuries earlier.

The coming of the English

The early settlers had the technical ability to plough the heavier and richer soils of Sussex, and with their keen eye for country, sought out the best-watered sites, shunning the wilder landscape of the Weald. No pagan burials have been discovered even along the Stane Street and other Roman roads, and early place-names are rare in the interior. By these two tests it must be concluded that the countryside in the northern part of western and central Sussex continued to wear its primeval appearance. It should be borne in mind that the fecundity of the virgin soils of the Weald was generally short-lived and that the common assumption that 'heavier soils yield heavier crops', whilst generally true, is not applicable to the Weald because of the physical deficiencies of the soils. Also despised were the thin soils of the downland, which had been under the plough for at least 2000 years. The early settlers' first preference fell on the intermediate soils of the loam terrains on the coastal plain and at the foot of the Downs escarpment which from the late Bronze Age onwards had attracted increasing settlement. When it is archaeologically possible to find them at work, the first English settlers are, as Cyril Fox put it, "turning the valley bottoms into water meadows, the forest margins into arable and pastures".[1] This is a very fair summary of the achievements in Sussex of the English colonists before the eighth century.

It is against this physical background that the English settlement can now be considered. Much obscurity still surrounds the kingdom of Sussex but knowledge has advanced to the point when it can be recognised as a combination of independent settlements, each making its own distinctive contribution to the landscape. The record of the English conquest in the *Anglo-Saxon Chronicle* appears to deal with only one of these. This assigns to the year 477 the landing of Aelle and his followers at *Cymenes Ora*, a place on the old seashore, since eroded and now represented by one of the shoals of Owers Bank, off Selsey Bill. Under 491 the *Chronicle* also records the massacre of the Britons in *Andredes cester* (Pevensey fort) which suggests a gradual advance eastwards. Other testimony is not inconsistent with the bald statements in the *Chronicle* but J. Morris has concluded that dates of a generation earlier would fit better into the context of the general European evidence.[2]

There are few signs of early Saxon occupation near the traditional landfall itself. This may be due to the close settlement which already existed in the environs of Chichester but dense colonisation occurred further east in the Littlehampton and Worthing districts. Here, on the fertile loams of the coastal plain, was created the heartland of the South Saxon kingdom. Group communities tapping the rich source of arable wealth were planted thickly in compact villages, as is shown by the distribution of place-names with the suffix *-ing*, from the Old English *-ingas*, long regarded

[1] Sir Cyril Fox, *The Personality of Britain* (1950), p. 80.
[2] J. Morris, 'Dark Age Dates' in *Britain and Rome: essays presented to Eric Birley*, M. G. Jarrett and B. Dobson (eds.), (1965), pp. 145–85.

as the most ancient stratum of English place-names. The loamy soils in the valleys through the Chalk, the ribbon of fertility below the escarpment of the Downs and the margins of the Lower Greensand were also crowded with little agricultural colonies from an early date. Few parts of England can have been so heavily populated. The consideration which most frequently influenced the siting of these settlements was ease of access by water. There is a particularly close correspondence between the former creeks and bays of the old shoreline and the *-ingas* place-names which so effectively record the exchange of one over-populated seaboard between the Weser and the Elbe for a similar one in Sussex.

Proceeding eastwards, another part of Sussex which bears the strong impress of early English settlement is the downland between the Adur and Beachy Head with slighter and more localised evidence on high ground as far as the Arun. In this district some forty pagan cemeteries have been discovered, of which Alfriston and Highdown Hill are the best known. The barrows yielded fifth-century brooches and other jewellery, coins, cinerary urns and other objects; most of the sites do not coincide with the distribution of *-ingas* names and J. Mc. N. Dodgson has concluded that the cemeteries mark still older settlements whose names are lost.[3] The related occupation sites remain undiscovered; very few, if any, survived into later times as villages or farms. These pagan cemeteries on the Downs raise more questions than they settle, for the Anglo-Saxon was seldom interested in the cultivation of the lighter soils. Their presence has been plausibly explained as the settlement of German federates amongst the Britons in late Roman times in advance of the folk migrations from the mid-fifth century. Such settlers may have received land allotments in

[3] J. Mc. N. Dodgson, 'The Significance of the Distribution of the English Place-name in *-ingas,-inga* in South East England', *Medieval Archaeology*, Vol. 10 (1966), pp. 1–29.

return for defending native farms, and later exacted tribute from the natives during a phase when, in R. H. Hodgkin's words, "they themselves were hill-dwellers before they cleared the land near the rivers and settled down to plough the heavy soils of the valleys".[4] It is perhaps significant that the cemeteries cluster most thickly between the Ouse and Cuckmere in a district remote from any sign of a villa-owning class. Some of the sites, such as Highdown Hill, are strategically placed to command the Channel.

The third element in the old kingdom of Sussex was the hinterland of Hastings. In its place-name vocabulary, its dispersed hamlet settlement and paucity of evidence concerning common fields, the district has strong affinities with Kent. The origin of these peculiarities seems to be the settlement of the area by the *Haestingas*, the tribal followers of *Haesta*. This name is still preserved in Hastings, a folk name, current before the creation of administrative units like the shire, hundred and rape, when the pattern of early settlement was still dominated by wild nature and other physical barriers. The *Haestingas* selected the dry land between the Romney and Pevensey marshes and, hemmed in by the sparsely inhabited forest inland, were able to preserve their identity within these natural frontiers even until the eleventh century. They have the distinction of being the only early English to make any significant inroads into the Wealden forest, so breaking its long and almost impenetrable obscurity. Even so, they mainly settled the coastal margins, particularly the heads of the then several valleys which were great inlets of the sea south of the upland known as the Battle Ridge. Only Brightling marks a colony well into the interior, a site on the natural highway of the Battle Ridge, probably a narrow belt of relatively open country that determined the movement of the colonists.

When the organisation of the inhabited space of Saxon

[4] R. H. Hodgkin, *A History of the Anglo-Saxons*, Vol. 1 (3rd edn., 1952), pp. 135–6.

Sussex emerges into view with the growing number of land charters from the eighth century onwards, it is revealed as one of remarkable complexity and distinctiveness. The most obvious characteristic is a conscious design in relation to the three main land resources, the arable and meadow, the sheep pasture, and the swine grazings. The English settler was equipped to deal with the heavier and richer soils of Sussex, and in his decided preference for the loam soils rather than the thin Chalk soils he confirmed evaluations made from at least the late Bronze Age onwards. This explains the striking symmetrical distribution of rural settlement at the foot of the Chalk escarpment and along the edge of the Lower Greensand, which since W. Topley's pioneer study a century ago, has become one of the commonplaces of Wealden geography.[5] This gives rise to the long and narrow strip-parish, comprising land suitable for cattle and swine grazing on the clay lowlands, the best arable near the site of the main settlement and sheep pasture on the downland. Topley observed perceptively that parishes in Chalk country invariably run up the escarpment to include downland, whereas plateau parishes on this formation rarely run down the escarpment to include the better arable and this supports the theory that the loam soils at the foot of the Chalk had become the main arable soils. It is still possible to reconcile this observation with the subsequent discoveries of pagan graves on the Chalk if we accept that these mark a military overlordship rather than an agricultural colonisation.

This orderly ground plan of settlement in southern Sussex, the outline of which has survived to this day, was paralleled by a systematic division of the great amount of uncolonised waste in the northern part of the old kingdom. By an ingenious system of land division most of the

5 W. Topley, 'On the Relation of Parish Boundaries in the South-East of England to Great Physical Features', *Journal of the Anthropological Institute*, Vol. 3 (1873), p. 32.

unsettled Weald was allotted to each of the manors between the forest and the sea in separate parcels located as directly northwards of the parent centre as was conveniently practicable and which interlock like the pieces of a jigsaw puzzle. This arrangement resulted in multiple estates with several detached outliers accessible from the more habitable coastal fringe only by the exercise of the ancient right of driving herds across the intervening land of the other manors.

The earliest record of this layout is a Saxon land charter of *c.* A.D. 675, relating to Stanmer on the Downs near Brighton which lists its outlying swine pastures in the present parishes of Lindfield, Ardingly and West Hoathly.[6] Other similar pre-Conquest documents permit the outline reconstruction of contemporary manorial topography. One of the most informative charters concerns the important manor of Washington which held appurtenant islands of pasture scattered over the breadth of the Sussex Weald, between ten and twenty miles from the headquarters on the verge of the Chalk above Worthing. In Kent such outlying pastures were termed *denns* (meaning 'swine pasture'), a name transferred to the settlements made later within them, to survive as the modern suffix *-den*. This word was little used in Sussex beyond the Kentish border; the equivalent term in west Sussex may have been the common suffix *-fold* (O.E. *falod*). These *-fold* names help to recall the ancient forest landscape for the word means staking off a clearing, the pioneer settler's first task towards making a home in backwoods.

The most conspicuous vestiges of this manorial organisation on the ground are the lines of natural trackways which developed owing to the separation of the outlying pastures from the principal centre (Fig. 5). Even a casual glance at the Ordnance Survey one-inch map will reveal the

[6] E. Barker, 'Sussex Anglo-Saxon Charters', *Suss. Arch. Colls.*, Vol. 86 (1947), pp. 85–90.

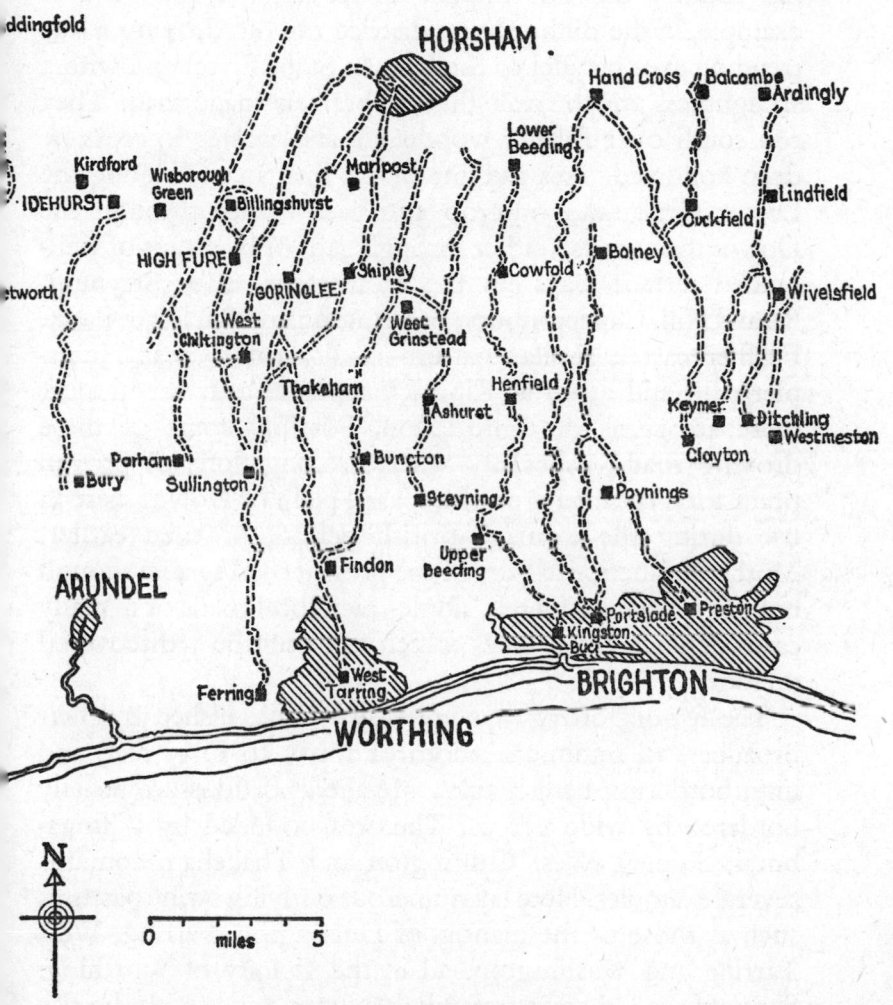

Fig. 5. Old droving roads.

closely-spaced pattern of sub-parallel roads on a north–south alignment. This pattern is particularly distinctive on the Weald Clay, where the physical configuration of the country did not impede direct communication. For example, in the Billingshurst district, the old droving roads trend on axes parallel to the Roman Stane Street and with a straightness which rivals that deliberately made road. They run south over former woodlands and wastes to cross by deep hollowed ways the line of the Roman road along the Lower Greensand outcrop and pass thence through the Downs to the coast, either through gaps or by means of well-graded terrace ways up the escarpment, as at Steyning, Round Hill, Chanctonbury, Storrington and Rackham Bank. Further east a similar pattern is discernible near Hurstpierpoint and again at Ripe where, as already mentioned, there are signs of centuriation. Possibly some of these droving roads, especially when prolongations of proven prehistoric trackways on the coastal plain or Downs were in use during the Romano-British period, or even earlier. Most still function as part of the present road system though not a few are now merely single-track local roads or in many cases derelict green lanes which can only be rediscovered on foot.

The former droveways are easily distinguished by their broadness (a minimum width of thirty to forty feet) and high bordering hedgebanks. Metalled portions are usually bordered by wide verges. The area bounded by Billingshurst, Shipley, West Chiltington and Thakeham contains several examples. Here lay numerous outlying swine pastures such as those of the manors of Durrington, Ferring, West Tarring and Washington, all in the vicinity of Worthing. Some of the old ways possibly lost importance with the rise of Horsham as a market town and the building of Knepp Castle, both of which were more conveniently served by the present A24 road. Whatever may be the reason, the old droveways which were probably the most direct routes between West Tarring and its outlier at Marlpost (a name perpetuated by a fragment of the remaining wood of this name) and that from Washington to the Crockhurst swine pastures in Horsham are only greenways for much of their length. A metalled stretch can be traced southwards as far as Green Street near Shipley ('the sheep clearing'). The continuation of the old track from this appropriately named settlement is a wide greenway, some six miles long, which aims for the Findon Gap through the Downs. Another interesting old droveway is the lane that links Amberley to Rackham, curves to avoid marshy ground in the Arun valley and then strikes for outliers formerly held by manors near Wisborough Green and Loxwood. The old crossing-point of the Arun used by this track has been superseded and the final section to Wisborough Green is a greenway. None of these old droveways, however, has yet been established archaeologically as being of Saxon or pre-Saxon origin, but circumstantial evidence is overwhelmingly in support of their early usage.

The infiltration into the Weald

It is hard to discern the sequence of events which led to the increasing pace of forest clearings in the woodland *denns* and the creation of new communities of woodland dwellers dispersed over the 'backwoods' of Sussex. Whence came the settlers, the means by which they prepared the land for cultivation, the extent of their reclamation and the nature of their fields are all matters about this major act of colonisation on which we know little. Nevertheless, suggestive hints are not entirely lacking, enabling us to visualise, if only dimly, the great achievement of taming parts of the claylands. In a concise summary of the course of events C. S. and C. S. Orwin suggested that

> the Weald men had settled at one time in the *denns* which were hollows or valleys in the woods, attracted to them by

the waters and shelter and by the ease of communication along the streams. From these centres began the attack by man upon nature and little by little as the population grew the woodland gave place to pasture and to cultivated land, the process continuing until none of it was left except in places associated with the wetter and more intractable soils.[7]

This assessment, though highly generalised and without precise indication in place and time, is essentially correct.

To obtain a more complete picture of this transformation we have to bring a variety of evidence to bear on the problem. Our answers may be gained in part from new archaeological techniques. Radio-carbon dating is expected to be one of the new fruitful lines of enquiry. It is very possible that in many *denns* the first exploitation of resources took the form of iron-mining, not agriculture. At present we do not know the extent to which the Saxons practised iron production in the Weald. Only three bloomeries have been subjected to radio-carbon analysis and one of these, at Long Gill in Mayfield, has been assigned to the period of the folk migrations. Further progress in this direction, which is dependent on suitably preserved charcoal, will greatly extend our knowledge of this aspect of the Saxon economy.

Another important aspect of the evolving Saxon countryside in the Weald is the antiquity of hedgebanks and belts of timber called 'shaws' which still commonly serve as field boundaries. It is not intended to anticipate the discussion of their origin, raised in the following chapter, but it must be stressed that the common assumption that all the older fields were defined in the first reclamation from the wilderness has yet to be tested. There is no reason to doubt that the Weald was individually cleared and parcelled into minute fields, individually farmed, at the height of the

[7] C. S. and C. S. Orwin, *The Open Fields* (1938), p. 16.

forest clearance in the thirteenth and fourteenth centuries. Nevertheless, it is by no means certain that this was the standard practice in remoter times; there are some grounds for suggesting that in the earliest English settlements in the Adur basin the land was communally farmed on the basis of large open fields which were not permanently divided into individually held closes until late medieval or more recent times. The evidence, slender as it is, will be discussed later for there is no contemporary Saxon source that can lead to certain proof. It does, however, underline the desirability of taking soil samples from old ground surfaces beneath ancient earthworks in the Weald to determine the extent to which they have been erected on formerly cultivated ground, woodland or pasture. Similar work is desirable at several places bearing woodland names compounded with the Old English element *-esce* or *-erse*, meaning 'corn stubbles', such as the modern Hazelhurst (in Ticehurst) and the unidentified *Birchen Ersh* in Cowfold,[8] meaning a corn field overgrown with hazel and birch respectively.

To what date the initial clearing is to be assigned we are at present ignorant. The names may preserve a primitive phase of shifting agriculture in the Weald preceding a phase of fixed fields. The archaeologist may eventually take up the problem to which the place-names can do no more than hint. For the time being we must not necessarily assume that the transformation of wood to individually held farms was the result of a single operation. The possibility is that around the old iron-working sites where there was a likely continuity of occupation from the Romano-British period, the primeval countryside underwent several phases of change of which we are at present familiar only with the last. It is by a combination of archaeological techniques, supplementing literary and other sources, that the story of the changing landscape of this difficult period will eventually

[8] A. Mawer and F. N. Stenton, *The Place-Names of Sussex*, English Place-Name Society, Vols. 6, 7 (1929–30), p. 252.

come to be written. Time, however, is short, and one is reminded of Beresford's comment that "if change moves fast across the countryside its historians must keep pace . . ."

From these speculations we must now turn to more positive proof of the developing countryside. A number of Saxon land charters surviving only as medieval copies, but possessing a generally accepted aura of authenticity, are amongst the earliest title deeds to landed property extant. They are concerned with boundaries rather than with rural economy or tenure, yet by implication they throw a vivid light on settlement and the extent of land improvement. Some of the earliest make references to actual habitation in the deepest recesses of the Weald, and one dated 765 provides circumstantial evidence of the earliest recorded Wealden settlement.[9] This relates to the *welinga stane*; 'the stone of the stream-dwellers', probably to be identified with the celebrated natural rock formation known as 'Big upon Little' near Stonelands in West Hoathly. Also mentioned is 'the barley clearing' and 'the clearing of Citta's people' (now the farms of Philpotts and Chiddingly in West Hoathly) and 'Wifel's open land' (the nucleus of modern Wivelsfield parish) and *Walcanstede* (Walstead farm in Lindfield). It is noteworthy that although both *welinga stane* and *Walcanstede* are enumerated in the charter as swine pastures of Stanmer, the place-names imply that some colonisation had already been effected there by the eighth century.

From other Anglo-Saxon charters we can obtain a glimpse of well articulated Wealden estates. A document assigned to A.D. 772 classified lands in Bexhill as 'inland' and 'outland' in the Kentish manner, the 'inland' being the most intensively farmed land of the lord and his tenants. Some landmarks mentioned as bounding 'inland' are still readily identifiable natural features in the present landscape, like Beda's spring (Bedwell field), Cooden cliff (partly eroded) and woods called Shortwood and Kewhurst. We can also

9 E. Barker, *op. cit.*, p. 87.

form a shrewd idea as to the location of the 'old boundary dyke' and the 'road bridge' (Fig. 6a). These landmarks bounded a compact block of land on a tolerably firm and fertile site just to the west of the present town of Bexhill. The 'outland' (an outlying dependency of the parent settlement) was the marsh and low-lying ground at Barnhorne, a little further west. Its territorial boundary ran mostly along streams and we can still trace them on the ground with little difficulty (Fig. 6b). The information as to roads, ditches, dykes and clearings on the 'outland' of Barnhorne leave us in no doubt that in the eighth century parts of this estate had already become permanently farmed and settled.

Not all the Wealden swine pastures were being cleared for farming as early as the eighth century. This is made plain by a charter relating to a 'grove of woodland' called Hazelhurst in Ticehurst. This property, bounded mainly by streams, can be largely identified from the landmarks given in the charter (Fig. 7). When granted to the Archbishop of Canterbury in 1018 it appears to have been still part of an extensive forest area occupying much of Ticehurst and Wadhurst.

These Anglo-Saxon charters of Sussex are of immense importance because whereas for most parts of England Domesday Book provides some idea of the settled land by the end of the eleventh century, the Sussex folios are disappointingly vague. This is because their data do not separately enumerate any colonists in the outlying Wealden properties or manors based on the coastal plain or at the foot of the Downs. Consequently, a map drawn from Domesday information misleadingly represents the Weald as almost empty, apart from the southern half of Hastings Rape, which is penetrated by tide-water and was the early home of the *Haestingas*. In one respect, however, Domesday gives a flood of light regarding eleventh-century Wealden settlement. By a fortunate circumstance some estates in

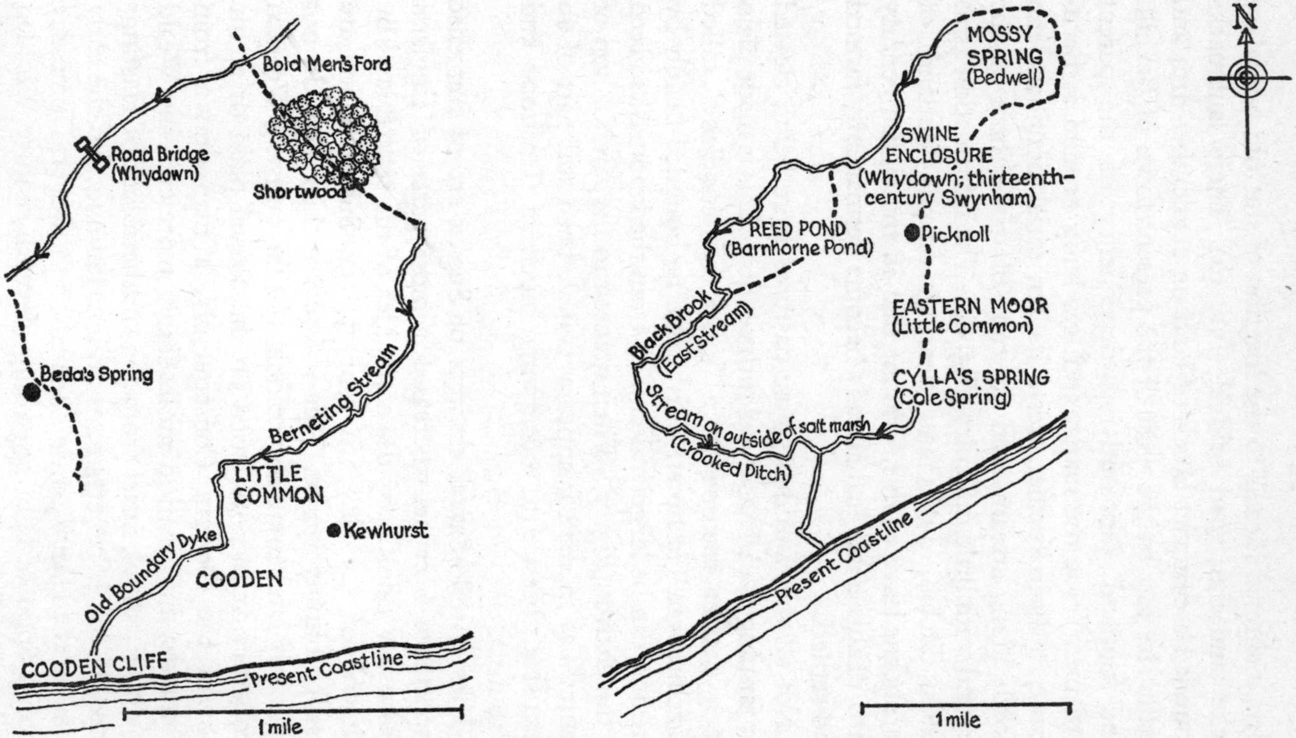

Fig. 6. The boundaries of early Saxon estates in Bexhill.

the north of Hastings Rape had been detached from their former manors in the Eastbourne and Lewes district and separately distinguished. These appear to have been isolated farms, thinly scattered over the bleak Forest Ridges. Some had not been previously assessed for taxation, and were probably recent clearings. The presence of new farms so early in this relatively unfavourable environment has never been fully explained. L. F. Salzman imaginatively suggested "that at some uncertain date claims in the Hastings backwoods were allotted to such of the lords of the Pevensey triangle as would take them up and that this forest district was deliberately colonised".[10] This hypothesis, though illuminating, does not explain why the Pevensey manors chose to settle their colonists in such distant wastes when most, if not all, had extensive and more favourably situated forest lands nearer at hand. The clue may be a geological one. The presence of sporadic ironstone situated at the base of the Wadhurst Clay may have induced prospectors from the Pevensey manors to work eastwards along the ridges into an almost empty Hastings hinterland and take up land on the strength of their ore discoveries.

Further information concerning Saxon settlement in the Sussex Weald is given by implication in the early monastic cartularies of Sele and Lewes Priories. It is only from these sources that we learn that a church and cultivated land existed at Shipley in 1081 and that churches had been founded in the northern parts of Lewes and Pevensey Rapes at Ardingly, Balcombe, Chiddingly, Cuckfield, East Grinstead, Slaugham, West Hoathly and Wivelsfield before the end of the eleventh century. When account is also taken of the church of Worth (the largest and most elaborate of the Saxon churches of Sussex, but unrecorded in Domesday) and the Saxon or very early Norman architectural features of the existing churches at Horsted Keynes and Bolney, it

[10] L. F. Salzman, 'The Rapes of Sussex', *Suss. Arch. Colls.*, Vol. 72 (1931), p. 23.

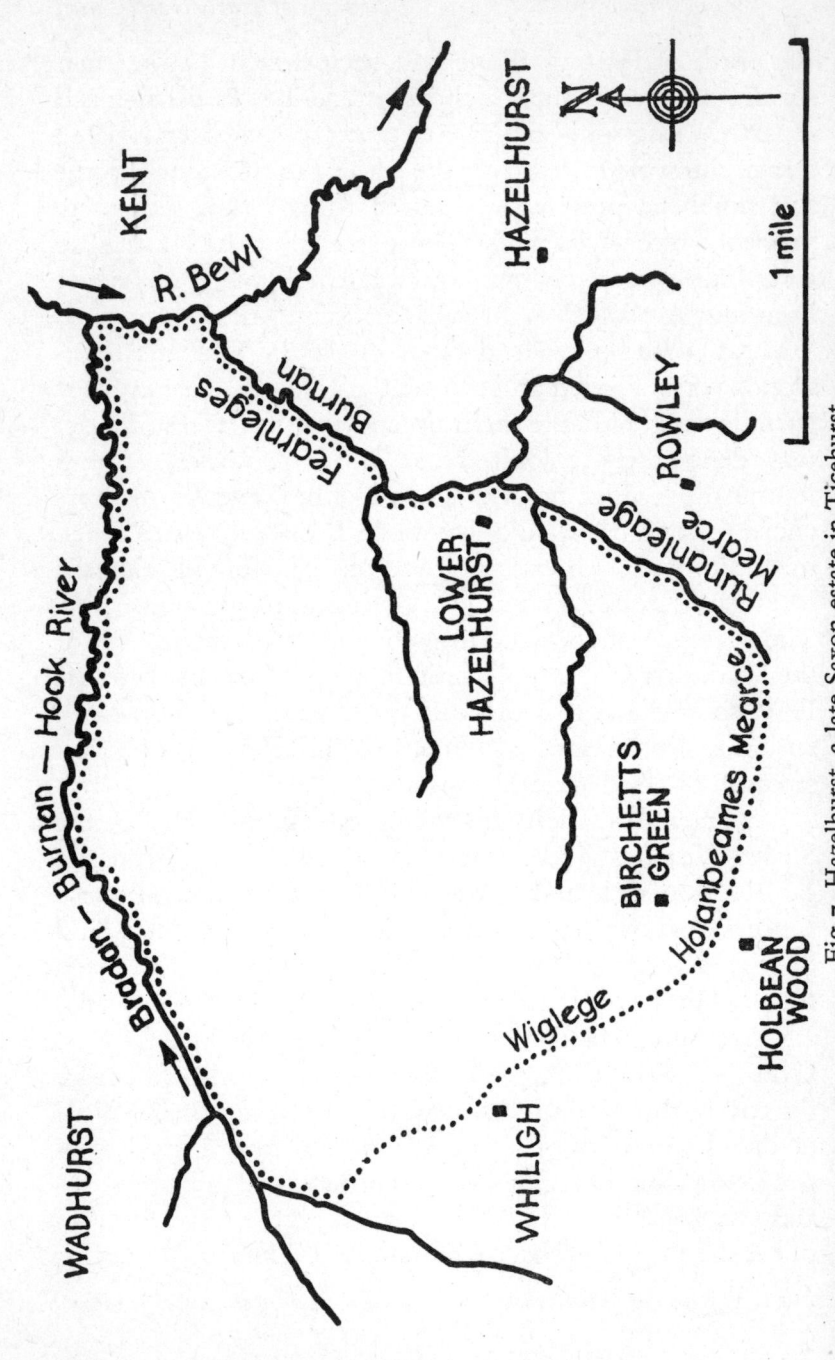

Fig 7. Hazelhurst, a late Saxon estate in Ticehurst.

seems clear that a considerable and well-distributed cultivation and attendant population must have existed in these
parts by about 1100 to sustain the parochial organisation
which had already developed there.

Another decisive impression of the considerable extent
and great age of much settlement in the Sussex Weald is
provided by the testimony of its place-names. The first
authoritative study of Sussex place-names was published
more than forty years ago, since when the interpretation
of linguistic material has acquired an ever-increasing
reliability and a cascade of new and unstudied Sussex
names has accumulated from local deeds not available to
earlier scholars. General conclusions regarding Sussex
place-names may therefore need modification in the light
of the reinterpretations and a more comprehensive survey
which may be possible in the future. Nevertheless, there
seems no reason to question the convincing evidence, not
fully appreciated until the publication of *The Place-Names of
Sussex* in 1929-30,[11] and even now given insufficient weight,
of the effect of the isolation of the South Saxons in preserving archaic word-structures of personal names. Many of
these names became unfashionable even by the ninth and
tenth centuries but, having been attached to places, are still
preserved, in a fossil form, in the local nomenclature of the
Sussex Weald. Such names relating to habitation-sites as
Ninfield, probably meaning in Old English 'at the open
land taken in for cultivation', Bromhill, Cleeve Axe and
Platnix in the extreme east of the county, derived from
South Saxon words for plum, ford and cornfield, as well as
many others, all testify to the great antiquity of some
Wealden settlement.

The cumulative evidence we have examined supports
R. Lennard's salutary reminder given in his *Rural England*
(*1086–1135*) that "we must not be too ready to fill the
Domesday map with imagined woodland and marsh".

[11] A. Mawer and F. N. Stenton, *op. cit.*

The origin, number and size of the pioneering settlements amidst the Wealden clearings, and their economic and social conditions are still shrouded in mystery. It seems, however, that settlement was much less sporadic and localised than has previously been assumed. The general advance of cultivation over woods, heaths and marshes assigned to the Norman period, and often cited in vivid contrast to earlier times, may have its basis not in actuality but in the slightness of the Saxon evidence. The old view, as expressed for example by J. H. Round, that by 1066 the forest had not been opened up for settlement "except in a few scattered spots"[12] is now in need of substantial modification. There is now every reason to believe that the new races from overseas were beginning to clear the Wealden woodland in earnest two centuries or more before Domesday so inadequately records their achievements. On the Low Weald of west Sussex the Saxons had probably occupied all the better-drained soils of a lighter texture, which are a common feature. This would have brought under cultivation large islands around the church and village sites, leaving the remoter waste until after the Norman Conquest. In the High Weald the Saxon population was probably sparser and confined to groups of farms along the natural highways running along the lower ridges. This, as we shall see, still left to swine and deer immense wastes reserved for the support of the rapidly increasing population after the Norman Conquest, but even in this difficult pioneer region the taming and colonising of the primeval wild has made considerable headway before 1066.

Early English settlement patterns and the question of continuity

In discussing some of the turning points in the evolution of the present Sussex landscape it has already been suggested that certain elements of the countryside possibly had their

[12] J. H. Round, *The Commune of London and Other Studies* (1899), pp. 1–27.

origins in remote prehistory or in the Romano-British period. In order to reach an assessment, however tentative, of the landscape consequences of the English conquest we must now consider in some detail how far the agrarian ground plan existing on the eve of the invasions was subsequently modified by the Anglo-Saxon settlers. This is a fundamental question because, as already demonstrated, the main English occupation of Sussex was located in areas which had already reached a relatively advanced stage of economic and social development, and must have possessed a territorial organisation, whether based on hillfort, villa or upland farm, which had evolved in the distant past. To what extent the English obliterated this pattern, or adapted it for their own usage, is one of the most enigmatic problems relating to the evolution of the Sussex countryside which still awaits solution. Sussex is one of those parts of lowland England where the indisputable intensity of the English settlement and the abandonment of the Romano-British hill farms were pictured as two aspects of a cataclysm which overwhelmed the old social order and the pattern of the rural landscape. Given the widest and most lasting currency was J. N. L. Myres' view that the English conquest "involved a complete break with the agricultural past".[13] Such a view represents a fair summing up of the evidence available in the first half of this century and the nature of the interpretations placed upon it. In recent years the whole question has been re-opened by fresh evidence and new ideas about the course of the invasions and English society. As a result several scholars have come to question the older view of the effects of the English conquest and to stress the continuity which seems to exist in the pattern of rural settlement in several parts of lowland England.

The present countryside contains so many ancient forms of rural community and puzzling features of early territorial

[13] J. N. L. Myres *in* R. G. Collingwood and J. N. L. Myres, *Roman Britain and the English Settlement* (2nd edn., 1937), p. 441.

organisation that it has long evoked discussion, showing no sign of abatement. Little research, however, has yet been done at local level, where alone solutions will be reached. It is not, therefore, the purpose of this chapter to present conclusions but simply to identify some of the anomalies in the settlement pattern which deserve further investigation. Much of the old pattern survives in the present landscape. Still more of its character is revealed by Yeakell and Gardner's map of southern Sussex, published between 1778 and 1783, on a scale of two inches to a mile, the earliest topographical map of the county.

Considering now rural settlements in the present landscape, using the eighteenth-century map for parts obliterated by modern housing, they begin to unlock answers, or at the very least make us deeply question the older views as to their origin. One of the fundamental characteristics of the Champion landscape is the rarity of the large centrally placed village with lands which by process of extension reached the utmost confines of its parish. More typical is the agricultural grouping which has lasted for many centuries in the parish of West Firle, east of Lewes. Here the big nucleated village of Firle is the 'head' of the parish which also comprised no less than four hamlets—Charleston, Compton, Heighton and Preston, each with their own separate common fields, two of which places are separately recorded in Domesday and the others have early place-name suffixes indicating an Anglo-Saxon origin.

This intermixture of hamlets and larger villages is often also associated with a third element, the single farms. Many of those on the Downs have never been more than single farms and are so distinguished in Domesday, such as several in the parishes of Binsted, Falmer, the Mardens and Up-waltham. Locksash Farm in the Mardens is one of these; its name in Old English means 'Locc's corn stubbles'. On the coastal plain of south-west Sussex there is also a marked dispersion of hamlets and isolated farms, many of ancient origin.

Clues to the origin of some of the settlement features of Champion Sussex may be found in the tenurial and topographical structure of the great ecclesiastical and lay estates. When St Wilfrid was endowed with lands in the Selsey peninsula by the king of the South Saxons in the seventh century, the 'inland' was worked by a force of 250 slaves. These, with other bondmen, dwelt at various named settlements. These can be identified with existing places such as Shripney, Bersted, North Bersted, Crimsham and the Mundhams. When this estate moved into the clearer light of the thirteenth century the compact fields of the demesne were worked by villeins and cottars dwelling in several of the appendant communities named in the seventh-century charter and were mostly hamlets. For the large royal manor of Bosham no charter evidence has survived but an identical pattern of small dispersed groups of servile cultivators is traceable from the early Middle Ages. Place-names help to confirm the antiquity of the topographical and social basis. Walton is considered to be derived from the Old English *wealh* and *tun*, meaning the vill of the native Britons. Here, apparently, the humble natives who supplied most of the labour had their own quarters. Creed is another hamlet with a most interesting social basis. Its name means a garden or small enclosure and this and the absence of larger fields here in the Saxon and medieval period thus seems to confirm the ancient existence there of a servile society.

The great Saxon estates in south-west Sussex therefore seem to have never comprised large central villages but contain many dispersed hamlets from which land-holders performed labour services on the demesnes. Similar patterns, as we have seen, exist elsewhere in the Champion but little Saxon documentary evidence for them survives. In this case the present landscape and medieval documents help to clarify their origin. Particularly instructive is the settlement pattern traceable in Ringmer, on the Archbishop's manor of South Malling (Fig. 8). Here four ancient hamlets are all sited with reasonable symmetry about Ringmer, a straggling village around its green. These settlements, Ashton, Middleham, Norlington and Wellingham, were hamlets each constituting a separate *borgh* and with their own common fields. By contrast, Ringmer had only closes and gardens. This indicates that the hamlets were the primary settlements and the village was the result of secondary colonisation.

The unusual importance of the hamlet is thus clearly demonstrable in Sussex. It plainly existed even in early times in a palimpsest which has never been completely deciphered, and it seems to have had a strong servile element in ancient times. The hamlets are frequently grouped in what, for convenience, are known as multiple estates. These generally comprised lands, as we have seen, on the periphery of the Weald and also within it, forming a little archipelago of estates under the jurisdiction of a single lord. Even the remoter land-holders of a multiple estate, as already mentioned, were not exempt from the labour services at headquarters. The origin of this distinctive form of territorial organisation is still shrouded in mystery and explanations as to date are conflicting. In the light of current opinion it is interesting to recall the remarkable prescience of W. D. Peckham, a local antiquary, who in 1925 regarded the hamlets near Chichester as survivals of Celtic *clachans* and discovered that some of the fields were measured in units similar to Roman *jugera*.[14] The multiple estates of Kent and Sussex, with their attendant hamlets and institutions, were the subject of an elegantly written monograph in 1933 by J. E. A. Jolliffe, who pronounced them Jutish and, in essence, derived from the Rhineland.[15] In 1934 Myres noted the similarity of the multiple estate and its institutions to the organisation in Celtic countries and in

[14] W. D. Peckham, 'Customary Acres in South-West Sussex', *Suss. Arch. Colls.*, Vol. 66 (1925), p. 155.
[15] J. E. A. Jolliffe, *Pre-Feudal England: the Jutes* (1933).

Plate 7 The hillfort of Cissbury Ring viewed from the south-west. The dimpled ground marks the Neolithic and Bronze Age flint mines. Traces of Roman-British and later fields are observable in the north-east corner. See p. 53.

Plate 8 The Iron Age ramparts of Caburn, above Beddingham, were probably a defence of a single farm. See p. 53.

Plate 9 Prehistoric field system on the Downs above New Shoreham, clearly detected from the air yet virtually erased on the ground by recent ploughing. The ancient trackway curving to the top centre cuts across the circular rampart of Thundersbarrow, an Iron Age hillfort. The small enclosures to the south of this hillfort were associated with a 'street village' settlement in the Romano-British period. See p. 63.

Plate 10 The little church of Coombes, folded into the shapely coombe which gives the settlement its name, serves a hamlet which has shrunk to little more that a farm. It is a symbol of the small size and poverty of many downland settlements in the past. See p. 92.

Plate 11 Sompting church with its Saxon tower and helm roof. See p. 92.

Plate 12 Although this aerial view of Wadhurst shows shaws in retreat, the small irregular and wood-bounded fields persist sufficiently to convey the atmosphere of the medieval pioneering scene. See p. 96.

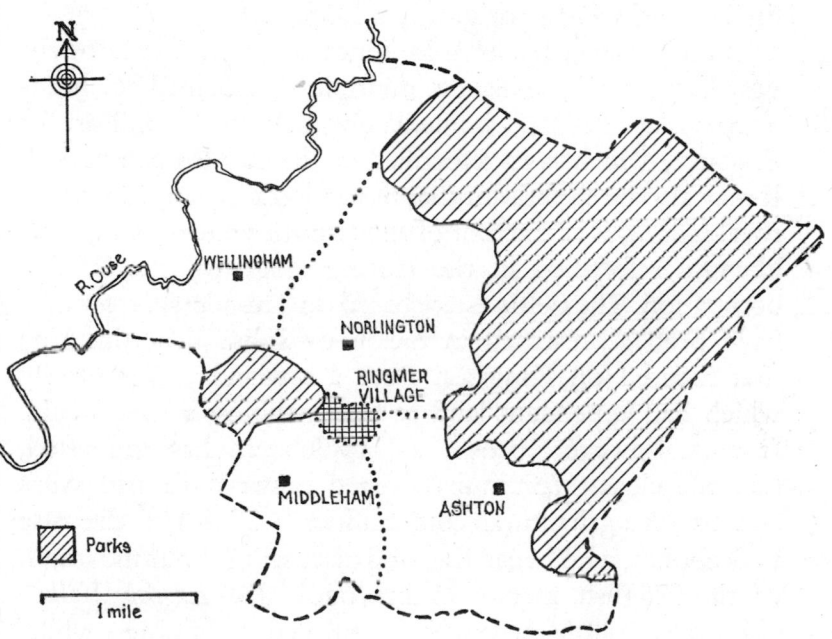

Fig. 8. Rural settlement in Ringmer parish.

words which have a prophetic ring today, remarked "can we be sure that he [Jolliffe] has not taken us back to something still older than the Jutes to the Celtic organisation?"[16] In 1961 G. R. G. Jones, following his studies of settlement patterns in early Wales, suggested that the multiple estate and hamlet structure of settlement evolved in Britain during the millennium before the advent of the Romans, often on the basis of a focus, originally a hillfort.[17]

There is much strength in Jones' argument. One of the very largest of the Saxon multiple estates had its headquarters at Findon, immediately below the hillfort of Cissbury, which was refortified in the sub-Roman period. It may also be significant that Saxon Beddingham, a notable royal manor, is at the foot of the Caburn hillfort, which was likewise refortified in the closing stages of the Roman occupation. The Celtic estate based on Thundersbarrow may have been represented in Saxon or subsequent times by that focused on Kingston Buci, a lowland village nearby which had appendant land at Shermanbury in the Weald. It may, however, prove, as Applebaum has suggested, that the closest continuity existed between Roman villas and Saxon agricultural communities.[18] If this is the case F. Seebohm, who began the long discussion about the origin of the English manor in his book *The English Village Community* (1883), may well be proved right. Meanwhile, everything we can decipher from the present pattern of rural settlement in Champion Sussex warns us against accepting without question the older view that the lineaments of the present countryside may be regarded as a legacy of the Saxons. To do otherwise could be to mistake a mask for a face.

---

[16] J. N. L. Myres, *Archaeological Journal*, Vol. 90 (1933), p. 159.

[17] G. R. G. Jones, 'Settlement Patterns in Anglo-Saxon England', *Antiquity*, Vol. 35 (1961), pp. 221–32.

[18] S. Applebaum, 'The Pattern of Settlement in Roman Britain', *Agricultural History Review*, Vol. 11 (1963), pp. 1–14.

Saxon churches

Apart from woodland clearance, another great legacy of the Saxons in the present landscape is their church building. Although the South Saxons resisted Christianity longer than any other English kingdom, they established churches in the See of Selsey more rapidly than in many other parts of the country during the later Saxon period. By 1086, even in the Weald, the parish church had already become characteristic of the Sussex village. More than twenty-five churches survive with substantial Saxon remains. The great majority display little of the more highly developed style of Saxon architecture, such as the use of 'long and short' quoins, double-splay windows and the embellishment of pilaster strips. Instead they are modest little structures built of local materials which rarely included good building stone and hence there is little ornament. Flint, chalk rubble and any other materials which came to hand, such as Roman bricks and tiles, were chiefly used. Stone, which was only roughly dressed, was used sparingly. In coastal churches this stone was mainly drawn from the foreshore of the Selsey peninsula where freshwater limestones in the Bracklesham Beds could be exploited easily.

The sites of the first churches were often determined by the continuous use of a place for religious and other community purposes over many previous centuries. A good example is provided by Berwick church, an unpretentious edifice almost dwarfed by a mound of great size in the churchyard which may well be a prehistoric burial place. A sepulchral urn was found beneath the foundations of the church of Arlington, which has much Roman brick and tile in its fabric. Its is probably not a coincidence that the church stands on the site of an important Roman building and the base of a Roman arch lies beneath that of the chancel. The graveyard of East Blatchington, amongst several others, has yielded evidence of pagan burials. A number of Saxon churches appear to stand on barrows, such as Southease and Piddinghoe. At Chithurst the church is erected on an even more formidable mound. Many of the churchyards surrounding the earliest churches were originally circular and ringed by a bank and ditch, usually later topped by a wall or fence. At Coombes, which has a primitive little church of about the eleventh century lying against the steep hillside, this original simple bank still survives, quite unchanged. At few other places can one still re-capture the Saxon scene to quite the same extent (Plate 10).

Of all the Saxon churches in Sussex that of Sompting, near Worthing, is the most remarkable and important (Plate 11). The main survival is the four-gabled tower, crowned by a shingled helm roof, now the only example of its kind in England, but which is still to be found in the Rhineland, the source of its architectural inspiration. It is a symbol of the strength of the continental cultural links which Sussex was establishing, probably through trade in corn and wool, in the tenth and eleventh centuries. The tower has none of the crudity usually associated with Saxon work. It is splendidly tall and slim, and although simply designed, is a delicate and elegant example of the more inspired ecclesiastical architecture which stemmed from the Carolingian renaissance. Distinguished from this church and the other Sussex churches with substantial Saxon work, such as Alfriston, Bishopstone, Bosham, Botolphs, Jevington and Old Shoreham, is that of Worth, lying deep in the Weald. Its large scale and boldness, its apsed chancel and characteristic motif of pilaster strips make it likely that it was the work of Surrey rather than Sussex masons.

Making as notable a contribution to landscape history, if not so architecturally significant, are the other simple little churches of about the eleventh century in which Sussex abounds. Such unpretentious buildings lie in many down-land hollows and are thick in the Greensand country. The churches of East Dean and West Dean near Eastbourne, Selham, Stopham and Sullington come readily to mind. Several are to this day aisle-less and lacking in towers. No single explanation for their remarkable survival can be offered but an important factor was the changing demo-graphic trend in the Middle Ages. They tend to prevail where village communities did not greatly expand after Domesday and many suffered dwindling congregations and increasing poverty during the agrarian recession of the fourteenth and fifteenth centuries. The presence of so much eleventh-century and earlier church building in Sussex is therefore a symptom of important social and natural pro-cesses operating in a distant past of which account needs to be taken by the landscape historian.

SELECT BIBLIOGRAPHY

Fisher, E. A. *The Saxon Churches of Sussex* (1970).
Poole, M. 'The Domesday Book Churches of Sussex', *Suss. Arch. Colls.*, Vol. 87 (1948), pp. 29–76.
Victoria County History, *Sussex*, Vol. 1 (1905), Vol 2. (1907).

4. The medieval imprint (1100–1500)

The landscape of woodland clearance

THE SUSSEX LANDSCAPE was most actively in the making in the twelfth and thirteenth centuries. Population was increasing appreciably, perhaps even spectacularly. Medieval peasants were more capable of reclaiming waste than improving the productivity of existing tillage so each human mouth meant more trees to grub, more marsh to drain, more heath to improve. Simultaneously, increasing population fostered trade and industry and this created new market towns and seaports. The most fundamental changes in the nature of man's surroundings were caused by the several generations of unceasing and progressive endeavour in taming and colonising the remaining cover of forest and marsh which gave way to a beautiful ordered pattern of fields, farms and villages. This creation of a landscape shaped by man from the primitive wilderness of the Weald unfolds a story of achievement without parallel in medieval England. Furthermore, it is still one of the most completely recognisable of the early English countrysides.

The year 1348 marks the most important watershed in the Sussex landscape before 1914. After 1348, little more virgin woodland remained to fall to the forester's axe; hardly any new hamlets or villages and very few farmsteads have since been added to the landscape and not a single new town was founded between the thirteenth and the eighteenth centuries. From 1750 roads, canals, and railways, it is true, opened up the Sussex countryside, but the greatest impact of modern transport on the landscape has been felt since the end of the First World War. In fact, the only period of change in the face of Sussex corresponding in its intensity to that of the twelfth and thirteenth centuries is that of the present. In examining the medieval appearance of the land, therefore, we are getting to the roots of the traditional Sussex countryside, that most English of landscapes. One word of caution must be sounded. As we have seen, although evidence of rural change is fragmentary before 1100 we cannot assume that this is proof of its unimportance. We must constantly bear in mind that we are now considering the closing stages of a drama beginning in remote times and perceptibly gaining in impetus from the eighth century.

When detailed manorial rentals survive, as for Rother-field in the High Weald, it is possible to assess the pace of woodland clearance. At Domesday this huge manor was credited with only four demesne plough-teams and fourteen villeins, each with a plough, which suggests that they held separate farms; in addition, there were six bordars (poorer peasants) who did not have their own ploughs. By 1346 this total of twenty land-holders had risen to no less than 294, an increase attributable partly to the sub-division of older holdings but mainly to the creation of new ones on freshly cleared ground. A similar great increase in land-holders occurred on the Archbishop of Canterbury's manor of South Malling, which stretched as a great corridor from the edge of Lewes north-east to Lamberhurst, now in Kent, but originally in Sussex. The increase in its number of villeins and freeholders assimilated waste during the twelfth and thirteenth centuries to the extent of several thousand acres (Fig. 9). Changes of a similar order took place in neighbouring manors of the Sussex High Weald. On the

Low Weald of east Sussex the frontier of settlement was pushed over the flat clay levels from the villages along the edge of the Downs. In the west Sussex Low Weald, where Saxon colonisation had been considerable, it was the more outlying woodlands which now began to retreat.

The clearing techniques of the first Wealden farmers have contributed much to the evolution of the contemporary Sussex landscape. The most distinctive feature of the Wealden landscape shaped by its pioneering medieval farmers is the patchwork of wood-bounded fields which still exist locally. The strips of wood bounding fields are known as shaws. Similar wide borders of wood were called *rewes* on the Low Weald of west Sussex. The singular absence of narrow, crooked hedgerows in areas where the original field boundaries persist, distinguishes the field pattern in the Sussex Weald from that of other English districts enclosed directly from the wild. The shaws frequently attain two rods (thirty-three feet) in width and comprise standing deciduous trees, hazel and hedge-maple, as well as the rich variety of shrubs and plants characteristic of ancient field boundaries today (Plate 12).

Considering their scenic importance, the shaws have attracted surprisingly little attention since William Marshall[1] and Arthur Young lamented their baleful effects on crops. In fact, the shaws provide evidence both for the nature of the new-won farmland and for the prevailing social and economic conditions which controlled the lives of the first woodland settlers. Marshall attributed this local custom (as distinct from the usual practice in wooded districts of clearing up to a narrow line of bushes or underwood) to the exceptionally large nursery of trees needed by Wealden farms virtually isolated by the execrable roads during winter. This may be one explanation for the practice of leaving shaws. Also, however, in the past, when shaws were more carefully tended than now, their trees and shrubs were

[1] William Marshall, *The Economy of the Southern Counties*, Vol. 2 (1798).

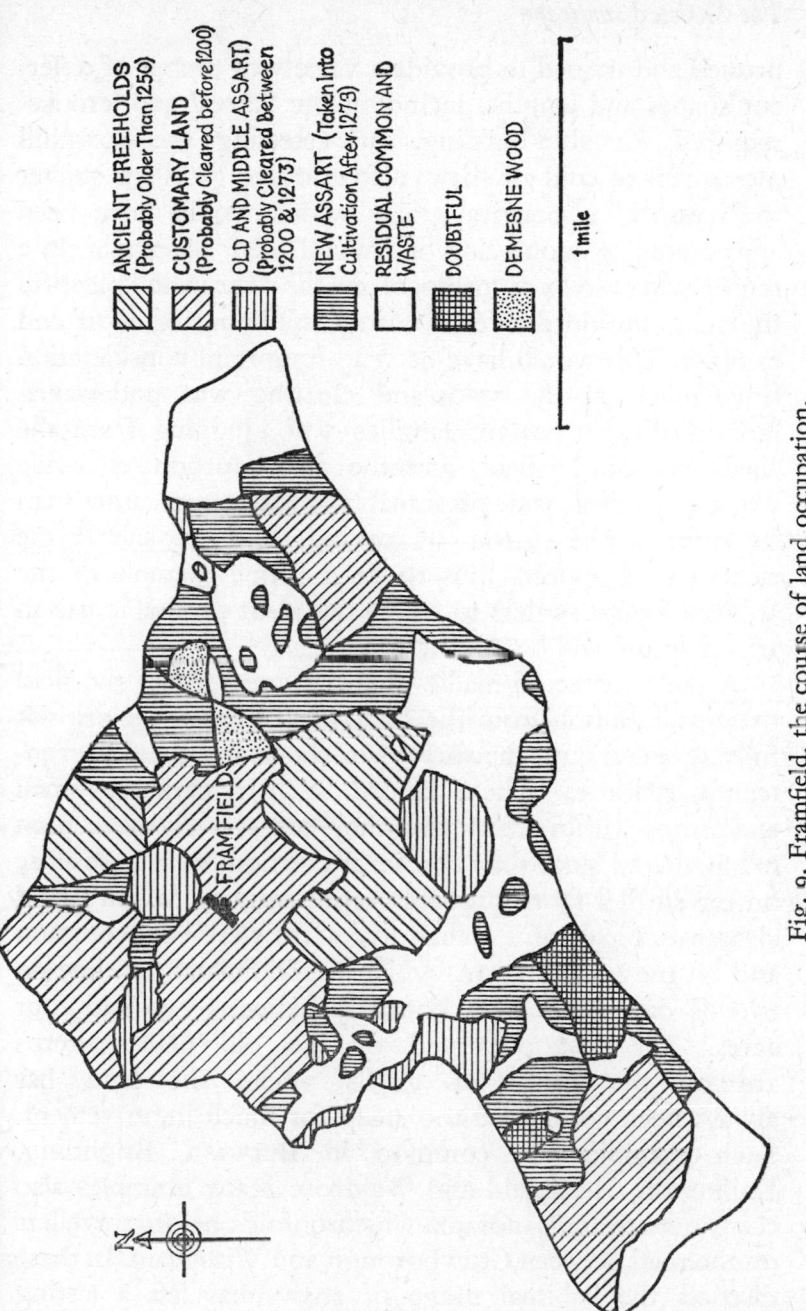

Fig. 9. Framfield, the course of land occupation.

pruned and trained to provide a variety of timber of different shapes and lengths, including the 'knees' and 'crooks' required for ship-building. By arresting the downhill movement of cold air shaws also afforded excellent shelter to livestock, a practical point which would have been appreciated by pioneering backwoodsmen. Moreover, in a region where soil was mediocre and land cheap and plentiful the shaw provided a fence with a minimum of effort and expense. This would have been an important consideration since much of the woodland clearing was undertaken individually by peasant families who, judging from the small size of the fields and the disproportionately wide wooded borders, were presumably stock-rearers rather than cultivators. The custom of leaving shaws to shelter the cleared land appears thus to be a prime example of the ability of early settlers to assess the most profitable use to which land could be put.

In the absence of medieval maps and terriers the field patterns resulting from the clearance of the waste are not fully revealed until the surveys of the sixteenth and seventeenth centuries. These record such remarkably small enclosures within shaws that they can scarcely have been much altered since their medieval creation, each little close on the smaller farms probably representing a season's land clearance. Fields of less than five acres were very common and on the smaller farms, which predominated, as they do to this day, fields were normally between two and four acres. The best preserved of the old field patterns are on the flanks of ghylls where the land has always been considered too steep for much improvement. Such examples are common in Burwash, Brightling, Dallington, Heathfield and Waldron. Many examples also contribute to the panorama which unfolds before travellers on the road between Crowborough and Withyham. In these districts the habitual usage of shaws has left a lasting impression of the ancient Wealden forest on the face of the present landscape, for to this day many fields have the appearance of woodland clearings.

One locality retaining much of its earlier aspect of a medieval clearing lies south-west of Mayfield, a beautiful hill-top village of medieval and sixteenth-century half-timbered houses overlooking the remote watershed of the rivers Ouse and Rother. In this deeply secluded pocket of the High Weald, where a tangle of narrow lanes and bridleways still preserve its air of quietness and mystery, are the scattered farms called Reed (a name derived from the Middle English *ridde*, meaning to grub trees)—Great and Little Broad Reed, Stile Reed and Wood Reed Farms. These were created by pioneers who took up successive grants of assart land from the reeve of the Archbishop of Canterbury's manor of South Malling and carved steep fields out of the wild during the thirteenth century. Seventeenth century developments helped to compose the present mine pits in the woods, hop-growing (so creating the need for the picturesque oast houses) and the farmhouse re-building which added tile-hung and weather-boarded fronts. Nevertheless, the rural ground plan with its thickly timbered shaws, wayside hazel coppice, greenways bordered by marl pits, and small fields sloping away to the humble, unregarded, farmhouses almost lost to sight amidst trees in the hollows is, in essence, the work of the Age of Clearing. That such unspoiled traditional countryside should survive within forty-five miles of central London is one of many unexpected delights of the Sussex High Weald.

The traditional sowing of tall trees in shaws or along the hedgerows furnishes the open park-like landscape which is so much of the beauty of Sussex. The oak is the typical tree of the Wealden scene. Heavy and handsome elms shelter farmhouse and village but the oak has pride of place in hedgerow, wood and coppice. This best known and most graceful of our native trees was indigenous to the stiff clays, growing densely on the broad levels of the Low Weald. For

centuries oak was planted to provide ship-building timber, beams for church and farmhouses, shingles for the church spires breaking through the trees, bark for tanning and acorn mast for swine. When as many as 2000 prime oaks were needed to build a single first-rate ship of the line in the eighteenth century, oak was profusely laid down on every Wealden farm. The Weald Clay formation stood so thick with them that early geologists called this 'Oak-tree Clay'. Until the recent past an oak was planted for every one felled. Most of the present standing trees were sown before their decline in economic value and as one by one they come crashing down in November gales we can expect fewer to be replaced. In this way the Wealden landscape will lose much of its distinctive charm and one more memory of the Wealden forest. For the present, the traveller between Hailsham, Horsham and Midhurst is never out of sight of Kipling's

> huge oaks and old, the which we hold
> No more than Sussex weed.

Punctuating the hedgerows a crown's distance apart, some as tall as sixty to seventy feet 'in the straight', they sustain the illusion that they have retaken possession of the landscape.

The rural settlement pattern of the Sussex Weald during Saxon and medieval times was constantly changing due to two basic influences. One was the familiar breaking-in of fresh ground along the margins of earlier 'islands' of cultivation, leading to secondary colonisation from mother townships. An invaluable clue to this lies in church organisation. The establishment of early churches in new, fast-growing communities as chapelries dependent on an older church was commonly practised. A notable instance is the chapel founded at the village of North Chapel which takes its name from a little church originally dependent on Petworth. Eastbourne had two such subordinate chapelries, Fernhurst and Lodsworth, both of which later became parish churches. Other churches which had a dependent chapel are Kirdford, Wisborough Green, Ditchling, Hellingly, Maresfield and Slaugham, the mother churches of chapels in Plaistow, Loxwood, Wivelsfield, Hailsham, Nutley and Crawley respectively. In each instance a more northerly 'daughter' community was hived off into the backwoods. Nutley, as we shall see, still retains the semblance of a pioneer settlement. Plaistow has also kept much of its old character as a little woodland clearing. Medieval Plaistow was a handful of scattered farms and a cluster of cottages around its chapel; its plan has been little altered since this initial modelling. The brick and tile-hung house fronts conceal ancient timbers which probably were the original house frames. The little 'village' green, fine oaks, the medley of shapely barns at nearby Rumbold's Farm (Plate 33) and the chequered fields and woodlands still owe much of their visual character to the distant past. In the same neighbourhood old Fernhurst has much the same character and one bears away a similar impression from Lurgashall and nearby Lickfold, both delightfully unspoiled settlements. The greens at these villages and also at such places as Rushlake Green in Warbleton, and Ringmer, originated with the colonisation of the waste by a group of smaller farmers and cottagers who valued a central clearing for grazing.

Another cause of changing settlement was intensified habitation on the old 'islands' resulting from gradual improvements of the soil by successive generations of human endeavour. The Rotherfield Custumal of 1346, which has much to tell on this theme,[2] explains that each of the original peasant farmers there had a *ferling*, a division of land varying from 100 to 150 acres. By 1346 each of these ferlings had been sufficiently improved to support several families and some of the once single farms had grown into hamlets, one being Hamsell. Another was *Gilderigge* (now represented

---

[2] S.A.T. LB 34.

by Gillridge Farm) in Withyham, provided with a chapel in 1292 because the inhabitants said they were unable to reach their nearest church at Buxted during winter.

The decline of *Gilderigge* is a reminder that many single farms today may also be the only surviving descendants of once prosperous hamlets. Moreover, C. F. Tebbutt's discovery of the abandoned settlements of Buxted and Buckham,[3] the first deserted villages to be identified in the Weald, should stimulate the search for other sites abandoned during the period of declining population in the fourteenth and fifteenth centuries.

During the fourteenth century a new form of woodland village began to appear on the face of Sussex, the 'waste-edge' settlement which grew haphazardly around the forests and the other major wastes. This initiated the endless scatter of houses straggling along the bordering roads and expanding here and there into shapeless hamlets, on the fringe of green and common, a sight repeated all over the Weald. This settlement pattern results from the long process of intermittent encroachment on the wastes in times of rising population. Coleman's Hatch, an early recorded settlement on the margins of Ashdown Forest, is a good example of a formless hamlet with cottages dispersed sporadically at the sites of springs. Rather unusually, Forest Row, first mentioned by this name in 1338, was a single street of houses.[4] The most interesting of the 'waste-edge' settlements is Nutley, where farms and smallholdings were being carved out of Ashdown Forest in the fourteenth century. The intermixture here of cottage gardens amidst gorse and bracken still demonstrates the appearance of a pioneering settlement when agriculture was making a penetration rather than a conquest.

For all the desperate energy of land-hungry peasants,

---

[3] C. F. Tebbutt, 'Two Newly-discovered Medieval Sites', *Suss. Arch. Colls.*, Vol. 110 (1972), pp. 31–6.

[4] P.R.O. E.372/182.

Sussex remains the most densely wooded county in Britain, about one seventh of its surface being under trees. Some of the fine vistas from the Forest Ridges, like the view eastwards from Nymans at Handcross, are still filled with deciduous woodland, ridge upon ridge. A similar impression of a great forested area is conveyed by the large woodland around Plaistow and Petworth, on the South Downs near Goodwood, or that viewed above the Low Weald at West Hoathly. Little of this woodland is 'natural' because almost every little patch of Sussex woodland in the past has been heavily grazed and exploited. Yet anciently enclosed woods or commons supporting mature trees still convey a sense of the 'dark and impenetrable wild' that early writers envisaged to be the untrodden depths of the Wealden forest. One of these is Mens Wood near Petworth where Ruth Tittensor has noted the presence of trees and shrubs characteristic of ancient woodlands, such as the Wild Service tree and Midland Hawthorn. Another is Ebernoe Common near Kirdford with many ancient oaks, thick stands of younger trees and a tangle of underwood, making a particularly vivid reminder of how laborious was the tree-clearing of the first woodlanders in making homes, fields and townships.

The most distinctive forest-craft to develop in Sussex was the enclosing of woods managed as 'coppice-with-standards'. This entailed the deliberate thinning of oaks to about twelve to the acre, so permitting the growth of thick underwood of hazel and alder, or of sweet chestnut, the present prevailing species. The underwood was cut in a cycle of about ten to twelve years to provide fuel, hurdles and fencing. This form of tree-farming is recorded on the Archbishop of Canterbury's manor of South Malling in 1273 and there are further reports of regular cutting from the fourteenth century. The combining of standards with coppice in the Weald was doubtless stimulated initially by the needs of ship-building and iron-making. When this market declined the demand for hop-poles and fuel for lime-kilns kept the coppices valuable. Now that charcoal is unwanted the surviving coppice is very neglected, as in Heathfield and Dallington, where it only exists because of the high cost of grubbing it.

Deer parks and forests

From the time of the Norman Conquest powerful landlords, members of the ruling aristocracy, set about the acquisition of hunting lodges set in extensive chases and deer parks (Fig. 10). With its immense woody wastes and diversity of scenery Sussex provided exceptional amenities of this kind. The great lordships were lavishly endowed in this respect, the Honour of Arundel having no less than ten parks and the Archbishop of Canterbury possessing nine. Imparking in Sussex began early; five parks are mentioned in the Domesday folios and by 1145 all the lords of rapes held parks. Many of these early parks were appurtenant to motte-and-bailey castles, such as Knepp and Pulborough. The lesser nobility also acquired parks, which multiplied rapidly in the late thirteenth century, a period when older ones were also being enlarged. Lords chose to curtail their agricultural activities on their Wealden estates at this time, even to the extent of imparking land previously improved with marl, and chose instead to be provisioned from their other estates in the Champion, where with the use of legumes productivity was rising.

Although most medieval deer parks have been converted to farms, their former usage still lends a distinctiveness to the countryside. The preservation of timber for the food and shelter of deer and swine saved many majestic trees now gracing the Wealden scene from the stroke of the forester's axe. The stiff cold clays nourished splendid oaks and mighty specimens with enormous crowns abound on naturally well-drained slopes in the old deer parks. Some of those in Sheffield Park, for example, may well have begun their

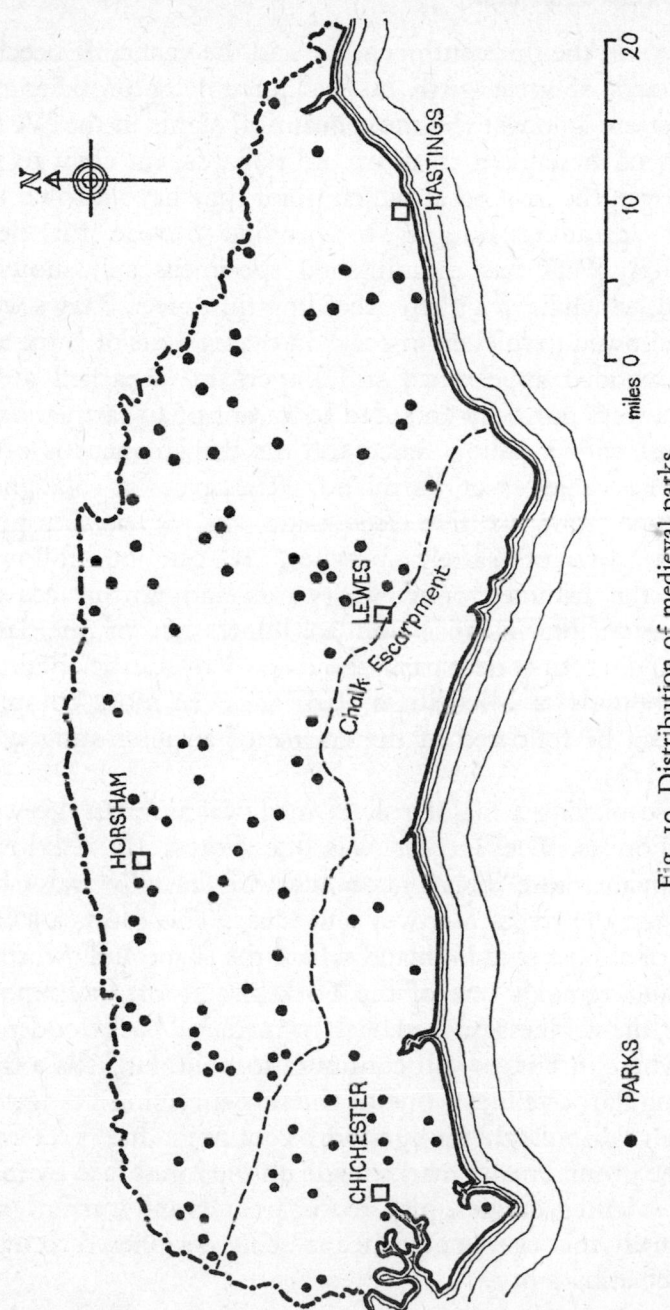

Fig. 10. Distribution of medieval parks.

growth in the thirteenth century and the venerable beeches and oaks of great girth in Buckhurst Park or Balcombe Forest are amongst the most beautiful sights in the Weald. Many of these giant trees are old pollards, cut eight to ten feet from the ground at which point they have thrown out great spreading boughs to provide browse for deer. Cowdray Park has monumental specimens still showing green, which have a girth exceeding thirty feet. Shaws were also allowed to thicken in parks in the interests of game and this wooded appearance still lingers in disparked areas. Parks were normally enclosed by means of an earthen bank topped with a paling fence and the embankment is often still traceable over farmland. The pale at Slaugham is some four to five feet wide and is now topped by a row of stately beeches. It can be followed from the hammer pond westwards and northwards for a considerable distance and an impression of the large size of the former deer park, about 500 acres, can be obtained. The bounds of Michelham Park are even more complete and can be followed in the course of an interesting walk (Fig. 11).

Also playing a major role in medieval agrarian life were the Forests. The largest was the Forest of Ashdown, occupying more than 15,000 acres of the hilly watershed between the rivers Medway and Ouse. This forms a sterile area of almost true highland where the shape and sweep of the hills reminds one of the Yorkshire Moors or Exmoor. Here, the wildness pushed back by medieval backwoodsmen elsewhere in Sussex still continues to hold out. It is a tract of singular loveliness, one of the few surviving vestiges of primeval England. Its age-long continuity has preserved on the ground many marks made on the forest face by man, such as banks, ditches, pits, roads, pounds and warrens, and gradually this visible evidence is being deciphered to make a fascinating story.

The word 'forest', denoting a hunting ground, is derived

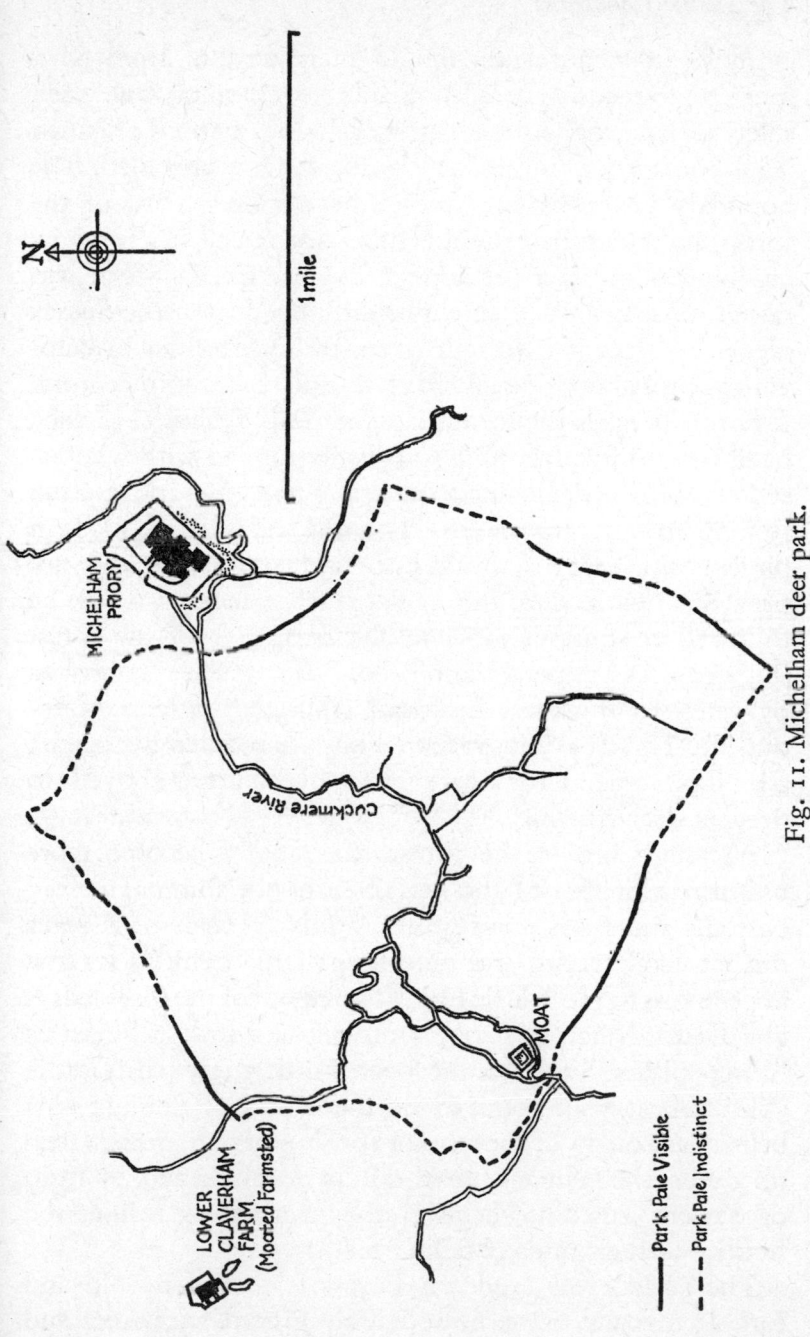

Fig. 11. Michelham deer park.

etymologically not from the Latin *foresta* but from *foris*, meaning 'outside', i.e. land outside the common law. Such tracts of land, not necessarily wooded, had strictly defined legal boundaries, within which Forest Law prevailed. The boundary of Ashdown Forest, the earliest record of the forest, and older than any surviving document, has survived on the ground to a remarkable degree. Ever since it was raised it has exercised an enduring influence on the Sussex scene. To trace it is to follow a medieval frontier of cultivation, probably originally fixed during the twelfth century. It normally takes the form of a 'deer-leap' fence, an earthen bank four to five feet high (originally topped with wooden stakes) with a deep ditch on the forest side and a bank sloping inwards to fields (Plate 13). This fence made it difficult for deer to break into farmland but it did not prevent them leaping out again. Such a fence can still be followed continuously round the perimeter of the forest (Fig. 12). At intervals the old boundary fence was broken by gates leading into the forest from the settled country outside. These have disappeared but are recalled by 'hatch', a local place-name for a gate with a high barrier above it to prevent deer straying.

Although life in the forest has rapidly become more uniform with that of the neighbourhood, some of its old customs and landscape features survive. Hard roads peter out into soft tracks, and mud-bespattered vehicles wallow in deep ruts to reach little farms carved out of the forest edge. Several fords across strongly-flowing streams still exist as 'water-splashes' and on the open heath a few hardy cattle still roam at will, betrayed by the sound of tinkling cow bells. Near many of the former forest gates are deep water-filled pits, the source of marl dug by local farmers by right of ancient custom whenever they needed to restore the fertility of their quickly failing fields.

The surface of Ashdown Forest is scored by old and forgotten roads, some now densely grown with trees and

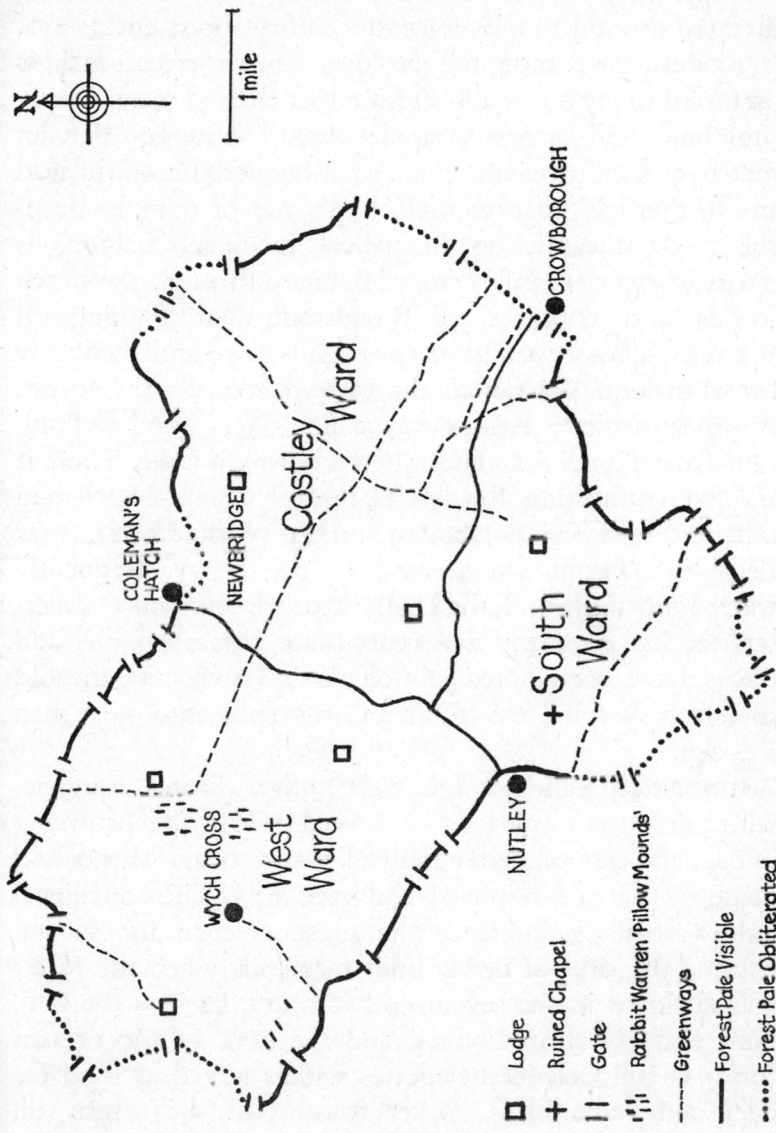

Fig. 12. Medieval Ashdown Forest.

Lodge □
Ruined Chapel +
Gate ‖
Rabbit Warren 'Pillow Mounds'
Greenways - - - -
Forest Pale Visible ——
Forest Pale Obliterated ••••

CROWBOROUGH

Costley Ward

NEWBRIDGE □

COLEMAN'S HATCH

South Ward +

West Ward

WYCH CROSS

NUTLEY

N

1 mile

brambles, but many re-discoverable on foot. Some stretches of deeply-worn track became derelict when routes were diverted around the seventeenth-century forest enclosures. In modern times more fell into disuse because road-makers preferred to lay out roads afresh rather than to metal deeply sunk lanes and narrow whapple ways. The longest derelict road over Ashdown is the 'horse road' between East Grinstead and Rotherfield, marked on Kelton's map of 1747. Its deep-cut track, meandering in typical medieval fashion, is traceable over six miles from Highgate through the beech woods and coppices of Broadstone and Pippingford Warrens, across open heaths near Gills Lap, and thence by Crowborough Warren to the eastern edge of the forest. Another medieval hollow-way which offers good walking runs from Kings Standing to Crowborough Gate. There is another connecting Reade's Gate and Chuck Hatch and others thread the north-west corner of the forest, near Legsheath Farm. On account of the heavy, frequently water-logged ground, the busiest roads branch into numerous tracks. As many as twenty-three separate paths and tracks have been noted at Coleman's Hatch, and the old road from Wych Cross to Birch Grove splits into more than a dozen.

In the deep valleys lodges were built for Forest Rangers, who cultivated a little land, preserved trees for the browsing of deer and encouraged the spread of such covert shrubs and plants as the wild raspberry and backberry. These medieval lodges strongly influence the present scene for several became the sites of newly built mansions when the forest was enclosed in the seventeenth century, such as the Old, New and Hindleap Lodges, and the flora of the present forest is still rich in the species which served as food for deer and game birds. Other features of the forest still visible are the old rabbit warrens. These were enclosed with a perimeter bank and ditch and contain earthbanks thrown up in the form of long, narrow 'pillow mounds' for the rabbit burrows. The 'berrys', as they are called, were described in the early eighteenth century as 'ancient'; probably, therefore, some were made when warrening was introduced into the forest during the later Middle Ages. They are visible in Broadstone, Pippingford and Pressridge Warrens.

The marsh landscape

No part of the Sussex countryside underwent such repeated change as marshes recovered in the early Middle Ages. Unlike the making of the landscape by woodland clearance, a permanent medieval accomplishment, farmland created from the sea was largely lost to successive floodings in the later Middle Ages and not regained until the more tranquil weather and expanding economy in Elizabethan and early Stuart times. Consequently, much earlier human action is buried under shingle, silt and peat, but the struggle of medieval marshmen to erect bordering dykes against the water and build sluices, tide-gates and water-lets, so turning soggy, black earth into rich fields, has left many visible vestiges on the ground.

The marsh known as the Pevensey Levels was the largest tract in Sussex to be enclosed with sea dykes (Fig. 13). In Roman times this was probably a wide bay studded with an archipelago of little clay islands. By the eighth century the eastward drift of shingle along the coast had given natural protection to the spread of saltmarsh overflowed by high tides which left upstanding islands (called 'eyes', from Old English *eg*, an island), such as Chilley, Northeye, Horse-eye and Rickney. Two Anglo-Saxon charters, one relating to Barnhorne in 772 and the other to Glynleigh in Hailsham in 947, both speak of 'fen' and 'marsh'.[5]

During the twelfth and early thirteenth centuries the Pevensey Levels gradually changed from saltmarsh to reedy

5 E. E. Barker, 'Sussex Anglo-Saxon Charters', *Suss. Arch. Colls.*, Vol. 86 (1947), pp. 90–5; *ibid.*, Vol. 88 (1949), pp. 59–64.

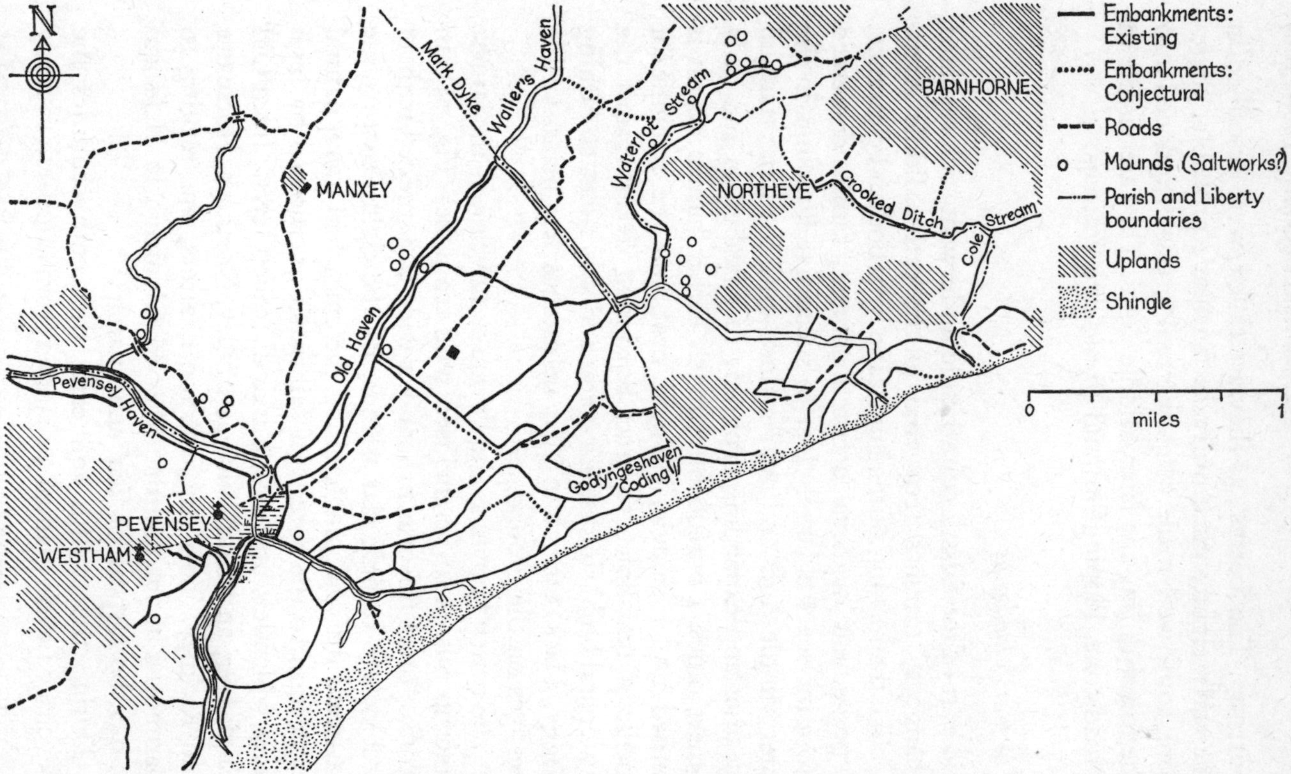

Fig. 13. Pevensey marsh.

and sedgy meadows and, ultimately, into arable fields. The reclamation was undertaken by opulent abbeys such as Battle, rich magnates like Gilbert, lord of Pevensey rape, and by many lesser men who built lonely farms on the hill islands, sheltering them with clumps of willow as they inned surrounding patches of marsh. Abbot Ralph of Battle (1107–24), for example, was an active reclaimer at Barnhorne. The large new fields created by him and his successors were so well dyked that they furnished heavy crops of corn. The Abbey's chief defence against the sea still remains clearly visible. It was the Crooked Ditch and the embankment, raised in the fourteenth century to ward off severe storms, which runs along its landward side. This old seawall provided a firm base for one of the trackways, locally known as 'trades', serving the Levels. The Crooked Ditch, running dog-legged round individual fields and not straight like later drainage channels, is just what one would expect of a patch of anciently enclosed marsh, created piecemeal by one or two land-owners. For several hundreds of years the Abbey carefully defended its marshland against flooding and its chequerboard pattern of ditched fields (mentioned by name in fourteenth-century records) has a virtually unchanged layout today, making it a fine 'period piece' of early medieval landscape shaping.[6]

Elsewhere, a similar pattern of new enclosures spread over the Levels.[7] One of the major new drainage channels was the Mark Dyke (*Merke Dik*) which ran as straight as early engineers could make it across nearly two miles of the lowest and most desolate part of the Levels. The upper course, no longer a major drain, is now a reed-filled, silted channel. The precise age of the Mark Dyke is uncertain but

[6] P. F. Brandon, 'Agriculture and the Effects of Floods and Weather at Barnhorne, Sussex, during the Late Middle Ages', *Suss. Arch. Colls.*, Vol. 109 (1971), pp. 69–83.

[7] L. F. Salzman, 'The Inning of Pevensey Levels', *Suss. Arch. Colls.*, Vol. 53 (1910), pp. 32–60. A. J. F. Dudley, 'The Level and Port of Pevensey in the Later Middle Ages', *Suss. Arch. Colls.*, Vol. 104 (1966), pp. 22–45.

it is clearly very old because it divides the Pevensey and Hastings rapes and acts as a parish boundary along its entire course. When constructed it ran presumably over swampy wastes with no visible boundary marks. We may be sure that Battle Abbey contributed to the cost because it held an outlying estate up against the Mark Dyke called *Marchaleslond*.

A medieval activity which has left its own impression on the Levels and other Sussex marshes is salt-making. Every summer the salt-boilers moved on to the rapidly retreating marsh edges and retained salt-water in trenches or temporary dykes, from whence it was led off into shallow clay-floored pans to await evaporation. The brine was then leached out and boiled in 'salt-houses'. Before the marshlanders reclaimed the marsh at the mouths of Sussex streams, and the great floods of the late Middle Ages deposited sheets of brackish water over them, the Sussex salt industry was a large one. Recorded in Domesday Book are 294 'saltworks', a larger number than for any other county. The salt-pans used for the collection of sea water have long been submerged and normally the only features of salt-making in the present landscape are the low mounds of residues, typically between three and five feet high and up to fifty yards in diameter. Several groups of these mounds have been discovered by A. J. Dulley on Pevensey Levels in the vicinity of Waller's Haven which probably derives its name from *weller*, the Middle English name for a salt-boiler. Another important salt-making district in early medieval times was the Adur valley where E. W. Holden has reported the sites of many mounds.[8] Several of his sites have recently been destroyed by ploughing but one group still lies in the meadows immediately upstream of Bramber bridge. Many more salt mounds have been found in the Manhood peninsula. All these sites afford valuable evidence as to

[8] E. W. Holden, 'Salt Works at Botolphs', *Sussex Notes and Queries*, Vol. 15 (1969), pp. 304–7.

past tidal conditions and the course of old shorelines.
The ravages of the sea led to the abandonment of much
of the Pevensey Levels during the later Middle Ages and
wreaked havoc at its ports. Pevensey itself was one of the
victims and the evidence of its losing battle with nature can
be pieced together from documents and on the ground. Its
prosperity was dependent on the daily tidal scouring of its
harbour at the main outfall of the Levels. As the inning of
adjacent marshes reduced the tidal flow the outfall became
blocked. This in turn prevented the discharge of land
drainage into the sea and widespread flooding resulted. The
first attempt to remedy the situation was the straight cut
between Fence Bridge and Wallsend, replacing the old
outfall at Pevensey. The former course can still be followed
between ancient retaining walls as far as the Crumbles
shingle spit where it peters out ignominiously. When this
artificial cut proved ineffective Pevensey was doomed. In
1402 the main outlet of the Levels was diverted eastwards
down the course of the Mark Dyke to the port of *Coding*
(Godyngeshaven), at the outfall of the Waterlot Stream
(Plate 14). Since this also became blocked by the eastward
drift of shingle, another cut was made still further eastward
in 1455 (Fig. 13). These two cuts explain the right-angled
bends in the present main drain of the Levels. Meanwhile,
the course of the Old Haven to Pevensey silted and, once
busy with boats, it has been desolate for nearly 600 years.
Looking back towards Pevensey from the banks of this
winding reedy channel one has the sight of the huge Roman
fortress and stone Norman keep rising dramatically out of
the flatness of the marsh. Nothing could give a better sense
of the time when Pevensey was the key to the whole of
Pevensey Level and consequently a major defensive point
along the Invasion Coast of England.

Other casualties of the late medieval floods were the little
ports of Hydneye towards Willingdon and Northeye, both
drowned by the sea. The site of Northeye, a limb of the

Cinque Port of Hastings, is recalled to memory by the local field-names of Town Field and Chapel Field and by traces of its main street and foundations of some of its buildings. Even so, it is hard to visualise its battered seawall, the noisy taverns, its chapel crowning the hill, ships at anchor, the excited cries of gulls and all the sights and smells of a once busy harbour. Yet every time we look at this seemingly featureless country it begins to give up a few of its secrets.

The soft rocks of the coastal plain also yielded readily to the sea's remorseless assault. Early maps, like the famous 'Armada' map of the Sussex coastline made in 1587,[9] show it fringed by sandy commons and salt-marsh, of which almost all trace has disappeared. By this date coastal erosion had been persistent for centuries and had destroyed several coastal settlements. A clue to the sites of these drowned villages is provided by still-existing local roads which no longer reach their original destination at some ancient port or quay but end abruptly on a featureless and inconsequential part of the coast. This trait of minor coastal roads is obscured by modern urban sprawl but if we continue the clearly rendered lines of local roads on Yeakeall and Gardner's map of 1778–83 and plot their convergence it is possible to ascertain the approximate site of several lost villages (Fig. 14).

The Ouse estuary also suffered from late medieval flooding. At Domesday the old defended Saxon town of Lewes was accessible to sea-going ships and the present agricultural villages of Piddinghoe and Rodmell engaged in the North Sea herring fishery (Plate 15). Gradually, seafaring gave way to farming as the marsh, locally called 'brooks', was inned. Despite the repeated raising of seawalls the Ouse valley was devastated by late-fourteenth-century floods and by the severe flood of 1421 which also destroyed much of the Netherlands.

The redraining of this marshland was deferred until the

⁹ M. A. Lower (ed.), *Survey of the Coast of Sussex made in 1587* (1870).

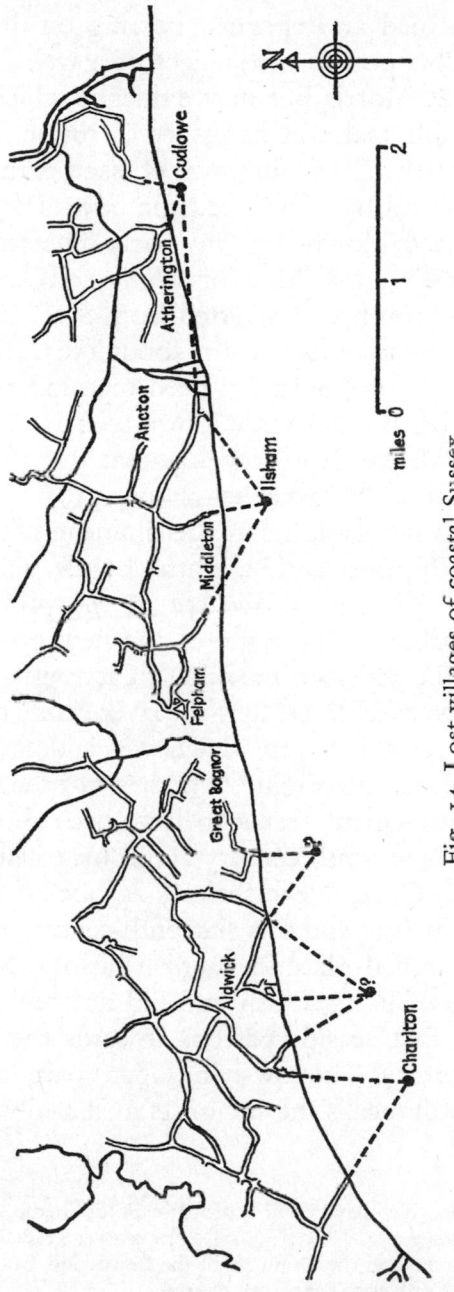

Fig. 14. Lost villages of coastal Sussex.

1530s when it had an important bearing on the origin of Newhaven. This port is the subject of a well-documented study by F. G. Morris but new evidence which has since become available makes it necessary to revise the story in several respects.[10] The main point at issue is the extent to which man's hand has developed the port. The traditional account, handed down by the early-nineteenth-century antiquary, T. W. Horsfield, in his *History of Sussex* (1835) is that the Ouse mouth was diverted from Seaford to the site of Newhaven by a violent storm about 1565. This version of the origin of Newhaven has been repeated on countless occasions since, but it is not borne out by the recently discovered evidence. It is now apparent that the diversion of the Ouse was a deliberate act about 1539 by local gentry to improve its navigation and the drainage of the estuary marshland in the Ouse and Laughton Levels. This involved making a cut directly to the sea at the present site of Newhaven harbour. The trade of the new port was long hindered by the repeated blocking of its outfall and for a time in the seventeenth century the river broke through the shingle at a point between Newhaven and Seaford. This probably explains the origin of the story of the storm. The drainage improvement seems to have been shortlived and not until the nineteenth century could man claim to have harnessed the Ouse. Nevertheless, as one of the earliest canalisations in England this sixteenth-century engineering has a well-deserved place in English history. Seaford was left in a state of living death and did not revive until the arrival of its first seaside patrons towards the end of the eighteenth century. The low-lying open space in the centre of the town still marks the site of its medieval wharves and warehouses.

[10] F. G. Morris, 'Newhaven and Seaford: a Study in the Diversion of a River Mouth', *Geography*, Vol. 16 (1931), pp. 28–33; P. F. Brandon, 'The Origin of Newhaven and the Drainage of the Lewes and Laughton Levels', *Suss. Arch. Colls.*, Vol. 109 (1971), pp. 94–106.

The landscape of high farming

The principal elements in the manorial organisation of the Champion were the great demesne farms worked by large bodies of dependent cultivators and grouped into extensive honours, estates of bishops and monastic lordships. The honour of Arundel was immense, comprising some 8000 acres of demesne arable scattered in more than fifty manors, most of them on the Plain and Down. The Bishop of Chichester cultivated some 3000 acres and the Archbishop of Canterbury a little less. Other huge estates, as has been aptly said, functioned as 'federated grain factories' and dominated the economy of Champion Sussex by the great scale of their enterprise. The emphasis on intensive farming is reflected, as we have seen, in peculiarities in settlement patterns which are still discernible to this day. By the end of the thirteenth century, the demesne fields had mostly been segregated and the common fields of the township peasants consolidated into a separately formed farm. This permitted innovation which resulted in technological achievements greatly surpassing the precariousness of the standard medieval husbandry.

The outstanding development was the suppression of the fallow on the best or the most easily manured fields, a practice much facilitated by sheep-folding but more particularly by the sowing of legumes in a continuous three-year rotation of crops. Barley (or oats), legumes and wheat, combined with a favourable climate and thick sowing of seed (partly to smother weeds and so reduce fallowing) to produce cereal yields substantially higher than the medieval norm. The Battle Abbey estates at Alciston gave harvests of wheat more than double the normal medieval expectation of six to eight bushels per acre, and other cereals yielded in like proportion. The monks of Battle Abbey belonged to the Benedictine order, a community famed throughout England for the excellence of its sheep-and-corn husbandry. The very uneven survival of evidence for the great lay estates compared with ecclesiastical properties has recently led historians to question the generally accepted superiority of Church over lay farming. But in Sussex the Battle Abbey yields surpass all the other known corn yields and we are probably correct in endorsing the older view that the Church built up model farms where the mode of high farming attained a rare distinction which was emulated with varying degrees of success in the surrounding countryside.[11]

It is still possible to recapture here and there something of this era of direct demesne exploitation. Very few manor houses and granges survived the 'Great Rebuilding' of the sixteenth and seventeenth centuries but below the downland escarpment a search for them amongst the very varied buildings on the old farms can reveal some notable medieval structures. One of the most rewarding ways of recreating the medieval past is to take the old track under the Downs to Eastbourne. This originally crossed the Ouse at Itford and lies south of the present A27 road which superseded it as a turnpike in the eighteenth century. This ancient road threads its way through hedgeless fields of corn little changed in appearance since the fourteenth century. Short diversions bring one to a succession of large manor farms especially rich in old, massive flint buildings. Most conspicuous are the enormous barns on the former ecclesiastical estates whose dimensions rival the nave of a big town church, a monument to the great scale and bountifulness of their tillage. Wilmington and Michelham priories each have large medieval barns as does Bishopstone manor farm, once an estate of the Bishops of Chichester. Another type of building

11 P. F. Brandon, 'Demesne Arable Farming in Central Sussex during the Later Middle Ages', *The Agricultural History Review*, Vol. 19 (1971), pp. 113–34. *Idem*, 'Cereal yields on the Sussex Estates of Battle Abbey during the Later Middle Ages', *The Economic History Review*, Second Series, Vol. 25 (1972), pp. 403–20.

Plate 13 The pale of Ashdown Forest near Newbridge. The view is of the outer side of the earthen bank. A line of stakes originally ran along its top. See p. 108.

Plate 14 Waller's Haven, the main drain of the Pevensey Levels. The natural channel originally drained to the south-west. The right-angled bend is due to the artificial drainage channel cut in 1402. See p. 115.

Plate 15 This maritime scene at Piddinghoe on the Ouse estuary recalls the fishing and trading activities of this little port when the mouth of the Ouse was a wide water-filled entrance. See p. 116.

Plate 16 The undercroft to the dormitory of Lewes Priory. See p. 126.

Plate 17 The cultural influence stemming from Normandy is evident from the broad similarity in architectural style between Lessay Abbey, Normandy (*above*), and the church of New Shoreham (*below*).

Plate 18 This huge, finely engineered tithe barn, achieves a beauty highlighting a cluster of medieval buildings at Alciston. It recalls the large scale and efficiency of monastic farming below the Downs during the Middle Ages. See p. 121.

surviving in considerable numbers in the district is the dovecote where pigeons were raised for the table during winter when fresh meat was scarce. At Charleston a circular, flint dovecote survives and at neighbouring West Dean there is a square one with sandstone quoins.

Alciston, one of the most fascinating of these downland settlements, possesses several old buildings documented in medieval records (Fig. 15). Here the grange buildings, once the property of Battle Abbey, are still remarkably complete. The most conspicuous is an enormous three-aisled barn with a high pitched roof supported on massive piers and rafters (Plate 18). Its precise age is indeterminable but the basic structure is almost certainly medieval. The beauty of its interior reminds one of D. S. MacColl's observation that the "mysterious welling of light amongst the old beams and timbers of a barn is one of the loveliest things upon earth".[12] The dovecote is now a picturesque ruin, with its nesting holes exposed to view. Fish stews still survive as a chain of artificial ponds along the course of a running spring behind the so-called Old Clergy House, itself a medieval building. Part of the medieval grange at Alciston is now incorporated in a wing of Alciston Court Farm and in the main cattle yard is a medieval cottage now used as a barn.

The distribution of common fields

The evidence for common fields in Sussex, both documentary and visual, diminishes northwards and eastwards of the coastal plain. A general belief has grown up that communal farming did not extend further north than the bed of *maam*, a fertile loam derived from the Upper Greensand, which outcrops immediately below the Chalk escarpment. Further investigation, however, has revealed fragmentary evidence that some kind of common-field system also extended on to the early-occupied Lower Greensand

[12] D. S. MacColl, *Annual Report*, Society for the Protection of Ancient Buildings (1904).

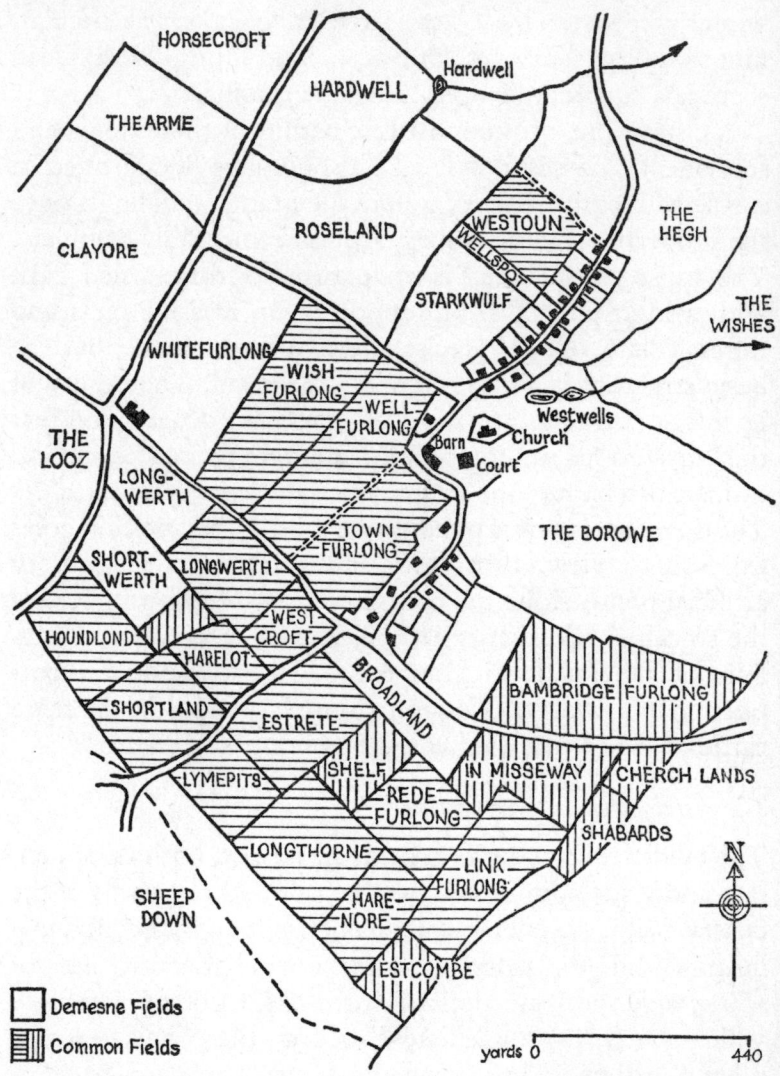

Fig. 15. Alciston, an estate of Battle Abbey.

formation supporting the second range of settlements north of the Chalk. Chalvington, Sherrington, Wellingham (in Ringmer), West Chiltington, Ashington and Petworth are examples of townships where the arable was originally worked in common. The enclosure of these common fields was well advanced by early Tudor times so that little is known about the farming system and the degree to which fields had been collectively ploughed and grazed. The historical development of the Petworth common fields can be unravelled from the surviving records and from an examination of the topographical features on the ground. Twelfth- and early-thirteenth-century charters refer to several unfenced strips (*helva inheia*), long strips of arable (*helva longa*) and headlands (*gara*) in the East Field of the town of Petworth. A North Field is also mentioned, together with strips scattered in other furlongs.[13] A system involving a biennial fallow on the basis of two large arable fields is probably implied. In 1444 the 'Townmansfield' was still farmed in common but all the town fields are shown as enclosed by hedges on the Treswell map of 1610.[14] On the ground the gently shelving fields on the eastern edge of the town bear traces of lynchets trending with the contours characteristically in the form of the inverted S commonly produced by a heavy ox-plough. This lyncheted hillside presumably marks the site of the East Field of Petworth. Superimposed on the lynchets are fields bounded by low earthen banks topped with quickset hedges and oaks and other standing trees several centuries old. It affords a good specimen of one of the early enclosed landscapes in the county (Plate 38).

In the Weald proper it can no longer be assumed that all fields were enclosed directly from the wild and cultivated individually within their own ring fence from the very beginning. Land won from the primeval forest in the twelfth

13 B.M. Cottonian MSS., Vesp. E xxxii, 47, 48, 50.
14 Petworth House archives.

and thirteenth centuries was undoubtedly individually farmed. All the facts irresistibly suggest this, but the nature of the fields reclaimed before 1066 remains an interesting source of conjecture. The existence of small patches of common fields in the High Weald no longer seems improbable in the light of the knowledge that even in the unfavourable environment of the heart of Dartmoor, hamlets containing only four or five holdings were worked on some form of common field system in medieval times. The Weald Clay, though more apt for pasture than tillage, had arable capabilities with regular fallowing as is proved by the land utilisation in the eighteenth and early nineteenth centuries. The 'rising lands' which W. Marshall noted as the earliest settled sites were reasonably well drained and therefore topographically suitable for common-field cultivation. Small common fields were probably dispersed on such sites in the Adur Basin where Shermanbury had demesne arable still collectively grazed when fallow in 1362.[15] There is no documentary evidence yet discovered concerning common fields on the more accidented country of the High Weald. Even here, however, the pattern of hedged fields may overlie former open fields at the sites of very early settlement. This possibility is strongly reinforced by a report from B. A. French, confirmed by a photograph, tracing lynchets observable at the hamlet of Brightling, one of the first Saxon colonies in the High Weald, running under, and at right-angles to, later hedged enclosures.[16] There is, therefore, the possibility that some Wealden fields represent the enclosure of long unfenced strips earlier ploughed along the hillsides and not down them as in parts of Devon. A wider field survey, carried out in all light conditions so as to take advantage of long shadows, would test this hypothesis.

[15] P.R.O. C.135/158.
[16] Private communication to the author. The field concerned lies immediately south of Brightling church.

Ecclesiastical building

Sussex has no surviving monastic remains comparable to Tintern or the great northern abbeys, and collectively its parish churches are modest, simple sanctuaries. It is the little unpretentious downland church that probably most typifies ecclesiastical building in the county. Yet Sussex also possesses a legacy of late Norman and Transitional churches which, stripped of the ivy which the Victorians allowed to cover them, are now revealed as amongst the most beautiful and majestic of their kind. They are attributable to a high-point of architectural inspiration and vigorous building activity after the Norman Conquest which reached its peak in the century following 1130. On account of its close military and trading connections with Normandy and the rest of the continent, Sussex, more than most parts of England, came under the influence of Norman art, learning and religious reform. Moreover, a county which had first provided the Conqueror's landfall, then the site of his famous victory on Telham Hill and was subsequently divided amongst his most influential supporters, could hardly have failed to occupy a special place in this great building movement. The impoverishment of the ports as harbours, silted in the later Middle Ages, and the fourteenth-century confiscation of alien priories founded by early Norman lords largely explains the very limited Perpendicular rebuilding in Sussex, except in Wealden districts where there was rapid growth of population. Consequently, the most sustained inspiration in the parish churches of Sussex is Norman.

This influence was still further strengthened by the habit of the early Norman lords of creating priories and cells as dependencies of Norman and other European abbeys. The plan of the church of Lewes Priory was based on the third church at Cluny, its mother house. The collegiate church at

Steyning, one of the finest specimens of twelfth-century architecture, was built under the supervision of the monks of Fécamp and its nave has a strong resemblance to the Romanesque churches of northern France. There is also a striking similarity of design between Lessay Abbey in Normandy (founded 1056) and the churches of Old Shoreham, New Shoreham (which was intended to be collegiate) and Boxgrove, which was established in 1117 as a cell of Lessay (Plate 17). These, and many other examples, demonstrate that in cultural respects much of Sussex was less a part of England in the twelfth and early thirteenth centuries than an outlier of Normandy.

Some notable monasteries mark the religious fervour of the twelfth century in Sussex. The King himself endowed the Benedictine abbey of Battle as a great war memorial, insisting that its high altar should be placed on the very spot where Harold fell. The Norman remains comprise part of the dormitory, cloister walls and undercrofts of the guest houses. The lords of the rapes combined piety with warlike enterprise and administrative flair, lavishly endowing religious houses with some of their newly-won gains. William de Warenne, lord of the Rape of Lewes, initiated the greatest building by founding Lewes Priory under the direct control of Cluny, then the fount of art and learning in Europe and the centre of monastic reform. Today the ruins are mere fragments but they are impressive enough to convey something of the scale and magnificence of the original buildings. Its noble priory church, larger than Chichester Cathedral, is almost completely razed to the ground, but the *hospitium*, now the parish church of Southover, and the remains of an infirmary chapel still exist (Plate 16).

This early foundation, with that of Sele Priory by William de Braose I, was followed by the Cistercian house of Robertsbridge and the lesser houses of the Premonstratensians at Bayham and Durford and of the Augustinians at

Michelham and Shulbrede. All these Wealden sites in the late twelfth and early thirteenth centuries provided the deep solitudes where the monks of these orders could renounce their life on earth. Bayham, the most inaccessible of all, has buildings forming an impressive group by far the most complete and instructive of the Sussex monastic sites (Plate 19). The plan can be fully traced and parts still stand conspicuously, presumably because there was a limited demand for building materials there at the Reformation. Of the Augustinian establishments the most impressive is Michelham Priory which stands on an artificial platform inside a moat that probably defended an earlier manor house (Plate 20).

All over coastal Sussex one notices examples of the great thirteenth-century rebuilding in the Early English style, but the finest are in the Weald reflecting the rising population and increasing prosperity of this region, which, with a dozen generations of human effort behind it, was fast outgrowing its 'colonial' character as an appendage to the earlier developed south. At Fletching, for instance, the tower has traces of Saxo-Norman work but the present large structure is the cruciform Early English style and was completed about 1230. The graceful shingled spire was added about 1340. Another rebuilding that symbolises a busy and prosperous Wealden community is at Lindfield, an important iron-working centre, at least from the thirteenth century. Extensive rebuilding was also required at Buxted, Heathfield, Rotherfield, Kirdford and Waldron. These large Wealden churches were built to accommodate the huge congregations which had come to settle in their parishes. West Hoathly church has had a particularly interesting evolution. Originally a little rectangular Norman building, it was progressively enlarged to keep pace with forest clearing. During the twelfth and thirteenth centuries an aisle and chapel were added and the chancel, most unusually, was extended to make it larger than the nave. In the fourteenth and early fifteenth centuries benefactors in the forest villages all over the Sussex Weald were setting up dainty shingled broach spires raised on newly-built towers. They gracefully crown the Wealden hills and must have been welcome landmarks for the growing number of travellers in this remote and still largely unknown region.

The retreat of settlement (*1348–1500*)

It has long been recognised that in the later Middle Ages former economic trends were sharply reversed; stagnation, decline and decay in varying degrees were countrywide. Equally significant, but scarcely appreciated until recently, were concurrent social and economic forces producing a marked increase in average wealth. Earlier views therefore are now being questioned and the later Middle Ages are no longer regarded as a time of unrelieved gloom, stagnation and recession. The Sussex landscape offers evidence in support of both points of view. The drastic fall in population following the Black Death and its recurrent visitations has left its mark in the form of deserted and shrunken villages. The contraction in the cultivated areas, though much obscured by later fluctuations, is still recorded in abandoned strip-lynchets. Woodland which has encroached upon medieval fields is another sign of an arrested economy. Some of the best examples of this are found in the deep ghylls of Burwash and Heathfield. On the other hand few counties have so many surviving buildings which attest to higher standards of domestic architecture and improving aesthetic taste.

Deserted villages are the most permanent memorials in the present landscape of severe population decrease from pestilence and famine (Fig. 16). All over the sheep-and-corn country of the coastal plain and downland the observant traveller will discern the visible evidence of settlements which have dwindled to insignificance. The dearth of Decorated or Perpendicular church architecture itself suggests a 'poor folk and a few' in the later Middle Ages and the many shrunken and rudely repaired churches indicate reduced congregations over many generations. The minute church of Lullington, which is not even the whole of the original chancel, is an extreme case, but the blocked thirteenth-century arcade at Botolphs, the shortened chancel at Alciston, the uncompleted tower and poorly repaired aisle of Kingston Buci are examples symbolising village decay which can be multiplied many times over. In some cases a solitary church may suggest vanished homesteads, as at Beddingham, Hamsey and Warminghurst. Many of these deserted or shrunken sites still retain evidence of building foundations. Berwick near Alciston is only a fragment of a large medieval village and Allcroft noted that "under its grass fields you may see the steads of a multitude of buildings . . . that have vanished".[17] These are still traceable in fields north and west of the church and in a field at the northern edge of the village. At Arlington the fields south and west of the church bear traces of unexamined earthworks and at the Lydds in Piddinghoe is possibly a deserted site still awaiting archaeological excavation. At Botolphs, which has dwindled to four houses, the foundations of former homesteads are still visible in a field opposite the church. This settlement lies in the Adur valley and the surviving earthworks about every farm and church in this part of the downland indicate that the river banks once teemed with country folk in contrast to its present empty state. Coombes demonstrates this very well. It simply comprises a tiny Saxon church, a fourteenth-century clergy house, a handful of old cottages and a single large farm, all nestling into the great fold of the Chalk which gives the place its name. These buildings overlook the sites of homes that have long since disappeared.

In some instances the changing morphology of rural settlement can be closely studied on the ground aided by

[17] A. Hadrian Allcroft, *Downland Pathways* (1934,) p. 60.

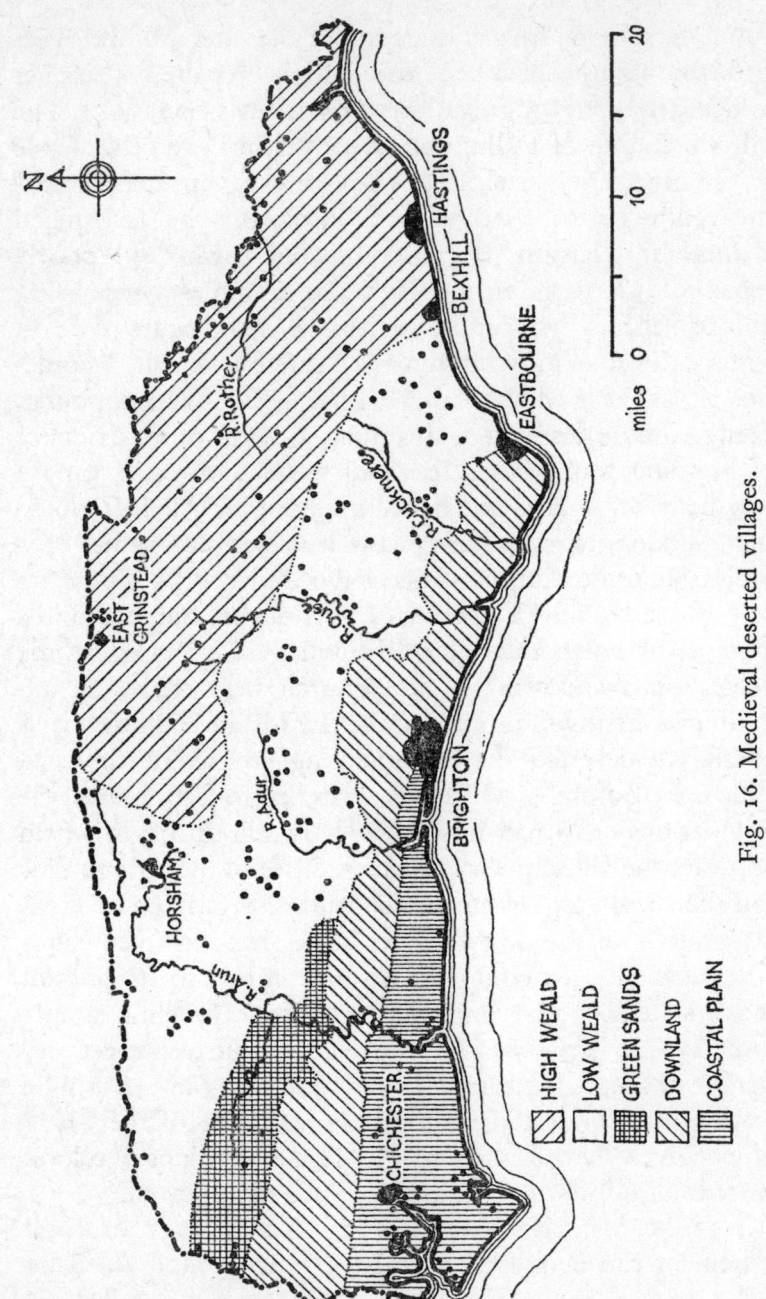

Fig. 16. Medieval deserted villages.

historical documents, at Apuldram, near Chichester, for example (Fig. 17). Since the sixteenth century it has become an anomalous settlement which includes an ancient church and an unusual fifteenth-century 'solar tower' house. There is also a manor house and a few other dwellings, none very old, sporadically dispersed about the parish. "There is no village" reads the categorical statement in the Victoria County History. This is certainly true now but Apuldram *was* a village when surveyed in 1433 by the monks of Battle Abbey.[18] It was then compactly clustered about 'ystrete', 'portstrete' and 'cotman strete' which converged at cross-roads in the village where today are wide verges. Two of these streets have subsequently decayed to mere footpaths and the little harbour of Apuldram has also vanished. The medieval silting of the Chichester Channel is possibly a factor responsible for the virtual abandonment of Apuldram.

Another shrunken village whose fifteenth-century plan can be reconstructed from medieval surveys is Alciston at the foot of the Downs between Lewes and Eastbourne. In 1433 the village comprised thirty-one dwellings (Fig. 15), but only about a dozen are occupied today. The homesteads, some mere cottages, others more substantial dwellings, were spaced randomly along the village street within large gardens.[19] Depopulation has left a rambling incoherent settlement, its street only half filled with houses in a long, straggling line. Alciston was divided into a 'south town' and a 'north town'. The former is now represented by only three houses. In 1433 a line of homesteads extended on both sides of the street to the Lewes–Eastbourne highway, now simply a bridleway. A fragment of flint walling of one of the houses is the only surviving masonry but the platforms on which the houses stood can be easily identified. Several of the surviving houses incorporate medieval structures.

Documentary and field evidence also amply attest to

[18] P.R.O. E.315/56: V.C.H. *Sussex*, Vol. 4 (1953), p. 138.
[19] P.R.O. E.315/56.

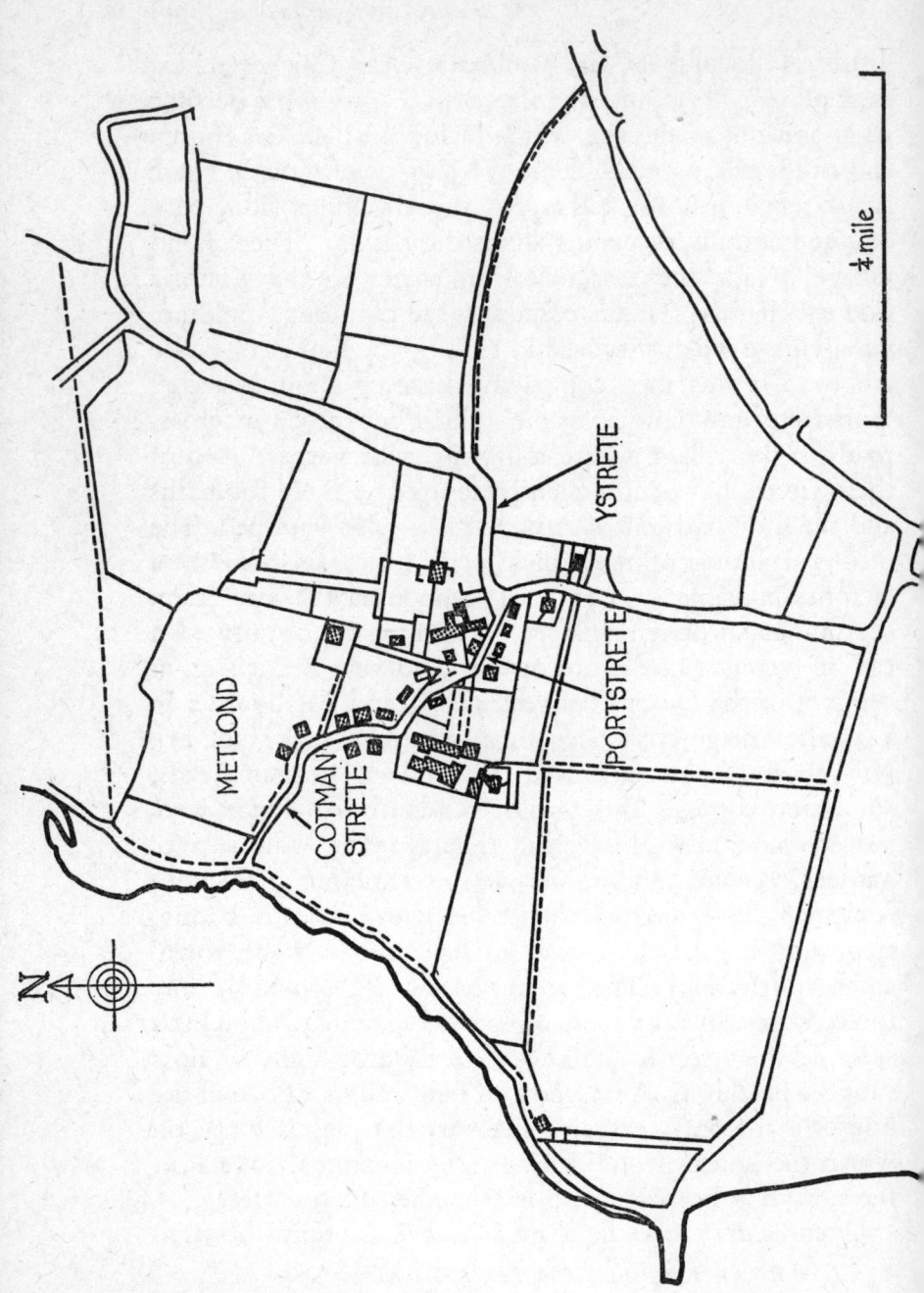

another phenomenon in the Champion region. This is the dwindling of innumerable settlement sites to an isolated farm, often the old manor house, and at most a cottage or two, where in medieval times communities of land-holding peasants co-operatively farmed the arable and had grazing rights on the sheep downs and commons. With the exception of a few farms on the Downs in the neighbourhood of Brighton, such as Mulstan, Hotsgrove and Patchway, and a few others in similar remote and lofty places, probably never anything more than single farms in the distant past, the vast majority of old farms in the Champion have gradually absorbed all the little peasant holdings which formerly existed there. The medley of rambling farm buildings—many probably dwelling houses at one time—help us to imagine a scene of peasant cots and little farms with their attendant hedged gardens, tofts and crofts often gathered about a small green. Not all of these decayed townships were small. Few visitors to Glyndebourne would suspect that at the nearby farm were fourteen peasant holdings in 1462. Sutton and Chinting near Seaford, now two large farms, had thirty-nine householders in 1327 and together constituted a separate parish. Kingston Buci near Shoreham today has only two old houses, yet had twenty-four taxpayers in the early fourteenth century at which time Winton in Alfriston, now a mere hamlet, had a minimum of twenty-five peasant holdings.

The economic and social forces responsible for depopulation were complex, and varied in nature and intensity over many generations. The retreat of rural settlement began apparently even before the Black Death for the *Nonae Rolls* of 1341 mention untilled land, rural poverty and French raids on coastal farms and villages. Centuries later small proprietors still clung to the soil in rapidly dwindling numbers but by the late seventeenth century the large downland farm, often occupying an entire parish, had become commonplace. In the first stage of this depopulation, up to about 1500, most of the old villages survived as communities, though most were already shrinking fast. The number of sites actually deserted, or reduced to extreme decay, in the Champion during the later Middle Ages amounts to about seven per cent of the vills enumerated in the tax schedule of 1334—a much smaller proportion than in the Midland counties, but appreciable enough to suggest the changing social circumstances.

Late medieval building

The heritage of late medieval building in Sussex is exceptionally rich both in variety and quality. It includes two specimens of feudal magnificence, Bodiam and Herstmonceux, which rank amongst the outstanding European legacies of medieval building. These show a divergent development, for the former is a traditional castle and the other a new style of semi-fortified country residence, but both symbolise the growing aesthetic taste and grandeur marking the culmination of medieval architecture. Much new building by Church, State and barons alike was to counter the persistent threats of invasion from France and of peasant revolt. Another powerful influence was the social movement which F. R. H. du Boulay in *The Age of Ambition* calls 'pastoralism', a new-found passion for building in the countryside distinguished homes still defensible by moat and gatehouses but giving precedence to relaxation and comfort, often involving the enlargement of parks. The "holy land of abbeys and Gothic castles",[20] as Horace Walpole described the Kent and Sussex border, was much enriched by these developments.

The wealthiest of the nobility built on a grand scale. The building of Bodiam Castle as late as 1386 is due to that conjunction of local and national causes which has so constantly diversified the Sussex scene. It was built by Sir

[20] Horace Walpole, *Letter to Richard Bentley*, 5th August 1752.

Edward Dalyngrydge, a veteran of Crécy and Poitiers, who had amassed immense wealth and prestige as a marauder in France. His influence at the court of Richard II and the urgent need for defence in a locality already twice sacked by the French made expedient his architectural pretensions. Dalyngrydge's castle represents one of the most perfect examples extant of the last age of purely military castles. Its overall plan is conventionally based on the Edwardian model of Conway and Harlech, omitting the keep, but giving prominence to gatehouses and having simple, massive curtain walls overlooking a deep moat. Its perfect symmetry and the beauty of its setting on an artificial platform makes it one of the noblest examples of military architecture.

During the fifteenth century the Lancastrian nobles closest to the Court had again made parks highly fashionable in which they added new amenities such as heronries and tree-lined avenues. The construction of Herstmonceux is an example of this trend (Plate 21). It is more than twice the size of Bodiam and was one of the stateliest and largest houses in the kingdom. Built *c.* 1440 of rose-red brick by Sir Roger de Fiennes, it is the chief of a group of houses in this novel material erected by wealthy nobles who became high officials at Court after campaigning in France. One cannot be sure whether their inspiration was derived from castles they had seen in France or from Flemish buildings; probably the latter. In his enlarged park Fiennes' house has a quadrangular shape with symmetrically placed polygonal towers at the corners and is be-pinnacled with smaller towers and turrets at intervals along the curtain walls. The whole is embellished with a noble gatehouse at the main front. The actual site lies very low; as Walpole observed in his letter previously mentioned, "the building for the convenience of water to the moat, sees nothing at all". Not yet did the greater magnates build a mansion to command a broad prospect.

Most of the larger medieval homesteads in Sussex were

moated. The word 'moat' invariably conveys the image of a castle-like house in stone or brick such as Bodiam and Herstmonceux, but large numbers of timber-framed dwellings of the lesser aristocracy, and even lower in the social order, were also protected by moats in the Middle Ages. Little research has been turned towards the Sussex moats. The Victoria County History listed only fifty-seven examples and regarded them as objects of little interest.[21] Emery's valuable distribution map of English moats draws on the same Sussex data,[22] but it is commonplace that such maps, covering the whole country, often reflect the intensity of local research rather than the real density and distribution of a feature. This certainly remains true of the Sussex moated sites because the published list is far from complete and the topic deserves urgent and detailed study. Allcroft put the number of moats at "more than sixty" in 1908,[23] but the number must greatly exceed this figure. E. Straker's unpublished papers[24] include a further thirty-eight unlisted moats and the present author has discovered more than 140 others so that the total at present exceeds 235. A systematic investigation based on place-names, documents, field-work and aerial photography would undoubtedly provide evidence of many more (Fig. 18).

One of the finest Sussex moated sites lies in Middle Wood, Waldron. It has an almost perfect circumference of about a hundred yards and traces of defensive earthworks inside it. This low-lying spot was the site of Herringdales manor and its chapel in the thirteenth century, before a new manor house was erected on a higher site nearby. One of the most accessible of the moated sites is Buncton Manor Farm, near Steyning, still surrounded by a small moat. The incidence

[21] V.C.H. *Sussex*, Vol. 1 (1907), pp. 477–8.
[22] F. V. Emery, 'Moated Settlements in England', *Geography*, Vol. 47 (1962), pp. 378–88.
[23] A. Hadrian Allcroft, *Earthwork of England* (1908), pp. 470–1.
[24] E. Straker's papers are now in the custody of the Sussex Archaeological Society, Barbican House, Lewes.

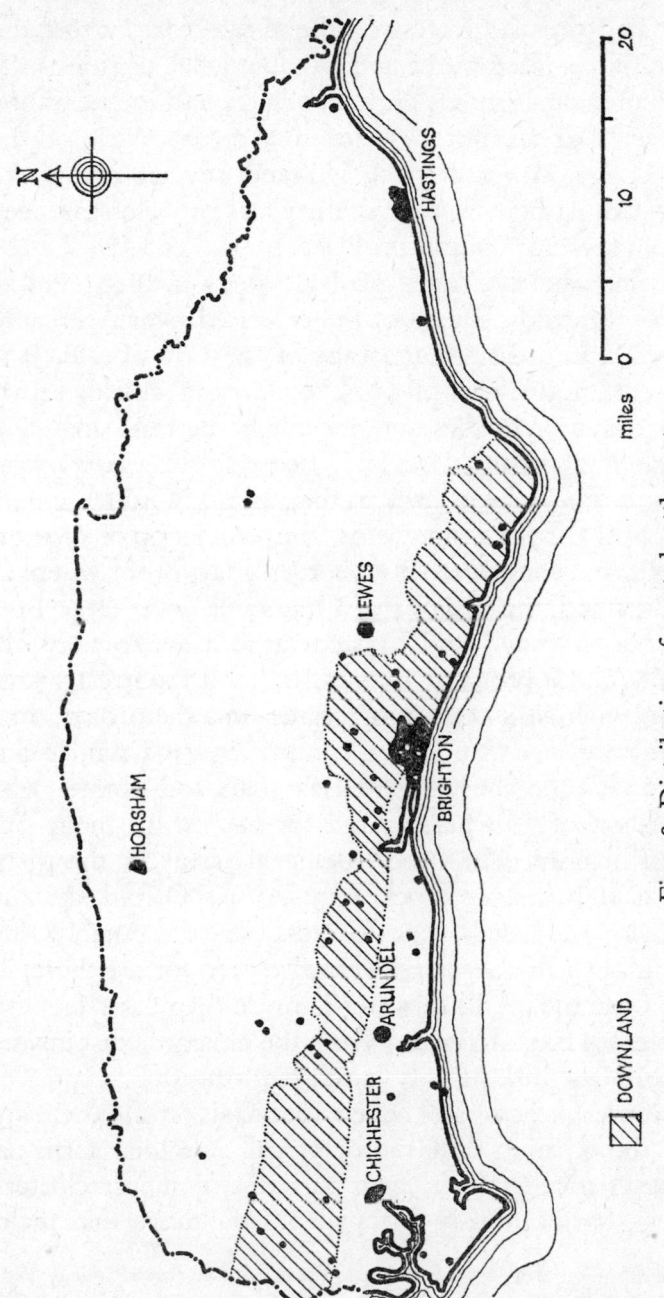

Fig. 18. Distribution of moated settlements.

of moated sites is greatest on the Weald Clay, where there was ample surface water and suitable level situations. The parish of Arlington has no less than six and the neighbouring parish of Laughton yields five more. Many of these moated sites are still occupied and several moats were renovated earlier in this century, as at Herstmonceux, Horselunges and Plumpton Place.

To find the most spectacular Sussex moated sites one follows the reedy course of the canalised river Arun across the gently undulating landscape of the Low Weald. It is a remote, tranquil, 'clay-pudding' countryside thickly set with decayed manor houses and ancient homestead sites. Their names—Pallingham, Harsfold, Lee, Orfold, Okehurst and Drungewick—take us back to the earliest Wealden colonisation, probably to a time before the foundation of surrounding villages. These were not yeomen's farms but where rich franklins and the bishops of Chichester once kept "bream and luce in stew" and moated large areas to keep their cattle from wolves and thieves. In 1256 the great moat at Drungewick, still containing water, was the protection for a large *staurum*, or stud farm, comprising 250 oxen, 10 bulls, 100 cows, 3000 sheep, as well as goats and horses, which the bishop of Chichester bred for use on his many other Sussex manors. The other medieval farms in the district were also primarily stock farms.[25] At Orfold the moat originally enclosed seven acres, so presumably large numbers of valuable cattle were also bred for use there. The part of the moat still in water is more than forty feet wide (Plate 24). The material dug from the moat was cast inside so the farm lies on a slightly raised platform.

These large farms still have a special air setting them apart from the smaller, and more typical, Wealden farmstead. Characteristically, they form part of a compact cluster of shapely, harmoniously-grouped old buildings that include

[25] M. Clough (ed.), 'Two Fitzalan Surveys', *Sussex Record Society*, Vol. 67 (1969), pp. 148–9.

great rambling, red-roofed and tarred weather-board barns. The hay barn, as for centuries past, is the most common building. In contrast, old granaries are small. Raised on stilts or occupying an upper floor to which sacks of grain were laboriously carried up flights of stone steps, these little granaries remind us that anciently the Sussex clays were pastures. The surrounding thick woods, formerly imparked, still harbour many deer which trespass on the winter crops, as did their medieval ancestors. Many fields are still parted by 'rews' up to seventy feet in width and even minor greenways are bounded, as were all old trackways, by wide verges. With their gentle slopes, brooks, groves of trees and orchards they form an exquisite man-made scene that is in essence medieval and retains the visual character which to the medieval mind was the perfect rural landscape.

The systematic investigation and recording of the legacy of medieval houses in Sussex is a very long-term task. Already it is clear that fourteenth- and fifteenth-century buildings—an era deserving to be called 'the first Great Rebuilding'—are much more numerous than was once believed. These vividly portray changing fashion in domestic architecture which clearly demonstrates the later Middle Ages as a period of actual development rather than stagnation.

The archaeological excavation of deserted village sites provides the opportunity, impracticable in a living community, for thorough investigation of successive layers of human occupation. By this means our knowledge of domestic architecture is being pushed back beyond the date of the oldest surviving buildings which are rarely earlier than the fourteenth century. The only major deserted site yet excavated in Sussex is Hangleton, a village on the downs north-west of Brighton, probably abandoned at the turn of the fifteenth century.[26] The interpretation of the maze of

[26] E. W. Holden, 'Excavations of the Deserted Medieval Village of Hangleton', Part One, *Suss. Arch. Colls.*, Vol. 101 (1963), pp. 54–181. J. G. Hurst and D. G. Hurst, 'Excavations at Hangleton', Part Two, *ibid.*, Vol. 102 (1964), pp. 94–142.

mounds and hollows before new roads and houses advanced over them has brought some important facts to light. One was the rebuilding or alteration of barns and dwellings on the same site between the end of the twelfth century and the abandonment of the site towards the close of the Middle Ages. The spade, in fact, revealed a complicated story of organic growth and decay which gives the lie to the still widely held assumption of the age-long stability of medieval village layout. In the course of several rebuildings, the timber-framed houses were replaced about the middle of the thirteenth century by new ones incorporating flint walls which in turn gave way to a fifteenth-century farmhouse orientated on a fresh axis.

Another result of the excavation of Hangleton which is of outstanding interest was the discovery of long-houses. They date from the thirteenth century and have affinities with similar long-houses still persisting in parts of upland Britain. There were two living rooms and a cross passage which separated a third room used for some farming purpose. The long-house is no longer part of the rural scene in Sussex today. All the oldest houses in the contemporary landscape probably originated as 'hall-houses', normally with a centrally placed living room and two smaller service rooms at either end. All three rooms were used purely for domestic purposes, animals and farm implements being housed in separate barns. Perhaps we should consider these hall-houses as representing improved standards of living in Sussex in the later Middle Ages.

In a region where the supply of good building-stone was highly localised, and high-quality wood plentiful, timber-framing was almost universal. But frame-building and plastering does not attain in Sussex the exquisite perfection exemplified by the clothiers' houses in Kent and East Anglia. The exuberance of the framed halls of Lancashire, Cheshire and the Welsh Marches is also lacking, the Sussex traditional style being one of self-imposed restraint and even austerity. Nevertheless, the remarkable durability of Sussex timber and the high standard of local workmanship, coupled with the strong tendency over the centuries to adapt and modernise rather than demolish, has preserved hundreds of dwellings with sufficient original features to allow us to visualise the layout and details of a medieval homestead.

By the fourteenth century the typical medieval dwelling had become a central hall open to the roof, often two bays in length, with small service rooms at either end. The highest level of attainment is represented by the 'Wealden' style which had the service rooms at each end jettied forward in the front elevation at first-floor level to make projecting wings, leaving the hall recessed, but with the whole roofed and framed as one unit. It has often been remarked that in its fully developed form the 'Wealden' must rank among the most aesthetic of vernacular building. The distribution of 'Wealden' houses is most dense in the Maidstone district of Kent, where architectural and other evidence suggests the form originated. But numerous examples exist in east Sussex and good specimens also occur in the Greensand district around Petworth; examples are Stonehill House in Chiddingly (Plate 23), a beautifully restored timber framed 'Wealden', and the 'Old Shop' at Bignor where the flint infilling was probably done later. In east Sussex, for reasons which are not yet clear, most 'Wealdens' are town or village houses rather than farmsteads. Possibly the greater buoyancy of the domestic textile industry compared with the depressed state of agriculture in the late Middle Ages explains this pattern.

More typical of central and west Sussex is the less elaborate T-shaped house with only one cross-wing and an unrecessed hall or even a singular framed house. An unusually large number exist in the villages of Albourne and Lindfield and in the towns of East Grinstead and old Crawley. Towards the close of the fifteenth century a number of larger and more spectacular framed houses were built in Sussex, marking a transition to the Tudor style, with more elaborate mouldings and more windows, such as Great Dixter, dating from *c.* 1470. An earlier moated manor site lies nearby. On the newer site was built an elaboration of a T-shaped 'Wealden', beautifully restored by the late Nathaniel Lloyd, an expert on the English house. Horselunges is another superb specimen of the new style, a 'continuous jetty' house constructed with two storeys throughout, the hall being retained but not left open to the roof. The flooring over the hall set a new fashion which was not widely adopted until more than a century later. Horselunges was later equipped with a fine staircase, a 'built-in' chimney stack and other exterior features but the sensitive restoration of Walter Godfrey in 1925 is faithful to the fifteenth-century structure. Another beautiful fifteenth-century framed house is St Mary's, Bramber, at right-angles to the road and probably merely the eastern wing of a courtyard dwelling originally belonging to the monks of Sele Priory, who were wardens of the bridge nearby. This house is notable for its continuous overhanging storey and the elaborate workmanship of its dragon-beamed angles. The Department of the Environment rates this as one of the best examples of timber-framing of the late fifteenth century in the whole of England.

Some remarkable early inventories drawn up at Hooe and Barnhorne in the 1460s give us a glimpse of the furnishings of one of the simplest Wealden houses. A typical example was William Creche's homestead on his little holding worked with two ploughs in 1462. It comprised three rooms, hall, bedroom (*camera*) and kitchen (*coquina*), apparently a single-storeyed house with a service room at either end of the hall. (Bell's farm in Slaugham and Nash-land farm near Horsham are but two similar surviving farmsteads.) Creche's hall was sparsely furnished with only the barest necessities—a table, two benches, a form and one chair. His kitchen housed the cooking equipment brought back and forth from the hall fire and the malt mill. In the bedroom were two plainly furnished beds, a bench and 'two coffins in readiness'. Here we have a revealing touch of medieval fatalism and a vivid impression of the frugal standard of living attained by the humble Wealden husbandmen in the fifteenth century.[27]

SELECT BIBLIOGRAPHY

Allcroft, A. H. *Earthwork of England* (1908).
Curzon, the Marquis of, *Bodiam Castle* (1926).
Du Boulay, F. R. H. *The Lordship of Canterbury* (1966).
Mason, R. T. *Framed Buildings of the Weald* (2nd edn., 1969).
Nairn, Ian and Pevsner, N. *The Buildings of England: Sussex* (1965).
Renn, D. F. *Norman Castles in Britain* (1968).

[27] Battle Abbey Court Rolls, Battle 1, folder 24, bundle 5, Henry Huntington Library, San Marino, California (microfilm held by E.S.R.O).

5. Tudor and Stuart legacies

The changing landscape of the Champion. The landscape of iron-making. The shrinking wilderness. Disparking. The second Great Rebuilding

TUDOR AND STUART times witnessed considerable change in the Sussex landscape. Remaining wastes shrank still further, but as we have seen, the main task of forest clearance was completed two centuries earlier. Most of the changes resulted from intensifying food production on farmland previously turned to limited account. During the long depression of the later Middle Ages the wild had been broken into many fields. The relatively prosperous Elizabethan and Jacobean farmers removed some of the neglect and decay by trimming back shaws and hedgerows, ploughing up old grassland and keeping more livestock. They also enclosed most of the common fields on the Champion and many commons, converted deer parks to agricultural use and modernised their farmhouses to such effect that W. G. Hoskins has styled this revolution in housing 'the Great Rebuilding'. Not since the early fourteenth century had land been such a scarce commodity.

Historians disagree about the relative importance of the several causes giving such momentum to the economy after 1500. The older view of a 'profit inflation' generated by an influx of specie which outstripped selling costs, wages and rent in England generally is now discredited and the most acceptable explanation of the rising demand for agricultural products is now considered to be increasing population pressure. The rapid growth of London also had a marked effect on land use in Sussex, it being within the ambit of the metropolitan food market and, locally, the meteoric rise of the iron industry added entirely fresh features to the landscape. Whatever the conjunction of causes—local, regional and national—impulses for rural change were most active in Sussex between about 1570 and 1640. Towards the end of the seventeenth century the period of prosperity came to a temporary halt with a depression in the iron industry and a marked decline in agricultural rents.

The changing landscape of the Champion

The most important process of landscape modification at work on the coastal plain and west Sussex downland was the piecemeal enclosure of the common fields by agreement (Fig. 19). This process left a close mesh of winding by-roads and farm-ways and a patchwork of small hedged and elongated fields, many with curvilinear boundaries. This "neatness and a sort of rural cosiness" which Thomas Sharp remarks upon in *English Panorama* is the particular charm of the Sussex countryside, is beautifully depicted on Yeakely and Gardner's map of west Sussex published in 1778. The imprint of the age of enclosure still remains in the present landscape, though it is being rapidly erased by twentieth-century mechanised farming. In 1724, when Daniel Defoe rode over the 'enclosed country' of south-west Sussex, some of the field patterns were already more than two centuries old, since even before 1500 enclosure of common fields in the county had made considerable headway. At Wiston, for example, one of the tenants was granted leave to enclose eight acres in the town fields as early as 1428, and by 1466 the common grazing over the remainder of the township arable was greatly reduced. Similarly, at Apuldram even by 1430 the tenants' holdings comprised both dispersed parcels and individually held arable fields, strongly suggesting the partial consolidation of former scattered strips.

Such instances of the supersession of the old communal

system of agriculture greatly multiply during the sixteenth century. This process was normally indicated by the gradual attrition of the common fields by the fortuitous amalgamation by exchanges among tenants of arable strips, which were then hedged to make a galaxy of tiny fields farmed individually, under more flexible rotations. The piecemeal enclosure of Graffham and Woolavington, below the Downs north of Chichester, occurred to form small individually held parcels before 1495, the date of the earliest records. In 1549 three of the Woolavington tenants were licensed to exchange their lands 'acre by acre' in two of the common fields, and to enclose their lands with hedges and ditches, subject to the approval of the lord and the remaining tenants. This was precisely the course of action staunchly advocated by J. Fitzherbert, the author of *The Boke of Husbandry* in 1523. By 1574 most of the common fields at the two villages appear to have been enclosed, but the redivision evidently did not meet with unanimous approval because several tenants were presented for tearing down the hedges dividing a neighbour's land.

That enclosure of this sort was active in Sussex during the sixteenth century is attested by a variety of documents, some of which assist us to date the final enclosure of the common fields. At Harting, Heyshott and Steyning (all in the west Sussex scarp-foot zone) and at East Dean, near Chichester, the main period of common-field enclosure was the reign of Elizabeth. At Middleton and the Ashlings, on the coastal plain, the enclosures can be assigned approximately to the first decade of the seventeenth century, by which date Bepton, Cocking, Ditchling, Keymer and Parham, all at the scarp-foot, and Ford, Merston, Portslade and Sidlesham on the coastal plain were enclosed. Records of Burton, Climping, Singleton and Warbleton indicate they were completely enclosed at some time between 1610 and 1640 (Fig. 19).[1]

[1] P. F. Brandon, 'The Commonlands and Wastes of Sussex', unpublished Ph.D. thesis, University of London (1963), pp. 307–10.

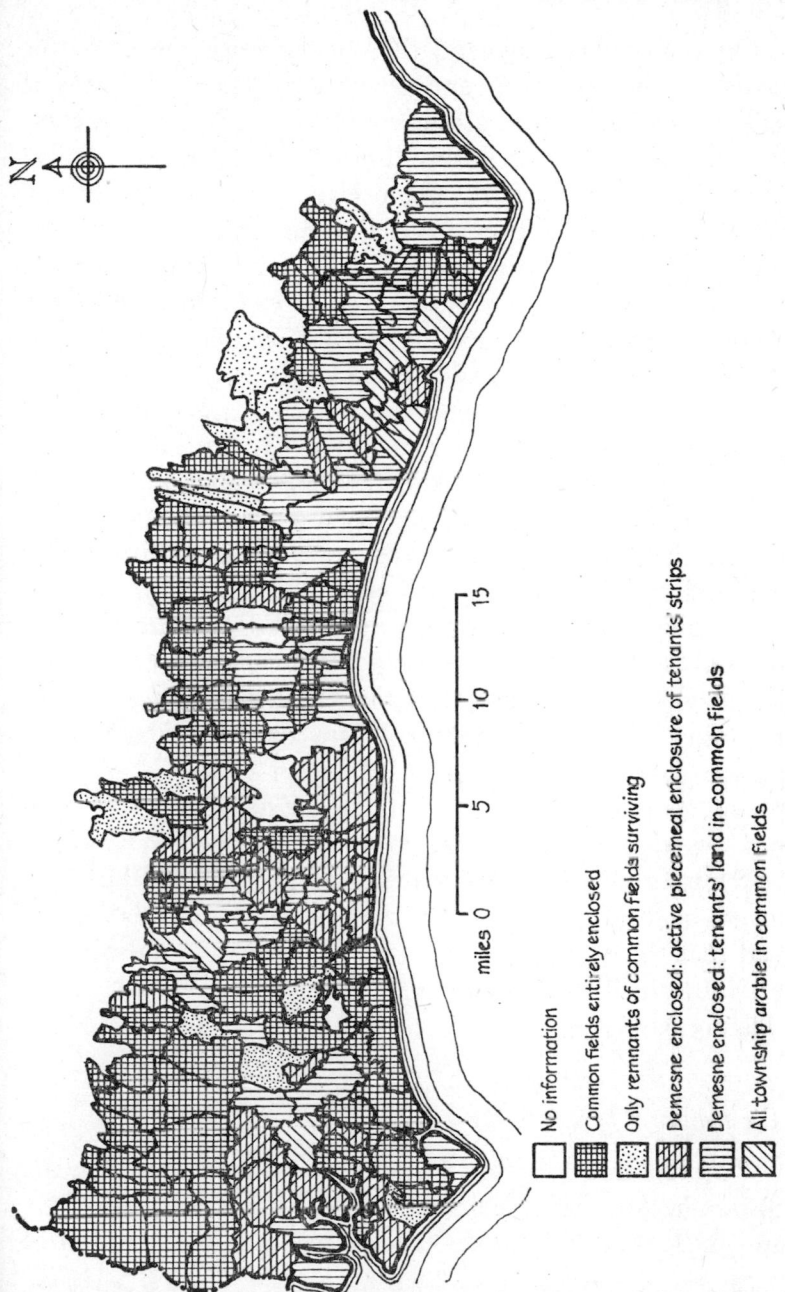

Fig. 19. Early enclosed common fields.

On the whole, however, the enclosure of the common fields in the sixteenth and seventeenth centuries was a 'silent revolution' unchronicled in surviving documents. Fortunately, the landscape itself has much to tell. Typically, the new fields were small because the standard holding of fifteen to twenty acres was often divided on enclosure into three arable fields, with an additional field proportional in size to the common rights exercised over the meadows. Another field was added to replace similar rights over the common, if this was also enclosed at the time. Most classes were created by exchanging old arable strips and hedging round not more than three or four of them. In consequence the characteristic new field was a 'long close', a term found in contemporary documents, often a furlong in length and curved in the inverted S-shape normal of arable that has been ploughed with heavy ox-teams for time out of mind (Fig. 20). High, massive hedges were planted, not only to shelter and provide good browsing for stock (an important consideration for a small farmer in a district retaining its arable emphasis), but also, in Fitzherbert's phrase, "to nurse up great quantities of timber . . ." This prospect of good timber growing in the new hedgerows was not the least of the advantages of enclosure. The resultant landscape still existed sufficiently at the end of the eighteenth century to impress Arthur Young junior, who observed that the whole coastal plain "is enclosed and divided up into small fields with high hedges intervening . . ." (Plate 32).[2]

The landscape of iron-making

For more than 2000 years from the prehistoric Iron Age the Sussex Weald was intensively worked for iron. The richest and most accessible ores were located near the junction of

[2] Rev. Arthur Young 'A Tour through Sussex', *Annals of Agriculture*, Vol. 22 (1794), p. 558.

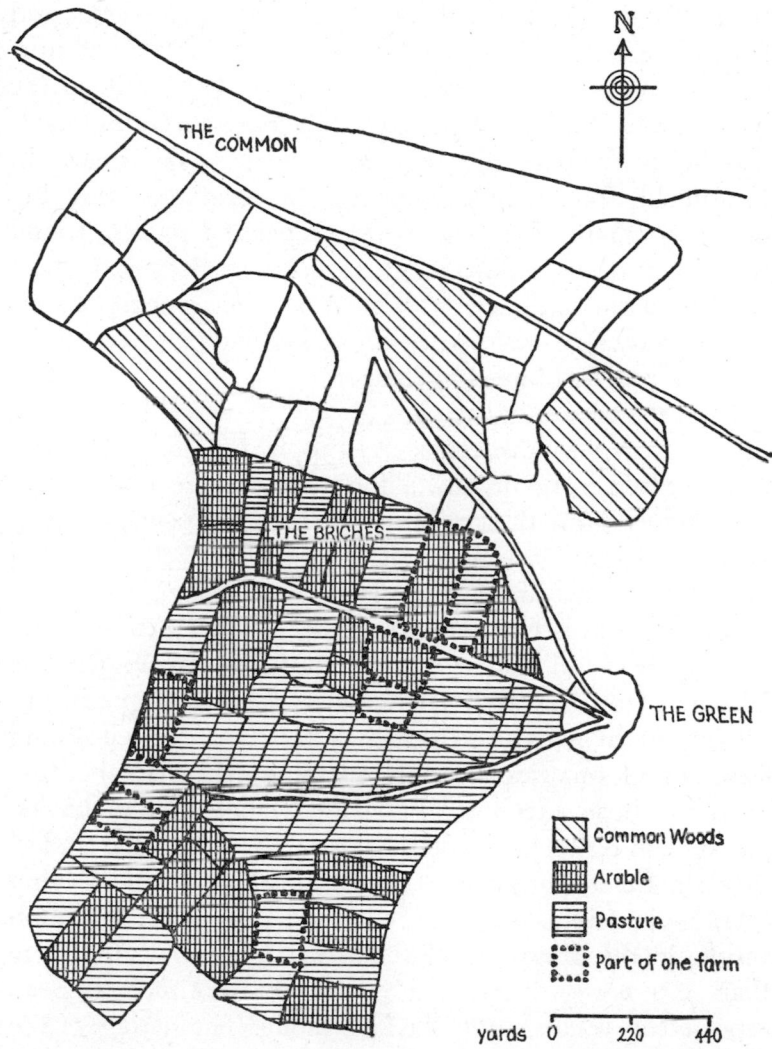

Fig. 20. Field patterns resulting from early enclosed common fields.

the Wadhurst Clay and the Ashdown Sand formation in the High Weald. Prospectors over the centuries patiently traced the ore exposures in the steep sides of the ghylls, and followed the beds by means of a series of shallow bell-pits, the age-old means of extracting the ore. On farmland the over-burden was shovelled back but invariably hummocks and hollows break the regularity of the old surface. In Heathfield, for example, almost every field has been dug over at some time for its iron. On steeper and poorer ground the old mine pits were more casually infilled, and many coppice woodlands are honeycombed with small, water-filled hollows, as at Minepit Shaw in Heathfield and Stilehouse Wood in Mayfield (Plate 26).

Until the advent of the blast furnace in early Tudor times, Sussex iron was made by the simple bloomery process, using only a crude hearth. The visible remains of the early iron industry on the ground are therefore usually inconspicuous heaps of cinder, slag, burnt clay, charcoal and partially roasted ironstone. The discovery of these old bloomery sites is far from complete, although enthusiastic investigation and field-work in industrial archaeology by the Wealden Iron Research Group and others is beginning to fill important gaps in our knowledge. The recording and study of bloomeries involves arduous field-work because most of those surviving lie hidden along stream banks, having lain protected from the plough by shaws and undergrowth. Investigation in the vicinity of stray cinder lying on ploughed fields or in the beds and banks of streams often results in the discovery of the actual bloomery site. More than sixty newly discovered bloomeries have recently been reported in Buxted and Mayfield alone. The dating of the sites depends on the nature of the associated pottery, often too simple and primitive to be precisely datable, and chance survivals of samples of charcoal suitable for radio-carbon dating. Mark Cross in Mayfield and Burwash Common, Burwash, are but two of many places in the Sussex Weald where iron-making by the bloomery process was a traditional occupation. All over the floor of Stilehouse Wood, for example, are extensive spreads of slag.

From the late fifteenth century the Sussex ironworks underwent an era of exceptionally rapid growth, establishing the county as the leading cast iron producer in the kingdom. Even following a sharp decline from the 1650s Sussex retained its virtual monopoly of gun-founding for another century, and the sole remaining furnace and forge did not cease working at Ashburnham, near Battle, until the 1820s. There are so few surviving buildings in the present landscape that it is not easy to reconstruct a picture of this industrial scene when the forges were turning out their handsome fire-backs, and the furnaces and mills cannon and shot that saw service in Canada, the American colonies and India. Nevertheless, the remodelling of the landscape to harness water-power has left a large legacy of relict features, many of which have yet to be fully investigated. Three major technical innovations have left their own individual impress on the ground. The earliest development was the forge hammer driven by water-power. Earthen dams were thrown up across narrow defiles to collect a head of water in hammer ponds. The mill itself was usually built of wood on a stone or brick foundation. The earliest documentary references to forge hammers in Sussex date from the 1430s when an iron mill (*ferrum molendinum*) in Burwash (probably at the site later known as Burwash Forge) and another at Ticehurst are recorded.[3] An even more important change was the introduction of the blast furnace into the Sussex Weald from France. The date of this event, though obscure, is believed to have been towards the end of the fifteenth century, when at least three furnaces were in blast in the county, Newbridge, Hartfield and Buxted, all on the fringes of Ashdown Forest. The blast furnaces needed a good head of water to work the bellows and water was therefore

[3] E.S.R.O. Ashburnham MS. 200A and Dunn MS. 9.

collected into ponds during winter, for use by the forges in dry summers. The third major technical change was the successful casting of cannon for the first time in England by Ralph Hogge of Buxted in 1543. Ordnance manufacture then became a staple industry in the Weald and water-power was needed to operate boring mills.

William Camden in *Britannia* (1586) gave a vivid description of man's handiwork at a Sussex furnace in its heyday: ". . . there be furnaces on every side . . . to which purpose divers brooks in many places are brought to run in one channel, and sundry meadows turned into pools and waters, that they might be of power sufficient to drive hammer mills, which beating upon the iron, resound all over the places adjoining." The ground both corroborates and amplifies this valuable statement. The blast furnace site at Broadhurst in Heathfield is one of the revealing survivals. Typically, it lies remote in Climpshurst Wood, which supplied it with ore, fuel and power. Only the stone foundations of the furnaces are now visible, but the black soil containing fragments of charcoal and roasted ore high up on the adjoining bank probably marks the spot where the charge from the furnace was mixed before being fed by means of a bridge to the top of the furnace shaft. The ironworks lay just below a wide, long dam, or 'bay', as it was known locally, across a headwater of the eastern Rother. Higher upstream are two, possibly three, other 'bays' which were provided with pen-stocks and dammed reservoirs. The ponds are now dry, partly because the erosive power of the strong stream has lowered their outlets. The abandoned site is now inhabited only by rabbits and foxes, but the deeply-sunk tracks and associated fields, long since encroached upon by coppice and shrub, are reminders of a once-thriving hub of industry (Plate 27).

Another old furnace site that repays study is Warren Furnace near Crowborough, lying deep in a valley still echoing pleasantly to the continuous sound of falling

Plate 19 Bayham Abbey, the most complete and instructive of the Sussex monastic sites. See p. 127.

Plate 20 Though one of the smaller Sussex monasteries, the Augustinian priory of Michelham was defended by its moat and fourteenth-century gatehouse. See p. 127.

Plate 21 Herstmonceux is one of the most sumptuous English houses of the fifteenth-century 'Age of Ambition'. Both as a precursor of the Renaissance house and as a source of inspiration to the Gothic revivalists of the eighteenth century, it is an artistic achievement of the first order. See p. 135.

Plate 22 The ruins of Cowdray, the earliest of the great Tudor 'courtyard' mansions of Sussex, still compose a memorable landscape. The house is connected by an artificial causeway to Midhurst, a delightful small town built of mellow sandstone. The 'estate' village of Easebourne lies discreetly on the north-west fringe of the old deer park, now largely devoted to golf and polo. The backdrop of tall trees form woods spreading to the Downs which fill the southern horizon. See p. 168.

Plate 23 Stonehill, Chiddingly. "The perfect timber-framed Sussex house of the fifteenth century" is Sir Nikolaus Pevsner's description of this dwelling in the Sussex volume of *The Buildings of England*. Originally roofed in Horsham Stone, the house has been carefully restored on three occasions this century. Apart from the bay window, an Elizabethan addition, the exterior is typical of Wealden hall houses. See p. 141.

Plate 24 Orfold Farm, Wisborough Green, is still partially moated. It depended on its water defences to protect large herds of cattle. See p. 138.

Plate 25 The mellow, harmoniously grouped buildings of Duckyls Farm, West Hoathly, set in the wooded 'up-and-down' country of the High Weald, are typical of the region. See p. 172.

water. The furnace was converted into a large stone-built mill at the end of the eighteenth century and the cleverly contrived diversion of several water-courses to feed the mill ponds has created a converging fan of little streams. Although the mill and its large buildings are in ruins, and steadily being robbed of their stone, the wide culverts and leats are still impressive, all the more because they are so unexpected in this empty landscape of heath and woodland.

One of the most historic and important iron-working sites in Sussex is Newbridge, on the northern edge of Ashdown Forest (Plate 28). 'A great hammer' operated by water-power is mentioned here in 1492 and ten years later six acres of land and a water-course were let within the forest in order to "construct a mill and forges with a great hammer and wheel for to make steel . . ."[4] Newbridge clearly became a complex of ironworks, for in 1658, by which time iron-working had ceased, old hammers, furnace ponds, bays and other buildings used in the industry still existed. Even now Newbridge retains a delightfully rural atmosphere. The little colony of iron-workers gave rise to the scattered cottages, tile-clad or weather-boarded, lying around the slopes overlooking the natural hollow where the mill waters were collected from a dozen different sources. The main furnace, later used as a corn mill, is now much altered and enlarged as a private residence, but the spillway and one of the hammer ponds, partially reclaimed, still exist. Rising steeply northwards are the bracken-covered slopes of the Forest, a centuries-old landscape.

The most beautiful legacy of the iron industry is the hammer pond (Plate 29). As the Wealden headwaters had such small volume, numerous 'bayed-up' ponds, constructed to serve the larger furnaces, interrupt the streams. These, on maps or from the air, resemble a chain of beads on a string. There are no less than eleven ponds on streams serving the famous Heathfield Furnace, operated by the Fullers of

[4] P.R.O. DL/42/21 f. 185.

Waldron, and another chain of ponds lies on the stream working Maresfield Mills. Lending particular distinctiveness to the Wealden landscape are the narrow finger-like ponds resulting from the damming of a narrow defile. Ridge-walkers in St Leonard's Forest are rewarded by sudden glimpses of these long and incredibly beautiful lakes, bordered by hanging woods clinging to their sheer banks. Several of these picturesque examples served St Leonard's furnace and forge, such as Bewbush, Tilgate, Hammer and Hakins' Ponds.

Also enriching the present scene are houses originally built for iron-workers—the ironfounders, the forge and furnace masters and the ironmasters themselves. Labourers unable to find accommodation in existing villages obtained a grant from the waste and built their home on a little plot enclosed from the common or village green. Poorer workers merely squatted on the commons, often in temporary shelters and hovels which have perished. At several places in the Sussex Weald permanent hamlets of iron-workers, as at Newbridge, sprang up. Others were New-pound in Wisborough Green, where nineteen cottagers were encroaching on the common in 1641, and Cross-in-Hand on Waldron Down. The larger houses of the forge and furnace masters were usually built beside the hammer pond bay. A beautiful house in St Leonard's Forest sited in this manner is Hammer Cottage. Basing in East Grinstead, Furnace Mill and Scarlet's in Cowden, and Furnace Pond Cottage at Slaugham are further examples of similar agreeable houses, built of local stone or timber. The ironmasters were generally accounted members of the local gentry and their houses equalled, or surpassed, contemporary manor houses. Streame in Chiddingly, the seat of the Frenches; Tanner's in Waldron, the home of the Fullers; Denne in Horsham, the Eversfields' residence; Gravetye, Stoneland and Chiddingly, the homes of the Infields, Paynes and Mitchells, all ironmasters of West Hoathly;

Idehurst in Kirdford, the Strudwicks' house, these, together with such outstanding Sussex houses as Bateman's in Burwash, Socknersh in Brightling and Middle House in Mayfield, were all built by Sussex ironmasters. The present scene would be greatly the poorer without these fine Elizabethan or Jacobean houses.

Another aspect of the landscape of ironworking was the abrupt and widespread depletion of tree cover in several places in the Weald. Hitherto Wealden society had lived in harmony with its landscape and peasant economy was dependent on the continuance of the woods and groves. Little wonder that the great damage wrought in the country-side by woodland clearance was considered by many contemporary observers as tantamount to devastation. The passions stirred by this decimation of the Weald's woodland sustained the earliest recorded conservation movement in England. All the agitation and anxiety, as is well known, has left a marked impression on Tudor legislation, on Commissions of Enquiry and manorial records of the time. It is doubtful whether any of this activity had much effect on the condition of the landscape. The first real victory of the conservation movement did not come until almost a century later when, under the influence of John Evelyn, land-owners began to plant trees to adorn the hedgerows.

The strong reaction of contemporaries against the removal of trees for use as fuel in ironworks gave rise to the long-standing opinion of later historians that great tracts of the Sussex woodlands were first laid bare for cultivation and settlement during the heyday of the Wealden iron industry. This conjecture does not stand up to a more balanced, systematic appraisal. The ninth to the early fourteenth centuries witnessed man's greatest impact on the Wealden landscape and only now is this medieval accomplishment becoming fully appreciated. As we shall see, the task awaiting the sixteenth- and seventeenth-century land-clearers was of quite a different order. They began to subjugate some of the residual woods preserved on commons, in parks, and, above all, in the forests. Much of this attack fell upon the wilder landscape of the Weald and the permanent, as distinct from the ephemeral, effects of this endeavour are relatively small in comparison with the gigantic scale of medieval and Saxon clearing.

The woodland speedily consumed as fuel for the iron-works was rarely on farms or in private woods which continued to be meticulously managed under customary rotations. It mainly lay in the Forests and on commons. John Norden lists ten localities, mainly commons, where the woods had been devoured in an orgy of speculation by 1607. Some clearances were spectacular—Dicker Common yielded 7000 oaks, of which 600 were mature, and Sir Thomas Gresham's similar destruction of common woodland aroused great local feeling. This wanton felling finally ended the traditional custom of pannage and interfered with the commoners' cattle grazing. On the Forests the marked decline in pannage revenues in the later Middle Ages suggests that woodland was even then severely reduced. The early Tudor surveys of Crown woods provide further proof of this deterioration, the normal result on soils as thin and as heavily grazed as the Sussex Forests. Less than one third of St Leonard's Forest was described as wooded in early Elizabethan times and in Ashdown Forest the only extensive area of mature trees was confined to the South Ward. In fact, the Forests had largely lost their tree cover before the large-scale development of the iron industry had ever begun. This explains the speedy removal of the remaining trees by the iron industry and the practice of rabbit warrening which prevented the regeneration of trees and encouraged the growth of bracken. St Leonard's Forest still wore a 'melancholy aspect' at the end of the eighteenth century and William Cobbett in *Rural Rides* reserved some of his well-known vituperation for Ashdown

Forest, describing it as a "heath with here and there a few birch scrubs upon it, verily the most villainously ugly spot I ever saw in England". He would not have much need to modify his description today, though the largely town-dwelling population of south-east England would scarcely accept his aesthetics of landscape.

The shrinking wilderness

Despite four centuries of medieval clearing, Gervase Markham could still single out for notice the "divers great forests . . . having five or six miles in length" which occupied the barren elevated lands on the Forest Ridges of the Sussex High Weald. St Leonard's Forest, the most westerly of these, with its bordering parks, comprised 9000 acres. The smaller Forest of Worth (including Tilgate) adjoined it, and beyond an embayment of improved land in the upper Ouse valley lay Ashdown Forest which occupied some 15,000 acres of the higher ground in the central Weald. Finally, Waterdown Forest lay close to the north-eastern edge of Ashdown.

Ashdown Forest was the scene of several important changes. One of its great attractions today is the remarkable diversity of its landscape. The open land is moulded into hills and deep valleys covered with bell heather, bracken, gorse and broom, relieved by the bright green of sphagnum moss in the boggy hollows. In the intermingled enclosed parts are such varied scenes as the beautiful groves of beech and oak in Five Hundred Acre Wood; the dark lines of conifer plantations at Pressridge Warren and about Old Lodge; islands of rich green fields at Pippingford and Broadstone; and the patchwork of little farms, many originated by squatters, carved out of the southern part of the forest near Fairwarp and Duddleswell, which give the landscape a charm of their own.

This wealth of scenery is largely due to the Forest's

history since the early seventeenth century. Under the Tudor monarchs it was robbed of most of its trees and was neglected as a deer park. The Stuart kings likewise showed little interest in it and encroachments began to multiply. During the Commonwealth the Forest was sequestrated, and through the advocacy of such writers as Adam Moore the first steps were taken to ameliorate it. A detailed scheme for the partial enclosure of the Forest was proposed in 1658, suggesting that most of it should be enclosed for the growth of trees. Much of the remainder was earmarked for pasture but tillage was recommended where marl was conveniently available.

Charles II was restored before this scheme could be implemented. He let the Forest, and large enclosures were made there under the management of Sir Thomas Williams. The commoners bitterly opposed this policy and insisted that several large parcels should be left open for their benefit. The face of the forest is scored by many banks and ditches recording the frustrated endeavours of 'improvers'. Two prominent banks, for example, extend across the Forest to the north and north-east of Camp Hill, near Duddleswell, probably attempted enclosures from the Old and Duddleswell Lodges. Another bank and ditch runs almost continuously along the northern side of the road between Wych Cross and Coleman's Hatch. It appears on Kelton's map of the Forest (1740) as the 'old ditch' and was set out before 1693, when almost all Broadstone Walk was being reserved for private use.

The commoners' fight to preserve the Forest as common-land, waged over more than forty years, earned them two significant rewards, both recognised in the celebrated Decree of 1693, a compromise finally bringing peace to the Forest (Fig. 21). One advantage of the fight was a large increase in the amount of land reserved for common grazing. The initial award of 1658 allocated only 4400 acres for this purpose; the award of 1680 increased this to 5000 acres, a proposal turned down by the commoners; the Decree fixed the amount at 6400 acres. The other benefit won by the commoners was more important than the increased grazing. In the Decree the principle was adopted that commons should be preserved on the edges of the Forest, convenient to the parishes using them. The award of 1658 had set out allotments of common without regard to this. For example, nearly all the south and north-east parts of Ashdown were intended for enclosure, notwithstanding the hardship this would have entailed for the commoners of the adjacent parishes of Hartfield, Withyham, Buxted and Maresfield. Basically, the Decree created the present layout of spacious open stretches of forest intermingled with equally large enclosures, thus laying the foundations for most of the constituents in the present forest scene. Now that the South Downs are mainly under the plough the unenclosed parts of Ashdown Forest have become the largest existing tract of wild scenery remaining in Sussex. For this lovely portion of England, increasingly used for recreational purposes, we owe much to the stubborn resistance of the 'Forest men' of three centuries ago.

The legislation of 1693 had little immediate effect on the face of the Forest for, as late-eighteenth-century maps disclose, most of the newly enclosed land remained simply rabbit warren. It was not until a century later, under the stimulus of war-time food and timber shortages, that the warrens were destroyed to make farms and plantations. Nevertheless, the Decree laid down the framework for the changes to come. One of these was the enclosure adjoining Buckhurst Park, which became known as the Five Hundred Acre Wood. Here, planting produced magnificent trees still lending beauty and grandeur to the local scene between Friar's Gate and Chuck Hatch. Its woodland glades are a reminder that by the eighteenth century man was becoming a preserver of trees, not, as he had been for centuries, a destroyer.

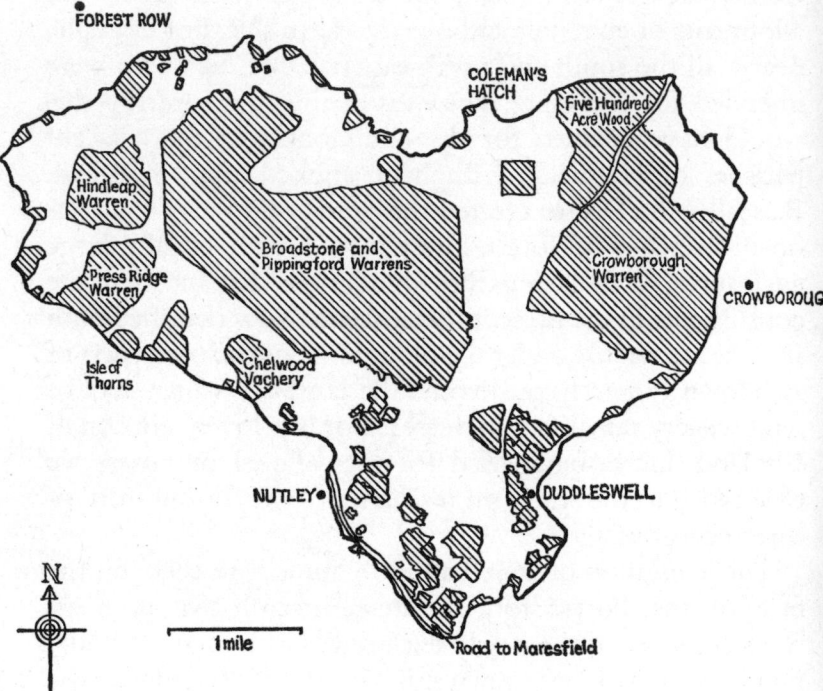

Fig 21. Ashdown Forest: the Decree of 1693.

Another major change in the Forest's southern aspect resulted from the enclosure of some 900 acres granted out in small sporadic parcels to be separately ring-fenced and farmed. These seventeenth-century grants followed the long tradition of piecemeal clearing along the Forest edge but were unprecedented both in scale and the effect they had in opening up the interior of the Forest to settlement. They produced Ashdown's curious semi-enclosed appearance with its scattering of cottages amidst heathland. To this day, the part of the Forest between Nutley and Duddleswell largely retains its seventeenth-century configuration and has become a thoroughly characteristic piece of 'waste-edge' scenery with little hedged gardens, well-stocked orchards and bright green meadows, pleasantly varying the expanses of intervening fern and heather.

The story of St Leonard's Forest in the sixteenth and seventeenth centuries is similarly one of steady nibbling at the Forest edge and a few larger enclosures for woodland. It would have been quite different if the bold intentions of two improvers had been realised. The first of the visionaries was Sir Thomas Seymour, who dreamed of founding a new town amidst freshly enclosed fields. He did not live long enough to embark on his Utopian scheme, but by one of the strange coincidences of history he anticipated by four centuries the New Town of Crawley, created in the radically different twentieth-century economic and social conditions. Seymour was the first of a long line of speculators who, lacking a farmer's eye, misjudged the nature of the Forest. Another was Sir Richard Weston who acquired land in the Forest about 1640 in order to experiment with agricultural techniques he had observed in use on the sandy soils of Brabant and Flanders. Weston failed to appreciate that the silty forest soils would be too wet in inclement weather for sheep-folding, the source of manure. In the early nineteenth century, when pressures for the expansion of cultivation were renewed all over England, the tile-draining of the

Forest was a prerequisite for its successful reclamation. This was the main lesson learned from Weston's futile experiments. More successfully managed were the little smallholdings proliferating around the edges of the Forest by 1609. Some 2500 acres of St Leonard's Forest were then let for farming at rack-rents in forty separate parcels containing twenty-two dwellings. Most of these new farms still included much unimproved ground, steadily taken into cultivation by paring off bracken or furze and ploughing in the ashes after burning.

It was the character of Worth Forest that changed most under the hand of man during this period. In climbing up to the high ground north of Staplefield Common towards Worth or Balcombe, the traveller enters the eastern half of old Worth Forest. At the beginning of Elizabeth's reign this tract of upland waste was enclosed and carved up into about thirty-five farms.[5] These farms were amongst the very last to be won from the heath and wood by small yeoman farmers. The sixteenth-century farmhouses were traditionally timber-framed, but several prospering families rebuilt their homes in the warm-coloured sandstone and thin bricks fashionable in the later seventeenth century. Frog's Hole, Gibbshaven, Nayland, Sandhill, Spicer's and Standing Hall farms originated in this spread of fields across the woodland glades and heaths.

Despite this, much of the former forest appearance persists in the present landscape. Take what road he will, the motorist enters beautiful avenues of high beeches, including gnarled and misshapen trunks, relics of the uncleared woodland cover. Many properties lining the roads are villas which sprang up in the early nineteenth century with improved communications. Older farms and cottages are generally down the slopes, several still approachable only by soft tracks. The rampant shaws, today actively retreating, and deep marl pits tell that Elizabethan

5 W. Scawen-Blunt, *History of the Crabbett Estate in Sussex* (1917), pp. 47-9.

162

and Jacobean reclaimers still used the well-tried techniques of earlier generations. The wealth of oak and other hedgerow trees is an outstanding characteristic of the scene. This deliberate planting was presumably a response to the need not only for fuel and fencing but also for the protection of men, cattle and crops from cold and heat. The presence of a thick warm wood at their backs and around the winter corn would have been a great comfort to the sixteenth- and seventeenth-century reclaimers, accustomed to harder winters than are experienced today. Perhaps, therefore, it is not too fanciful to see elements in the present landscape reflecting our changing climate.

Disparking

The reclamation of deer parks was another source of improvable land. The nobility still continued to cherish their private hunting reserves and some lords extended them at this period, like the proud Coverts when they built their magnificent Palladian mansion at Slaugham in the early seventeenth century. Similarly, some of the wealthy merchants who purchased religious estates aspired to the dignified possession of a park, notably the Palmers who acquired parks at Angmering and Parham at the Dissolution. But the chief trend of the times was to reduce the acreage under parks taking advantage of rapidly rising rents. The aristocracy, still fortunate enough to retain possession of vast lordships, frequently disparked one or more of their estates thus increasing their revenues without seriously compromising their pleasure. The break-up of the great ecclesiastical properties such as the Archbishop of Canterbury's lands in the Lewes district, or those of Lewes Priory, facilitated the transfer of parks into speculators' hands.

The conversion of a park into productive farmland was a daunting prospect involving manifold stages of timber clearance, denshiring, marling and liming, hedging, ditching and fencing, as well as the provision of farm buildings and dwellings. Such work was not normally undertaken by park owners themselves but by several lessees in turn, each progressively improving and consequently paying a higher rental than the previous tenant. The disparking of Petworth Great Park illustrates the process perfectly. This was initially leased for grazing at a yearly rental of £60 in 1593. In the second stage beginning upon the expiry of the lease in 1614, the tenant was empowered to divide and enclose the park "as he should think meet and convenient" at a yearly rental of nearly £70. In a third phase of reclamation, which began, as before, with fresh leases in the mid-seventeenth century, the land was in good enough heart to be let to ten tenants at a combined yearly rental of £265.[6] A similar record can be pieced together from the parks of Cuckfield, Ditchling and Hayley near Lewes. Little wonder that lords were 'harnessing their barrens' wherever they found it convenient.

The most helpful evidence on the ground of this Tudor and early Stuart disparking is the presence of aged, freestanding or hedgerow trees, growing on the land when the park was enclosed. The fine trees on lands enclosed from Petworth Great Park, for example, still stand in all their glory. Furthermore, the former use as a deer park has stamped itself architecturally on several of the old farmhouses which began their existence as lodges or wardens' houses.

Other important sources of exploitable land were the commons. Generally speaking, every Wealden manor still retained spacious commons, lying mainly in remoter parts which survived the attack on the virgin lands ending in the fourteenth century. In some districts the proportion of commons to improved land was very high. Along the Downs scarp-foot between Albourne and Lewes, for example, the traveller going northwards quickly entered a belt of almost unrelieved commons and wastes on the Weald

---

[6] Lord Leconfield, *Petworth Manor in the Seventeenth Century* (1954), pp. 64–5.

Clay. In parts of the High Weald commons were even more in evidence. Fletching, Framfield, Laughton and Mayfield were but a few manors with commons exceeding 1000 acres each.

Traditionally, Wealden farmers had pastured cattle on the commons and fattened them on enclosed fields before sending them on the hoof to Smithfield and other markets. Gradually, however, needs were changing. The late-seventeenth-century grazier-farmers, like Sir John Fagg of Wiston, on whom Daniel Defoe has conferred immortality in his *Tour through England and Wales*, brought young Scotch or Welsh stock and devoted more attention to their weight and quality. This required ample fields with good grass, not unregulated common grazings. Moreover, as tillage increased in the Weald the stored-up fecundity of the 'uplandish' commons which guaranteed several years' good returns was sought as a replacement for worn-out fields. Yet another motive behind enclosure in this period was anxiety about fuel stocks. Nothing short of fenced enclosures and the eviction of commoners could facilitate the spontaneous growth of fresh timber.

As the desirability of enclosing commons and similar wastes became insistent, the overall changes in some parts of the Weald resulting from this amounted to a major contribution to the present landscape. Around Lewes the enclosure movement was active for more than a century following 1530 (Fig. 22). The earliest enclosures at Clayton, Ditchling and Laughton provoked agrarian unrest in Edward VI's reign. In the first years of Elizabeth there were protests about the large share of the enclosed Plumpton Common appropriated by the lords of the manors involved. Later enclosures in this district met with more general approval and proceeded more peacefully and steadily. By the late sixteenth century the commons of Alciston, Barcombe, Beechwood, Heighton, Novington and Wivelsfield had been enclosed. These were followed before the

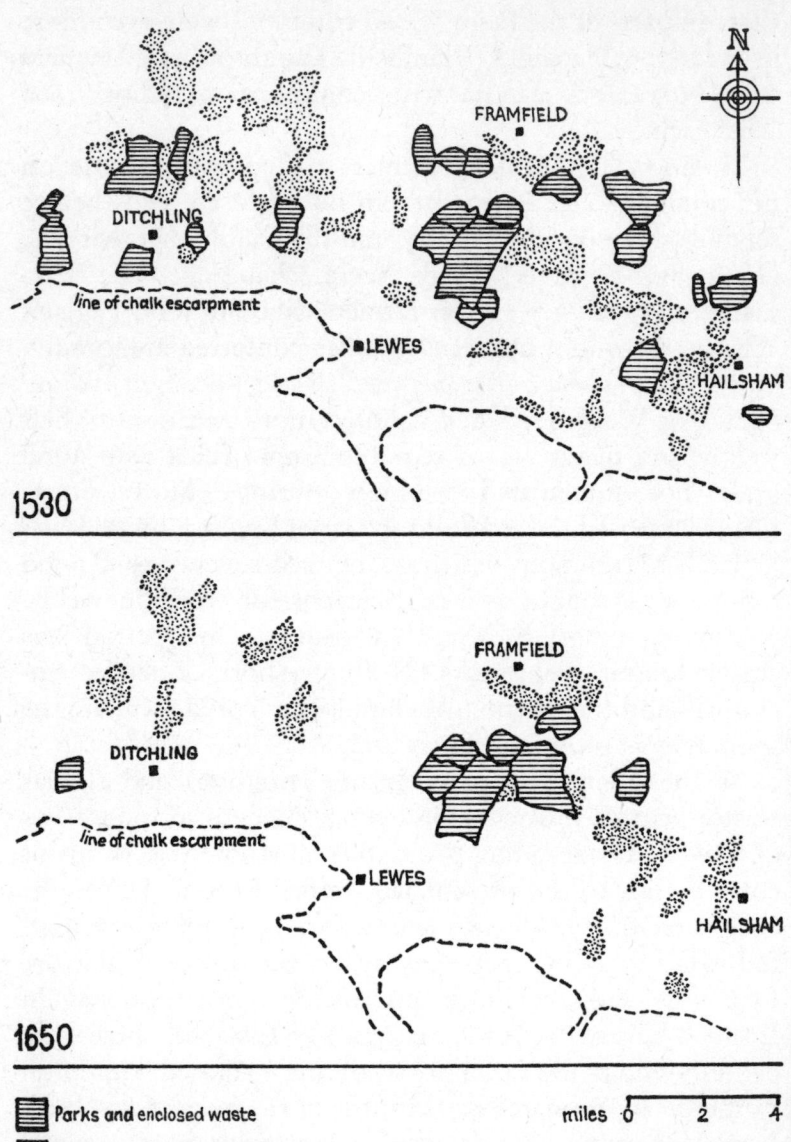

Fig. 22. Enclosure of commons in the Lewes district in the sixteenth and seventeenth centuries.

mid-seventeenth century by those in the manors of Allington, Balneath, the College of South Malling, Houndean, Middleton, Streat and Westmeston.[7]

These extensive enclosures have imparted a distinctive field pattern to the scene. Medieval fields have an irregularity of outline attributable to the hand clearance of trees or the age-long swing of the ox-drawn plough. By contrast, straight-sided, evenly sized fields were laid out by the Elizabethan and Jacobean improvers, using the new instruments of land survey, the theodolite, plane table and measuring chain. In this manner a neat grid of rectangular or square fields was created, each enclosure being divided by low earthen banks on which were planted hedgerow trees. Such 'chessboard' farmland falls within the view of the traveller coming from the high ground of the Weald towards the Chalk escarpment north of Brighton. At the junction of the A272 road in Chailey and the local road from Wivelsfield Green, for example, there is a wide prospect of planned fields. This resulted from the enclosure of about 600 acres of Chailey Common by the manors of Allington and Houndean in the first half of the seventeenth century. A similar pattern is observable near St Helens Farm, representing the division of the old common of Streat. Another instance is seen west of the B2112 road between the common at Ditchling and the older enclosures near the village itself; here was the medieval chase of Frankbarrow. Walkers can easily gain a closer acquaintance with these early enclosed landscapes by taking to the numerous footpaths, including that leading eastwards across the old Plumpton Common from Heath Farm, a name which recalls a long-vanished feature of the landscape.

The second Great Rebuilding

The "great bravery of building which marvellously beautified the realm" that Camden observed with such pride, extended

7 P. F. Brandon, thesis cited, pp. 157–62.

into Sussex, as it did into most of England. An important factor contributing to marked changes in domestic architecture was the rising living standard to which W. Harrison alludes in his brilliant contemporary account of Elizabethan social life.[8] When the Tudors were established in 1485 domestic life in Sussex, as elsewhere in England, centred on the open hall and the basic plan of vernacular building had been unchanged for generations. By the first decade of the seventeenth century houses had taken on a completely new shape. This period of change is unparalleled in the history of the English house. In the course of reconstruction much use was made of brick, stone and tile, materials hitherto available only to the wealthy, for infilling between ancient frames or even for completely re-fronting. As a result an older façade of lath and plaster often lies hidden behind a newer facing, and careful expert investigation is needed to unravel the complicated architectural history of many older houses. The great houses of the late sixteenth century displayed more revolutionary innovations. Their fortress-like character was abandoned and old moated sites generally deserted in favour of higher and healthier residences of stone, brick and glass, set in formal gardens surrounded by parkland rich in oaks and abounding in deer. The stately mansions erected in this manner satisfied the soaring ambitions of the new Tudor and Stuart nobility who wished to rival the grandees of France and Italy.

The most magnificent sixteenth-century house in Sussex, setting the fashion for two generations or more, was Cowdray, outside Midhurst. It has been in ruins since a disastrous fire in 1793 but enough is still standing to attest to its former grandeur (Plate 22). Characteristically, Cowdray faces east, regarded in Tudor times as a much healthier aspect than south. Its builders in the reign of Henry VIII, the Earl of Southampton and Sir Anthony

[8] F. J. Furnivall (ed.), *Harrison's Description of England in Shakespeare's Youth* (1877–98).

168

Browne, were both courtiers and office holders. Southampton has left a memorial of this by emblazoning in 1537 badges on the fan-vaults of his gatehouse porch commemorating his new appointment as Lord High Admiral and the birth of the long-yearned-for prince, later Edward VI. Browne acquired immense additional wealth at the Dissolution, being granted not only Battle and Bayham Abbeys and Easebourne Priory in Sussex, but also Waverley Abbey in Surrey and a London nunnery. The two Cowdray owners began building in the new style adopted by the king, himself an enthusiastic rebuilder, at Hampton Court and Nonesuch Palace. The building enclosed a central quadrangle, the archetype of a great house still in vogue when William Morley built Glynde Place in the late 1560s. Cowdray's notable gatehouse, incorporating the same style of central oriel as at Hampton Court, still forms the central piece of a symmetrical west elevation some 180 feet in length. Cowdray was also famous for its magnificent hall, again modelled on that of Hampton Court, and its regular ranges of mullioned windows. Its ruins help to compose a memorably romantic landscape. Set off by a backdrop of tall trees, it encompasses a view of woods stretching away to the foot of the Downs which fill the southern horizon.

After Cowdray a spate of building began in Sussex and few counties can rival the generous legacy of Elizabethan and Jacobean mansions and smaller houses. Of these later Elizabethan houses none embodies more of Elizabethan taste in its architecture and surrounding landscape than Parham (Plate 31). The estate, originally held by the Abbey of Westminster, was purchased from the Crown by Robert Palmer, whose family had local connections but owed its wealth to trade in London. His great-grandson was an adventurer with Drake who sold Parham to Thomas Bysshop, a London barrister who enjoyed a meteoric rise under James I. The house of mellow grey stone from the Lower Greensand nearby lies on the site of a medieval grange, probably incorporated into the east wing. The front has such a close affinity with those of Loseley, Surrey, and Wiston, built a little earlier, that all three mansions were probably the work of the same mason. The elevation has the characteristic E-plan with projecting wings and ranges of well-proportioned mullioned windows possessing the symmetrical regularity so strongly favoured by Elizabethan taste. Above the Great Hall is the Long Gallery of some 160 feet, another indispensable feature of a great house at the close of the sixteenth century, with splendid views of the surrounding countryside. The park is a particularly interesting survival from the past. The eighteenth-century landscape designers are responsible only for the vista from the west where they added a lake, opened up views to the Downs and planted numerous exotic trees on the West Plain. This scene greatly contrasts with the remainder of the larger park which is pure Tudor and something of a rarity, with its disorderly ensemble of bracken and grass interspersed amongst copses and coverts. These wilder and 'untamed' prospects convey a good impression of the character of early deer parks and provide a strong sense of continuity in the local landscape.

Strongly influenced by the Court, the older established Sussex families now became active builders. Among them we find William Morley, who used local flint and imported Caen stone when building Glynde Place. This is one of the most charming of the early Elizabethan houses. It was drastically altered by Bishop Trevor, whose family inherited it in the eighteenth century, and who built a new east front. The original west front was altered slightly at this time but the original entrance with its beautiful stone arch and flagstone floor opens into a small courtyard reminiscent of some of the smaller Oxford Colleges (Plate 30).

A new development in Sussex is marked by Chiddingly Place, built in 1574 by Sir John Jefferay. This was the first

Sussex mansion laid out on an E-shaped plan, characteristic of Elizabethan domestic architecture. Thereafter the court-yard house gave way to this new fashion. Three other fine houses on the E or the H type plan, each more fully evolved than the last, quickly followed Chiddingly Place. Wiston, where the original east front still survives, was completed by Sir Thomas Shirley in 1575. Parham was begun by Sir Thomas Palmer in 1577 and Sir George Goring began building Danny in 1582.

Towards the end of Elizabeth's reign the older Sussex families were still building; Sir Edward Culpeper, for example, built Wakehurst Place in 1590, but by this time they were being rivalled in the scope of their enterprise by many immigrant families, who generally spread the cost of property purchase and its conversion over two or more generations. The proximity of Sussex to London made it a favoured place of residence by parvenus and the most ambitious of the gentry, as it enabled them to combine local activities with their professional life in the metropolis. Many settled in the county on lands put on the market after the Dissolution. The Fords were Devonshire clothiers who bought Uppark, originally an estate of Durford Abbey. J. E. Mousley has shown that almost half these immigrant families were unknown in the county before 1500.[9] As early as 1565 the expanding ranks of the gentry permitted Sussex to have its own sheriff instead of sharing this office with Surrey as it had earlier.

Moving down the social scale, one of the distinguishing features of the manor houses and homes of the smaller gentry was the continued virility of the vernacular tradition of timber-framing in which Sussex abounds. Some Wealden villages such as Lindfield, near Haywards Heath, are incomparably rich. The splendid examples in the village street are reckoned by Sir N. Pevsner, a leading authority

---

[9] J. E. Mousley, 'Sussex Country Gentry in the Reign of Elizabeth', unpublished Ph.D. thesis, University of London (1956).

on English domestic architecture, as the finest group in Sussex. One of these, Barnlands, has the close-studding and transomed windows characteristic of this era. It was originally a delightful medieval hall house which underwent the customary modernisation in the sixteenth century, when an imposing chimney stack was fitted to an external wall and ornamented with ashlar stone. Another fine example in Lindfield is the spectacular Thatched Cottage, much larger and elaborate than its name suggests. Other good timber-framed houses, built or modernised in the Tudor or Jacobean period near Lindfield, are East Mascalls, Old Place and Wapsbourne. Lady Wolseley has given excellent accounts of these, and other similar houses.[10] Amongst other notable framed dwellings in the county are Yeoman's in Hamsey, Pashley in Ticehurst, Brickwall in Northiam and Socknersh Manor in Brightling, perhaps the most attractive of them all.

In Sussex, as in all the counties around London, the Great Rebuilding movement eventually pervaded all classes of society. Yeomen and husbandmen, no less than nobility and gentry, substantially improved their houses. Many of these remain, adding distinction and charm to the present landscape. In the Weald, the late sixteenth and early seventeenth centuries were a period of relative prosperity and most of the farmsteads were modernised at this time. When the Rev. Arthur Young observed them in 1794 he noted the lack in the Weald "of those substantial buildings that so strongly characterise wealthy affluence and successful ease, directly flowing from the prosperity of good husbandry". This generalisation is borne out by the surviving farmsteads in the present Wealden landscape, most of them having modest exteriors with little trace of luxury. As H. Kenyon has remarked of the old farmsteads in Kirdford, a parish of the west Sussex Weald Clay, "they are exactly the type of house to be expected in a relatively poor forest

[10] Countess Wolseley, *Some of the Smaller Manor Houses of Sussex* (1925).

country and fit beautifully and without pretence into their surroundings".[11]

The improvement most generally adopted by smaller householders was the provision of a fireplace and chimney making practicable the 'lofting-over' of the medieval hall by the insertion of other rooms often filled with their own fireplaces.[12] Previously this had been precluded by the necessity to allow smoke to escape through the roof. Timber-framing continued to be the cheapest method of house construction in the Weald and the basic method of house construction did not change during the Great Rebuilding. The main difference between the Tudor and earlier framing practice concerns the subsidiary members which were not close-studded, i.e. set vertically at a distance of one width apart but widely spaced in 'post and span' style and infilled with wattle and daub, plaster or brick. This change and the general practice of re-using medieval timbers in newly built houses as at Horncombe in West Hoathly and Woodland Farm in Lindfield suggests that the increasing scarcity and cost of building timber may well be responsible. The use of brick for infilling became highly fashionable. A favourite technique called 'brick-nogging' was to set bricks at different angles in successive layers, in decorative patterns of which the herring-bone and chevron were the most popular. The weathered fronts of houses treated in this way have a delightful mottled effect between the silver-tinted timbers which greatly enhances their beauty. The most exquisite examples are found along the foot of the Chalk escarpment in west Sussex as at West Burton or Bignor, where cottages have been repaired over the centuries with a variety of local materials, including flint, stone and brick.

A practice not common in medieval times, but now

[11] H. Kenyon, *Kirdford: Some Parish History* (1971), p. 10.
[12] C. Hannah, 'Old Buildings on the Brookhouse Estate', *Suss. Arch. Colls.*, Vol. 83 (1942–3), pp. 15–34.

becoming more general, was the weather-proofing of exterior walls by hanging tiles or weatherboard cladding. At Shoyswell Old Manor the south wing is tile-hung to prevent harm from the sun's rays, whereas the less vulnerable east front has been left in its original close-studding. At Wardsbrook in Ticehurst the three sides most exposed to the prevailing winds—east, south and west—are protected with tiles. Weatherboarding is most characteristic of Wealden villages on the Kentish border, such as Burwash, Ticehurst, Wadhurst and Northiam. Elsewhere the tile-hung cottage, for many travellers the epitome of the Sussex countryside, is traditional and its cladding invariably protects older timbers.

Not all domestic buildings were converted during the period of the Great Rebuilding. Open halls survived into the late seventeenth century even in parsonages such as East Blatchington near Seaford which had "a hale open to the toppe" in 1675. On many small farms in remote parts of the Weald the 'lofting-over' process was deferred until the eighteenth century. More evidence of this later conversion is provided by views and plans of properties on an eighteenth-century Buxted estate.[13] One house at Laughton had three rooms on the ground floor styled dairy, kitchen and 'old kitchen', suggesting alterations completed not long before, and this is not a solitary example. Several farmsteads still had rooms styled 'halls'. The late-eighteenth-century Buxted estate plans are particularly interesting, for they help us to put farmhouse building into the local and social economic setting. They strongly suggest that most homesteads in this part of the High Weald originated as medieval hall houses, the nucleus being commonly a two-bay hall with a service room on either side. Most of the buildings on the Buxted estate had extensions of one kind or another, the familiar 'disorderly accretions' which make old buildings so interesting. The wings sometimes provided extra living

[13] *Views and Plans of Houses in the Buxted Estate* (1798), S.A.S.

space—a 'great parlour' for example—but more commonly additional room for a dairy, buttery and wash- and brew-houses, all of which provided services originally centred on a single room, the kitchen. The increasing number of rooms in the smaller farmsteads reflects, therefore, not only improved living standards but also the larger size of families and more regional specialisation in dairying. The growing demand of the farmer for a more elaborate homestead is one of the most marked developments during the Great Rebuilding and its immediate aftermath. The fact that this occurred in the last age of local building materials renders the surviving old Sussex farmhouses a particularly handsome addition to the countryside.

SELECT BIBLIOGRAPHY

Cornwall, J. 'Agricultural Improvement, 1560–1640', *Suss. Arch. Colls.*, Vol. 98 (1960), pp. 118–32.
Gulley, J. L. M. 'The Great Re-building in the Weald', *Gwerin*, Vol. 3 (1961), pp. 129–46.
Leconfield, Lord *Petworth Manor in the Seventeenth Century* (1954).
Mason, R. T. *Framed Buildings of the Weald* (2nd edn., 1969).
Nairn, Ian and Pevsner, N. *The Buildings of England: Sussex* (1965).
Straker, E. *Wealden Iron* (1931).
Wealden Iron Research Group, Bulletin (in progress).
Wolseley, Lady C. *Some of the Smaller Manor Houses of Sussex* (1925).

6. The reshaping of the countryside in Georgian and early Victorian times

The opening-up of the Weald. The extension of tillage. Wealden squatters and cottage-keepers. Designed landscapes

A NEW CHAPTER in the history of the Sussex landscape opened in the eighteenth century. By 1750 centuries of colonisation in the Sussex wastes had left little more wilderness to tame and in the long cultivated lands of the Champion enclosures had largely superseded communal farming. Continuity, therefore, was more notable than revolution in the pattern of farm, field, shaw and hedgerow during the eighteenth and nineteenth centuries. Even so, this period saw considerable economic development and constitutes an important phase in landscape evolution. Under the impetus of rising corn prices (the response to a fast-growing population) and food shortages exacerbated by war, there was a great arable expansion based mainly on cultivated grasses but also on new crops. The increased mobility conferred by greatly improved communications was an additional stimulus. Under these influences the Weald was transformed from a grassland into a largely arable province relatively destitute of cattle apart from the 'starveling' beasts observed by W. Marshall on the remaining commons. On the Downs, too, pastoralism declined during this period.

Inevitably, these changes involved much human handiwork in remodelling the landscape. The great landlords eagerly invested in turnpike roads and canals, and later in railways. All farmers, great and small, broke up rough pastures and upgraded worn-out fields. The extra labour required for arable economy explains much new cottage building in the landscape and a great number of country houses were rebuilt or refronted in this period. Another important landscape change in Sussex arose from the adornment of country estates. Successive generations of Georgians developed a growing appreciation of natural beauty, and with taste and energy set about the embellishment of their estates in the informal manner practised by 'Capability' Brown, and Repton. Their aim was the re-creation of the romantic kind of scenery idealised on the canvasses of Claude Lorrain and Salvator Rosa. Sussex contains thousands of acres modelled according to this new approach to landscape art, and in many parks designed about 1800 the groves, woods and individual trees still flourishing today in the splendour of their maturity are amongst the most beautiful legacies of any age in the visible present.

The opening-up of the Weald

After centuries of isolation, the Weald still retained an underdeveloped and backward character. With modern communications its fuller exploitation became possible. Until the later eighteenth century the deficiencies of the roads were a great obstacle to rural advancement. So appalling were the ways across the seemingly bottomless clays and the finely-grained soils that visitors rarely ventured into the region after September, and markets were often impossible to reach for several months in the year. The carriage of heavy bulk goods, such as timber and ordnance from the gun-founders, was confined to the summer months when, however, the roads were quickly made treacherous by rain. "The roads grew bad beyond all badness, the night dark beyond all darkness, our guide frightened beyond all frightfulness," complained Horace Walpole after a descent of Silver Hill on his way from Bayham Abbey to Robertsbridge in August 1752.[1] Private travel, in fact, demanded great fortitude and patience; the saddle-horse was normally the only practicable manner of transport. Thomas Turner, the shopkeeper diarist of East Hoathly, travelled in this way through the claylands with great foreboding, never failing to record his intense relief after a safe return.[2] Even in Cobbett's day, by which time 'macadamising' had begun in Sussex, it was prudent to keep to high ground if rain threatened, and the miry condition of the local roads was observed by W. Topley in his *Geology of the Weald* as late as the 1870s.

The few high roads in Sussex, especially those traversing the Weald, are attested by *Britannia Depicta*, a revision of Ogilby's road-book published in 1720. Only three main routes between London and the coast are mentioned, two of which led to the ancient port of New Shoreham. Richard Budgen's map of Sussex (1724) is another invaluable source of information about the roads on the eve of improvement. It shows that the water gaps through the Downs did not then attract the routes joining the Weald to the coast. On the contrary, their low-lying marshy floors hindered roadmaking. Instead, a crossing over the high ground of the Chalk was made to the coastline. A good site to examine the local topography of the old roads is Saddlescombe, north of Brighton, where the ancient trackway which became an early coaching route is traceable along the upper edge of a steep valley slope, well above the modern roadway. Another stretch of old coaching road can be followed over the Downs from Fulking to Portslade, a route avoiding the Adur valley. Its straight, slightly cambered surface, offers

[1] *Letter to Richard Bentley*, 5th August 1752.
[2] F. M. Turner (ed.), *The Diary of Thomas Turner of East Hoathly* (1754–65).

dry, breezy walking. Near Lewes a similar road ran over the Chalk to Glynde, by-passing the Ouse flats at Southerham. In its descent round the flanks of Caburn it becomes a fine hollow-way containing a profusion of wild flowers. Budgen's map throws much light on contemporary roads showing that, for example, the customary route across Sussex into Kent, at least for travellers on horseback, was still the prehistoric trackway along the summit of the South Downs.

Between 1749, the date of the first turnpike road in Sussex, and the opening of the London to Brighton railway in 1841, a close network of public roads opened up, and laced together, the Weald (Fig. 23). The hub of the new system was Brighton, the rapidly growing coastal resort, but the other watering-places were equally dependent on improved road connections with London. Each was served eventually by a new highway traversing the Weald. The new roads did much to stimulate the Wealden economy, though this was subordinate to their main purpose. The best known of these roads were the successive shortenings of the London to Brighton route, which as late as 1779 provided no direct connection. The first of the new coach roads to Brighton was built through Cuckfield (the present B2036 road). In 1810 it was superseded by an even shorter cut from Pyecombe to Bolney avoiding Clayton Hill, a triumph of road-making, marking the first successful crossing of a wide stretch of Weald Clay. Another road, offering a better route to Brighton, followed the Adur valley, replacing in 1807 the ancient track over Beeding Hill. The toll cottage once at Upper Beeding is now in the Open Air Museum at Singleton near Chichester. Another new road reached the Weald from the coast by means of a water gap in the Chalk, leading from Worthing via Findon and Ashington (the present A24). Meanwhile the old roads were much improved. The Act of 1752 for turnpiking roads north of Lewes stated that ". . . the roads are in so bad

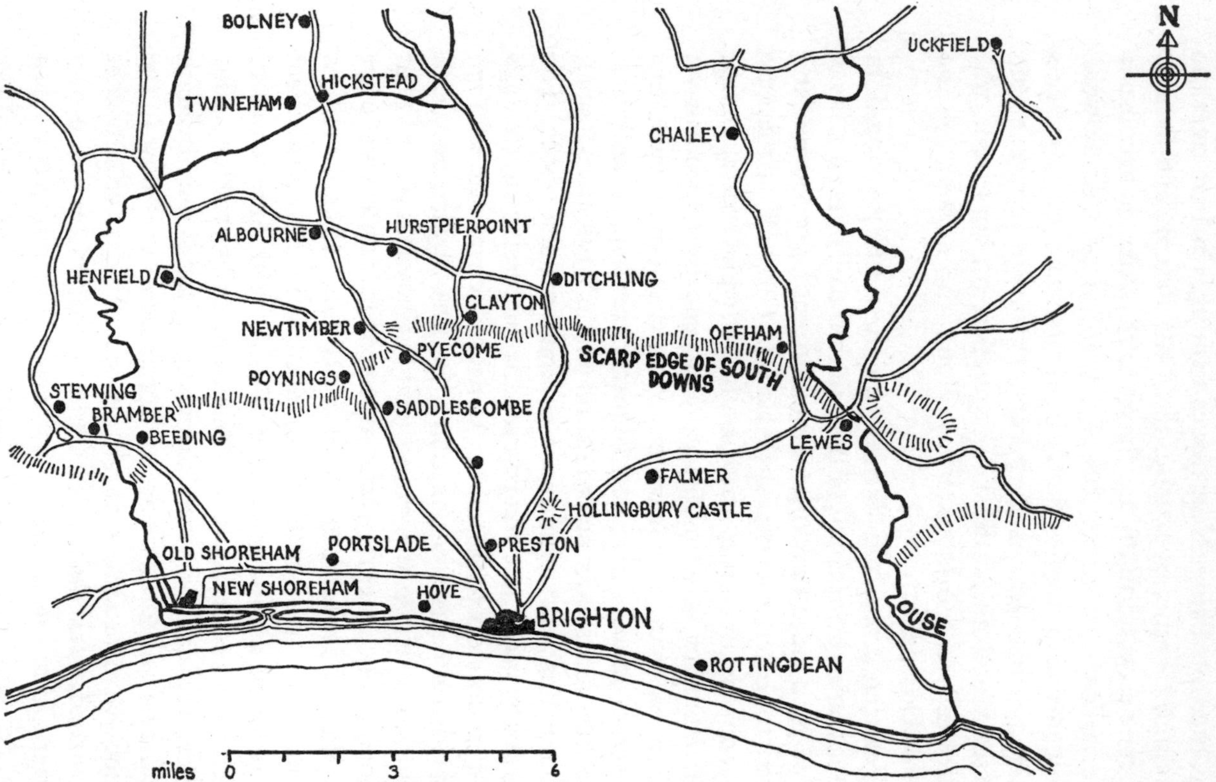

Fig. 23: Turnpike roads converging on Brighton.

a condition that they are impassable to wheeled carriages in winter and very dangerous and difficult for persons travelling on horse-back." Some of the turnpikes replacing the narrow clay ditches that passed as roads over the Weald were not always kept in much better repair, but by 1820 a hard macadamised surface had become usual in Sussex which brought land carriage to a perfection undreamt of in Walpole's day.

Although the turnpike system greatly facilitated travel, permitting fast public services by stagecoach, the frequency of toll gates made carriage of bulk goods very expensive. A local land agent in 1769 observed that improved water navigation was needed in the clay country about Lewes "so as to bring corn to market in winter from a dirty country surrounded with turnpike gates" and for carrying chalk and other manures for land improvement.[3] It became the avowed aim of river navigation and canal-builders to provide transport for agriculture. The Act of 1791 authorising the making of the western Rother navigable to Midhurst expressly stated that the proposal would improve the lands and estates near the waterway. Again, the prospectus for the Chichester Canal, cut in 1817, declared as an aim "the promotion and improvement and better cultivation of the circumjacent country by the conveyance of manures". Another consideration which lay behind canal-building in Sussex was the strategic value of an artificial cut between Portsmouth and London, by-passing the sea route round the North Foreland, then a prey to storms and enemy shipping. Beginning with the improvement of the Arun as far as Arundel in 1732, involving a direct cut to the sea at Little-hampton, successive schemes embraced navigation on the rivers Ouse and Adur, and similarly on the western Rother (1794). Three other canals were built: the Wey and Arun (1813), the Chichester (1817), and the Arundel and Portsmouth Canals (1823). No person was more identified with

[3] E.S.R.O. Glynde MS. 2731.

canal construction in Sussex than the third Earl of Egremont (1751–1837). During his long and influential life he espoused the cause of, and committed his large fortune to, agricultural improvement. He personally financed the Rother navigation, which served his great estates at Petworth, and projected the west Sussex canals. Like his contemporary, the first Earl of Sheffield, another distinguished patron of Sussex agriculture, he attached the highest importance to transport—the greatest single problem, it seemed, hindering the development of the Weald.

The Sussex canal-building era was brief indeed and its effects short-lived. The restoration of peace in Europe in 1815 and the policing of the Channel removed the need for an inland water-route to London. From 1840 railways steadily sapped the canals' trade. One after another the canals closed and by the 1870s only the Chichester Canal survived as an active waterway. Saltern's Lock on this canal is still in working order but the rediscovery of the other Sussex canals takes the field-worker along dry or reedy canal beds, such as the Wey and Arun near the Surrey border (Plate 48) and the Arundel and Portsmouth Canal near Barnham. Here and there fragments of masonry or old timbers mark the sites of locks—for example the Brewhurst and Drungewick Locks on the Wey and Arun Canal. More imposing monuments of the old waterways are the Hardham tunnel, built in 1790 to avoid the wide meander of the Arun near Pulborough, and the Orfold aqueduct, which has partially collapsed, that took barges to Guildford and northwards to the Thames. Early-nineteenth-century warehouses and wharves survive at Newbridge and Midhurst, but they have long since been converted to other purposes.

The effects of improved communications on agriculture, industry and trade, and consequently on society and the landscape, have never been systematically assessed. Contemporaries were in no doubt about their stimulating effects, especially in the Weald, opened up from its seclusion after centuries of inaccessibility. Arthur Young noted that before the construction of the Horsham to London turnpike in 1756 "whoever went on wheels was forced to go round by Canterbury". He declared that there was no one "who does not acknowledge and date the prosperity of the country to this road".[4] Young traced a direct relationship between the turnpikes and the rural economy. "Before the communications with London, low rents, low prices and confined consumption and no improvements; open the communication and high rents, high prices, a rapid consumption and numerous improvements." Before the turnpikes and canals the only commodities relatively easy to transport in the Weald were those coming in and out on the hoof—meat, tallow, hides. This had been so for generations. With improved transport the Weald was more effectively linked to the growing markets of London and the coastal resorts.

Nor should the social effects of the improved communications be underestimated. The turnpikes brought country estates in Sussex within two or three hours' travelling distance of London compared with a day, or even longer in bad weather, previously. The sale particulars of Rowfant House at Worth in 1810 drew attention to its landscaped grounds and "Gothic elevation" together with "its easy remove from the Metropolis, being within a short morning's drive . . ."[5] This epitomises the social change permeating the landscape of the Weald generally. The penumbra of London, after a long-foreshadowed tendency, was now cast more sharply across the region. In the words of a contemporary newspaper advertisement Sussex now possessed "every requisite for either residence or investment". As proof of this, the nobility and gentry, and those newly enriched by trade and industry, began buying up many

---

[4] Arthur Young (ed.), *Annals of Agriculture*, Vol. 11 (1789), p. 292.
[5] S.A.S. F.439.

small copyholds as hunting boxes, villas or *fermes ornées*. Windswept ridges, the bane of the cultivator, were now eagerly sought after by these newcomers for the sake of the bracing air and wooded prospects, delights which were an outcome of the Romantic appreciation of wild scenery. As a result some country estates were broken up and sold off in plots for 'cockney boxes' as early as Regency times. In this way Tilgate and St Leonard's Forests, long the purview of the speculator, and the Wealden areas near Brighton and Lewes were becoming parts of 'villadom' in late Georgian times. In his gently mocking verses the Rev. S. J. Pratt (1749–1814) in his *Cottage Pictures* ridiculed this middle-class invasion of the countryside:

> no village dames and maidens now are seen
> But madams and the misses of the green!
> Farm-house, and farm too, are in deep disgrace,
> 'tis now the lodge, the cottage, or the place!
> Or if a farm, *ferme ornée* is the phrase!

The extension of tillage

In the Weald the response to buoyant markets and new communications by land and water was sharp and immediate. The rural economy was caught up in the broad sweep of national events and underwent a fundamental change of emphasis from livestock to cereals. As late as the third quarter of the eighteenth century much of the Weald, especially that close to the perimeter of cultivation along the high ridges, was poor quality 'wild grass' pasture which had never been broken up in the memory of contemporary farmers. In the most backward districts, such as the parish of Horsted Keynes on the margin of Ashdown Forest, grass seeds and turnips were unknown in the 1760s, a century or more after their adoption on farms further south. The still poorer country on the clays was let at low rents as stubborn land unprofitable to plough before the

Plate 26 Old water-filled mine pits in coppice woodland at Minepit Shaw, Heathfield. These workings supplied iron ore to Waldron and Heathfield Furnaces in the late seventeenth and eighteenth centuries. The woodland also provided fuel for the local iron industry. See p. 150.

Plate 27 Woodland near the site of the Broadhurst furnace, Heathfield, has encroached upon former fields still traceable by means of bordering earthen banks. See p. 152.

Plate 28 Newbridge, Ashdown Forest, near a site of one of the earliest blast furnaces and for long an industrial site engaged in iron-making, forging and boring. The mill shown was built after the closure of the ironworks. The grassy bank in the extreme left is the result of recent infilling but the mill pond is still a picturesque feature. See p. 153.

Plate 29 Furnace Pond, Ebernoe. The furnace served by this pond is said by the seventeenth-century writer John Norden to have been one that "devoured many famous woods". Ebernoe Common (in the background), however, is again well clothed with wood which includes ancient oaks and beeches. See p. 153.

Plate 30 The original entrance in flint and Caen stone to William Morley's courtyard house at Glynde, built in 1569. See p. 170.

Plate 31 Parham, a fine Elizabethan E-plan house on the site of the medieval grange of Westminster Abbey. The mullioned windows of the Great Hall are original. See p. 169.

Plate 32 The long, narrow fields depicted on this map by Yeakell and Gardner (1783) resulted from the piecemeal enclosure of strips of arable by means of exchange amongst tenants in the sixteenth and early seventeenth centuries. The small rectangular fields in the north mark enclosures of commons made in the same period. See p. 148.

late-eighteenth-century era of rising corn prices. The hungry soils of the sandstone ridges were in a still more beggarly condition. The extensive commons and wastes, notably St Leonard's and Ashdown Forests, were regarded by W. Marshall "as bleak and barren as moorland in Yorkshire and Westmorland".[6]

Yet by Marshall's tour of the southern counties in 1798, the Sussex Weald had undergone rapid metamorphosis into an arable province. Acute contemporary observers were highly critical of the change. Although best fitted for grass, Marshall observed that "excepting the commons and some narrow strips of brookland there is scarcely an acre of natural herbage or old grassland in a township". This reversal of the traditional Sussex husbandry was accomplished in two ways. Old enclosures were improved by burning, liming or marling and with expanding prosperity farmhouses and buildings were modernised. Simultaneously, the field area was increased, requiring the land clearance which had been a regional inclination for generations. Both processes made a substantial contribution to the reshaping of the landscape.

The first type of operation is well illustrated by the changes at the Broadhurst estate, Horsted Keynes,[7] some of which are still evident today. There were two phases of improvement, one affecting the lighter soils and the second concerned with under-draining of the clays in the 1840s when cheap tile-drainage became practicable. The first stage was the more important. When the estate changed hands in 1764 the land was in poor heart and abounding in timber. The obstinately conservative tenants were "backward in the modern improvements", particularly "in changing grass, turnipping, etc.". The inhabited farmhouses with earth floors were in a bad state of repair; those on hillsides were

---

[6] W. Marshall, *The Rural Economy of the Southern Counties* (1798), Vol. 2, pp. 102–47.

[7] E.S.R.O. Glynde MS. 2170, 2177, 2731.

without water supply "besides what is catched in ponds".

The description of this estate probably exemplifies the condition of the more backward parts of the Wealden countryside following the mid-eighteenth-century depression in agriculture. The new owners of the Broadhurst estate were the Trevors of Glynde who were advised by their agent to bring in tenants from "a country that abounds in improvements in husbandry". This hope was unrealised, but the diffusion of new progressive farming methods was effected by means of unusually detailed husbandry clauses in the leases. These prescribed for the sowing of temporary leys, wheat cultivation and other improved techniques. This, we may be sure, is how enterprising landlords improved a neglected estate and educated tenants in the Sussex Weald during the second half of the eighteenth century. Today farm buildings prove to be the most lasting memorial of this eighteenth-century agrarian revolution. The farmhouses on the estate, such as Oddynes, were repaired or rebuilt in late-eighteenth-century style with stone taken from the demolished Broadhurst manor. Cinder Hill and Ludwell Farms were renovated and enlarged and the thatched roofs of all three gave way to tile or Horsham Stone, the latter probably re-used stone from Broadhurst.

The rural advancement documented on the Broadhurst estate was multiplied many times over the Weald and was at once transmitted to the face of the land. Lack of communications was no longer an impediment to agricultural development and pride, profit and patriotism were now powerful incentives for a new exploitation of the meagre resources of the lime-deficient Wealden soils. Some of the most intense activity was concentrated along the forest ridges between Cross-in-Hand and Burwash and between Heathfield and Battle. The reduction of the waste by smallholders will be discussed later in this chapter; here we are concerned with the larger operations of farmers and land-owners. One of these was John Fuller, ironmaster, of Waldron, whose daily journal and other farming records for the 1770s and 1780s reveal his attentiveness to enclosure and improvement of the waste.[8] Fuller tackled annually a parcel of heath, sometimes 'waste' already legally and physically enclosed but still in a natural state, or a new intake from the commons authorised by the lords of Laughton or Heathfield manors. Adopting the standard practice of his day he grubbed up the old beech stems, denshired the heath and applied lime made in his own kilns on Hungry Hill in Heathfield. Men were employed for the more laborious work, women burnt heather and bracken and heaped up rubbish. Meanwhile, other farms further east, notably Holbran, Kingsdown, Rounceford, Westdown and Park-hill pushed their fences further out at the expense of the Heathfield and Burwash Downs. All the great land-owners engaged in this activity and the example was not lost on the smaller farmers. The outstanding contributions were those made by the Earl of Sheffield near Fletching and Lord Ashburnham and General Murray in the Battle district, but these were only a few of those responsible for the shrinking waste.

The greatest challenge was reserved for those who attempted the conquest of Ashdown, St Leonard's, Tilgate (the residue of Worth Forest) and the Waterdown Forests. Ashdown was an expanse of poor, light soils, so sterile that even during the Second World War supplies of scarce lime needed for its amelioration were diverted to more eligible areas. Its altitude made harvests more than usually precarious. The improvement of St Leonard's and Tilgate Forests presented even more difficult problems because much of this land was gently sloping silty clay, badly in need of under-draining before good timber or crops could be secured. The total area in these Forests awaiting improvement at the end of the eighteenth century could not have been

[8] S.A.S. RF/15/1, 21.

less than 25,000 acres. Even most of the land previously enclosed was devoted to little more than rabbit farming and was let between 1s. 3d. and 3s. an acre. The reclaimers of this waste were large-scale operators whose creation of new farms out of the wilderness attracted the attention of contemporary observers. Many of the enclosures in the present agricultural scene owe their origin to them. In Ashdown Forest the main improvers were Bradford, who owned Pippingford Warren, and Howis who worked in Crowborough Warren. To this day the great contrast between the fresh green appearance of the improved land there and the heath on the remnants of common is striking. In Tilgate Forest Seaton's pioneering earned him the Gold Medal of the Board of Agriculture, but a similar reclamation of St Leonard's Forest proved a failure and had to await tile-draining in the 1840s.[9]

The new fields resulting from eighteenth-century expansion were quite distinct from the small, irregular, timber-bound closes originating from ancient clearances. The latter lay "scattered amongst the woodlands in dabs", as the fields at Foxhunt in Waldron were described by an eighteenth-century surveyor. The new farming landscape was characterised by large square or rectangular enclosures, bounded by quickset hedges, standing on a little ditched bank, which began to appear in the Elizabethan period. Changing methods of cultivation account for the different shape and size of fields. Instead of the occasional ploughing by oxen, frequent tillage by horse-teams was becoming usual, producing large, geometrically shaped fields. This kind of farming scene, sharply contrasting with the older enclosed landscape, can be identified at many places in Sussex. It is very evident on the straight road between Ringmer and Halland where the road and 2000 acres of Broyle Park were laid out by parliamentary commissioners.

9 Arthur Young (ed.), *Annals of Agriculture*, Vol. 34 (1800), p. 133; C. Leeson Prince, *Crowborough Hill* (1898), p. 238.

The geometrical grid of the enclosure awards is noticeable in the Lower Dicker district near Hailsham where enclosing was busily in progress on the Laughton manor lands in 1818. Another interesting conjunction of old and new landscapes occurs in Framfield parish between Lewes and Heathfield. Here, ancient farms, resulting from medieval clearing, for centuries forming little islands in the waste, now lie embedded in a more regularly planned landscape that did not originate until 1862. After the Framfield Enclosure little more common land in Sussex was enclosed by Act of Parliament. There was by then a general agreement that with the rapid increase in London's population the remaining commons in south-east England should be preserved as open space.

The landscape of the English Chalklands was also greatly changed during the eighteenth and early nineteenth centuries. In Lincolnshire and Yorkshire, as also in parts of Wessex, the carpet of grass on most of the old sheep walks was enclosed and broken up for arable. In Sussex much chalk turf was converted to tillage, especially under the impetus of soaring corn prices during the Napoleonic Wars, but the Downland yeomen remained faithful to their traditional calling as graziers and most of the pasture was preserved for summer feeding of the much improved native breed of Southdowns. The Sussex sheep flocks actually increased in size during the eighteenth century; about 1800 no less than 200,000 ewes were kept between Eastbourne and Steyning, a stocking rate which Arthur Young junior regarded as "one of the most singular circumstances in the husbandry of England".[10]

The conversion of sheep down was therefore a more gradual process than in most counties and escaped the notice of contemporary observers until the late eighteenth century, when the pace of change was hastened by war. One of the

[10] Rev. Arthur Young, *A General View of the Agriculture of Sussex* (1813 edn.), p. 301.

best documented of these later reclamations of sheep down is that at Brighton where the common field proprietors in the 1760s broke up a fresh tract of pasture each year and added strips to their traditional holdings. The extra furlongs in this instance were presumably needed to feed the growing population of the town which was then just entering on its career as a seaside resort.[11] Simultaneously, landlords were enclosing downs which had not been fenced-off earlier and were breaking up parts of them by degrees, especially during the years 1800 and 1801, years of unprecedented corn prices. To this day downland farmers can identify steep slopes unploughed since the Napoleonic Wars, such being the extreme threat of famine at that time.

The conversion of the downland continued apace in the first half of the nineteenth century when it was finally halted by tumbling corn prices. Little of the reclamation is recorded in documents but the evidence is still plainly visible in the landscape in the form of distinctive vegetation. When the tilled downland was allowed to relapse to pasture the colonising grasses were tall, wiry, coarse and thinly-strewn, turning brown towards August. Such grass was called 'gratton' grass by the old shepherds and contrasted with the springy, close-matted turf of the untouched sward which remained freshly green and nutritious throughout the summer. Most of this 'gratton' grass has yet again passed under the plough in our own lifetime but in the eastern downs near Eastbourne and Jevington one still meets large expanses of it—a valuable witness to the extent and site of an earlier breaking-up of the downland.

The extension of tillage on to old meadows, heaths and commons has left many minor relict features on the ground, such as the widespread imprint of ridge-and-furrow, marks of old ploughing which have given a corrugated effect, resembling a gigantic washboard, to the surface of the fields. This feature is most pronounced on the heavier soils where

[11] E.S.R.O. Map and terrier of Brighton (1792).

ridging into 'lands' for wheat was the customary method of land drainage until superseded by tile-draining from the nineteenth century. Arthur Young, who described Wealden agriculture in very disparaging terms, nevertheless strongly commended the care taken by Sussex farmers in this preparatory ridging of the ground. Although A. H. Allcroft drew attention to this landscape feature as long ago as 1908 in his *Earthwork of England*, it has not drawn a comment from any other writer on Sussex and its systematic mapping and description has yet to be attempted. The ridges are best visible with the aid of the long shadows of evening light or when picked out by a thin powdering of drifted snow. Much ridge-and-furrow is traceable in the Arlington and Chiddingly districts on the Weald Clay and B. A. French has reported to the present author its widespread distribution at Brightling, Dallington and Warbleton in the High Weald. It is doubtless eighteenth- and early-nineteenth-century ploughing, in the main, which has left this record but the possibility that some is older cannot be ruled out.

Other vestiges of human action in the landscape leaving a clear imprint on the ground resulted from the constant search for fertiliser, always a prerequisite of Wealden and downland agriculture. Over the centuries marl, then lime, and finally artificial fertilisers, have superseded one another in turn as indispensable adjuncts to Wealden farming. The practice of marling is responsible for a pit or pond at the corner of almost every field. Lime was first extensively used in the seventeenth century, but since its source lay in the chalk pits of the South Downs, up to thirty miles distant, its usage did not supplant marling until the transport improvement in the late eighteenth century. A. Beatson, writing of changes in Mayfield in his *New System of Cultivation* (1821), noted that marling had ceased in the area "about forty to fifty years ago" when the new turnpikes made land carriage feasible. By the time W. Topley wrote the *Geology of the*

Weald (1875) marling had almost died out. Immense tracts of summer fallow, in readiness for wheat, were regularly whitened with lime up to the last quarter of the nineteenth century. Cobbett noted this singular sight with astonishment and Arthur Young considered that the practice was so costly that "by lime in the Weald they spend the value of a crop of wheat to get one".[12] Nevertheless, until alternative manures became available the ritual of liming for wheat was followed meticulously. It has left numerous quarries on the face of the South Downs escarpment (several of which yielded important fossils to Mantell, the celebrated Sussex geologist) which grew into impressive large workings where navigable water was available for transport inland, as at Houghton, Arundel, Lewes and the famous Holywell pits near Eastbourne which supplied chalk for the lime-kilns at Hastings (Fig. 24).

The breaking-up of the sheep walks on the Downs at this period also depended upon the application of chalk and lime in great quantities because the thin leached soils were especially acidic when derived from the overlying Clay-with-Flints. Consequently, the Downs are dotted all over with pits from which chalk has been dug for lime-burning or for use in its raw lumpy state. The Berwick and Alciston Downs, for example, bear several large pits which are almost certainly attributable to late-eighteenth-century reclamations (Fig. 25). On Applesham Farm in the Adur valley, pits are adjacent to all the fields most in need of lime. Gell, who was the tenant here in Young's day, applied about 1½ tons of raw chalk per acre to about 150 acres of his farm during a spell of about twenty years.[13] Although this amount appears to have been exceptional, other downland farmers sought fertility by the same means. Fertility once given by lime or marl has usually long since been exhausted but recent soil analyses at Applesham have proved that

---

[12] Arthur Young (ed.), *Annals of Agriculture*, Vol. 11 (1789), p. 212.
[13] Arthur Young (ed.), *Annals of Agriculture*, Vol. 24 (1796), p. 529.

Fig. 24. Lime-burning at Southerham.

Gell's work nearly 200 years ago still has an improving effect on the soil. This long-lasting effect is unlikely to be unique since most chalk seems to have been applied in a lumpy raw state in which condition it is extremely slow-acting.

Flint-built barns, widely scattered across the face of the Sussex Downs, were another addition to the Georgian landscape. They usually bear the name of the parent farm on the centuries-old arable in the valley below and date from *c.* 1780 to 1840, before working oxen were displaced by horses. These roughly built barns were necessary to house larger teams working extended arable and to store heavier harvests. Sited on remoter parts of the downland, manure was made in these barns where it was most wanted. New farmhouses and farm buildings also appeared in the Georgian landscape on arable farms newly reclaimed from the down and warrens, such as Halcombe and Hodden in Piddinghoe near Lewes.

Wealden squatters and cottage-keepers

An aspect of the Wealden commons leaving a permanent impress on the Sussex scene was the trimming back of the wastes by squatters and other cottagers. This was no new development. Growth of the Wealden population creating renewed pressure on land had always been relieved by encroachment on the uncolonised wastes. The empty spaces were being filled up in this way during the thirteenth and early fourteenth centuries. In the next period of population increase at the turn of the sixteenth century, the poor again began to set up house frames around the edge of Ashdown Forest and along the high ridges in the Burwash and Heathfield district. In another upsurge of population between 1770 and 1830 many of the rural poor solved the problem of food and housing by squatting on the commons, thus proliferating hundreds of small holdings and

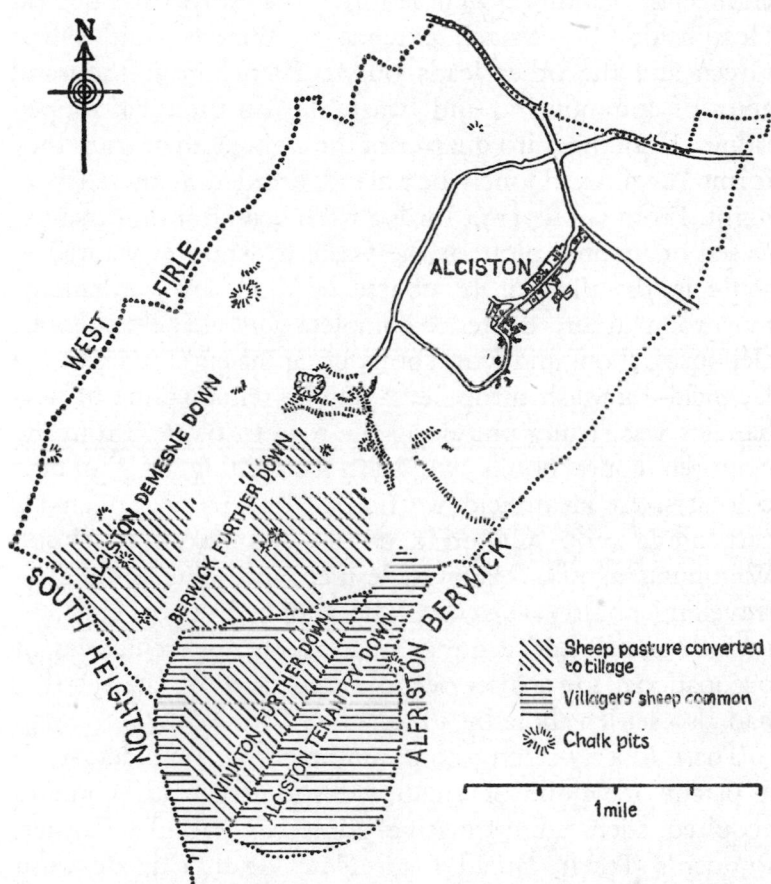

Fig. 25. Conversion of downland to arable: Alciston and Berwick.

cottages located indiscriminately at the whim of the squatters (Fig. 26).

One area of fast-growing settlement at the end of the eighteenth century occupied the ridgeways dividing at Heathfield. One branch extends to Burwash and Hurst Green and the other leads out to Battle. Four thousand acres of commonland and 'waste' lay on these flat-topped ridges. Until the third quarter of the eighteenth century they formed a wild and lonely heathland, dreaded by travellers at night. From about 1774 lords of the neighbouring manors leased or granted plots of the waste to whoever wanted to settle in the district. In course of time new settlements mushroomed into existence complete with chapels, schools, alehouses, shops and workshops along the eight miles of the Uckfield–Burwash turnpike. A similar tenuous line of new hamlets was strung out along the road to Battle. From the manorial court books we learn something of the new colonists. At Heathfield we find that Hunt had erected a carpenter's shop, Gilbert a chapel, the Bakers a school, Wilmhurst a mill. Many tradesmen, including a higler (a travelling poultry salesman who supplied young chickens to 'crammers') and a nurseryman, both representatives of occupational groups to become important in the district, had also settled there by 1780.

These loosely-strung communities of smallholders with a patchwork quilt of small fields dotted with cottages acquired such unimaginative names as Wood's Corner, Punnett's Town, Broad Oak, New Heathfield, Burwash Weald and Burwash Common. It is still possible to recapture some of the atmosphere of Punnett's Town in its pioneering days around 1800. Its only foci are the little Nonconformist chapel and several alehouses, one of which still survives. The chapel at Punnett's Town was founded in 1767 but the present building dates only from 1809. Gilbert, the first pastor, built the adjoining cottage, and the oldest tombstones in the graveyard are distinguished by simple terracotta

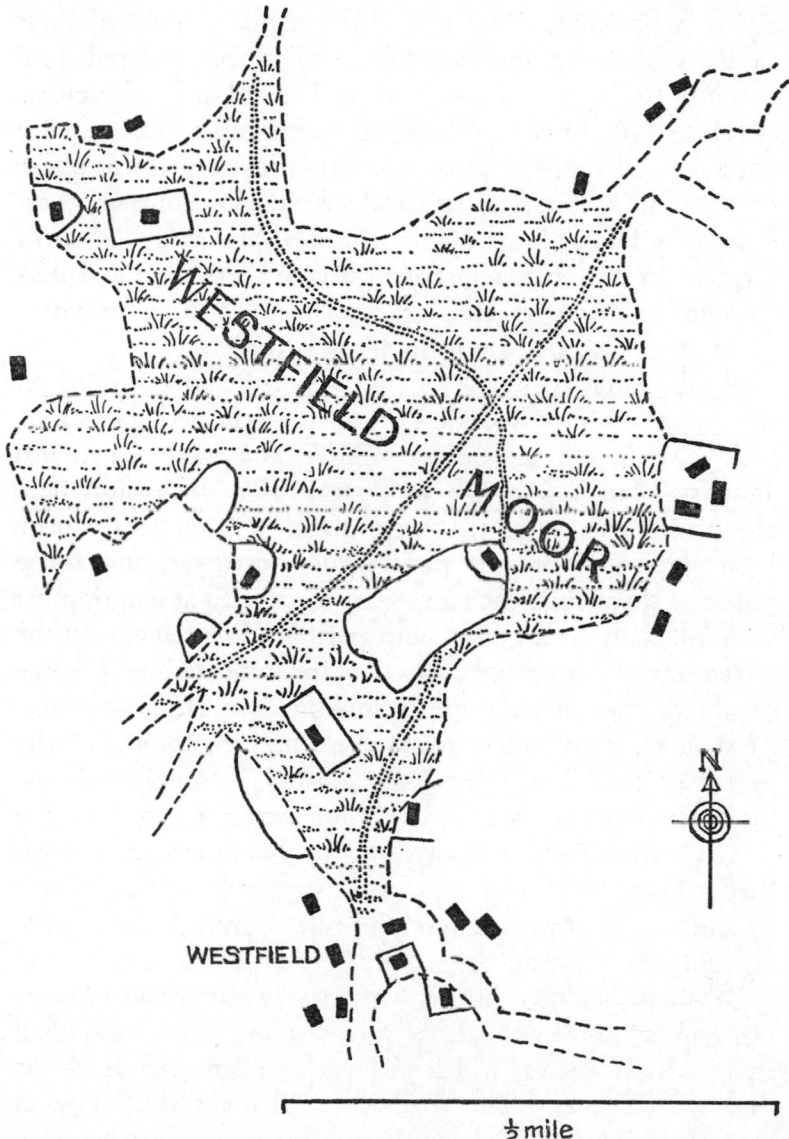

Fig. 26. Squatting and cottage-keeping at Westfield.

reliefs by a local craftsman. Most of the original houses in Punnett's Town were built by the occupiers themselves. Those who built a house illicitly normally replaced their cabins with more durable edifices when they secured legal recognition. Few of the original dwellings, therefore, survive, but there are several early-nineteenth-century cottages and shops at Punnett's Town to record this phase of rebuilding, many in the local vernacular white weatherboarded style. Many of the houses are built in short terraces to minimise construction costs. Potatoes and oats formed the cottagers' chief crops, as want of lime for wheat meant that the poor ate little white bread.

Similar encroachments of the former waste occurred on the margins of Ashdown Forest in Maresfield parish. A local newspaper, the *Sussex Weekly Advertiser*, dated 7th January 1810, reported 130 separate new enclosures here alone. The great majority were made by 'squatters' whose hovels and hedges were periodically destroyed only to be raised again around the hard-won acres until at length most were officially 'recognised' and permitted to remain. In the 1820s many fresh enclosures were reported and some obstinate encroachers were imprisoned in Horsham gaol. "I shall have an Indian town close to me of some of the greatest rapscallions that ever existed," complained one local land-owner. Many dwellings being erected in the parish were merely huts of turf and thatch over a floor of earth. These 'sod' huts were still being built in rural slums as late as the 1870s because the new Sanitary Acts were not enforced beyond the legally settled districts.[14]

By the early nineteenth century these squatter and cottage-keeping settlements had acquired their own individual shape and character, which in large measure they retain to this day (Fig. 27). The roadside settlement at Nutley in Maresfield on the Ashdown Forest edge is due to modern traffic on the Eastbourne road (A22). The older settlement

[14] E.S.R.O. Ashdown Forest MSS.

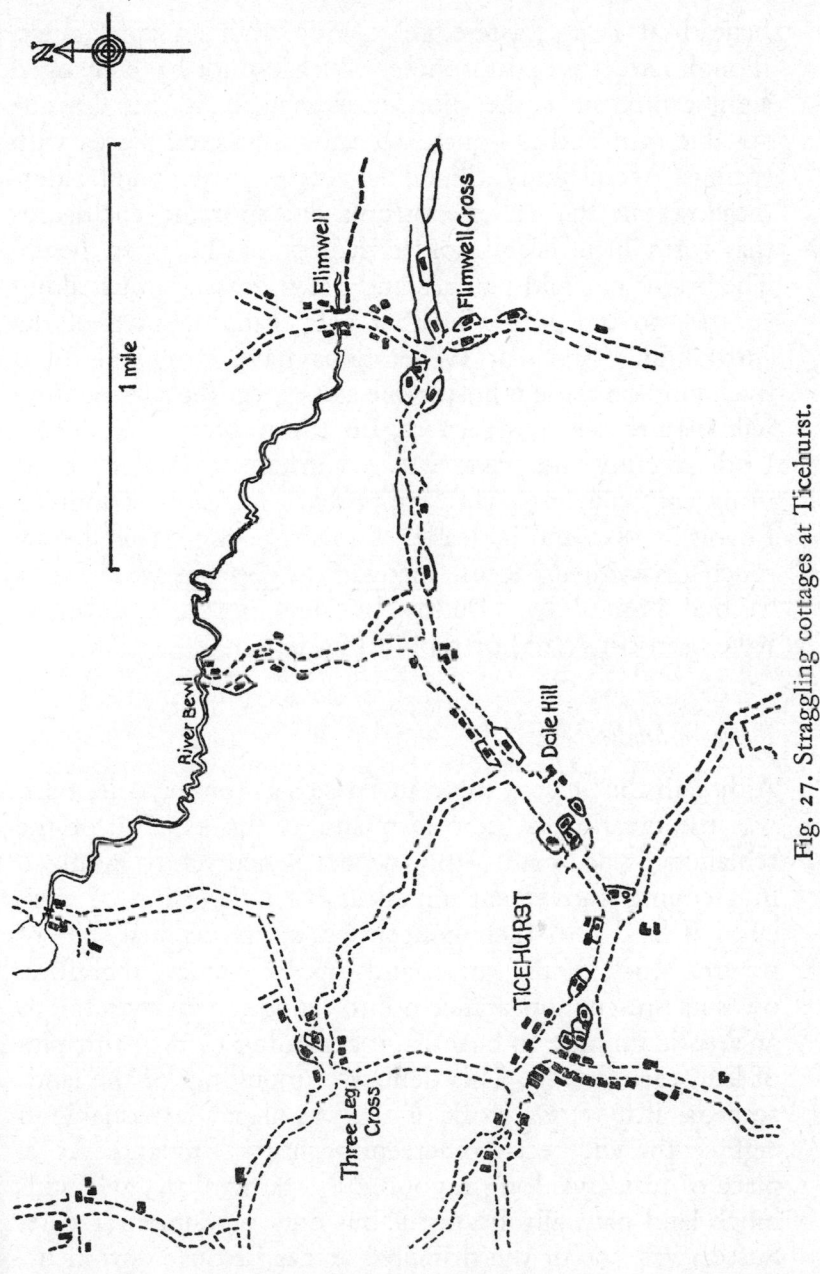

Fig. 27. Straggling cottages at Ticehurst.

beneath it is a 'waste-edge' colony with an appearance, though hardly an atmosphere, which cannot have changed significantly since the pioneer clearings. At this altitude suitable farmland is limited to a few sheltered places with springs. Accordingly, the fields, cottage gardens and water-meadows in the valley bottoms are sporadic enclosures that form little islands of settlement in the open heath. The bright emerald patches and green grass are in striking contrast to the purple heather and changing tints of the surrounding bracken. Generations have struggled for a livelihood on these inhospitable slopes, yet the surrounding wild nature seems set to regain the mastery completely. Until recently the scene was a constant reminder of the insurgent villagers who supported the last Labourers' Revolt in 1830 and its leader 'Captain Swing'. This is now much less evident because many of the cottages are in use as 'second homes' by London business people and others have been converted or rebuilt into larger residences.

Designed landscapes

Although the general trend in Sussex, as for centuries past, was the creation of new farmland at the expense of the remaining wild, many land-owners concurrently indulged in a counter-movement aimed at the conversion of agricultural land into their conception of its original state of nature. Much of the rural landscape of Sussex, therefore, owes its present appearance not to economic motives but to an artistic impulse to beautify it according to the principles of landscape design. This deliberate moulding of the landscape, as if it were a work of art, was highly fashionable in eighteenth- and early-nineteenth-century England. As a place of residence long favoured by the wealthy, and with much land naturally beautiful but only moderately fertile, Sussex was one of the principal arenas of this adornment. The philosophic basis underlying the redesign of the land-

Plate 33 A stilted granary, old hay-barns and ox-stalls at Rumbold's Farm, Kirdford. The pond was probably a fish 'stew' in the Middle Ages. Modern farm buildings lie behind those shown. See p. 101.

Plate 34 The aesthetic qualities of the landscape have long been the primary consideration in the broad and deep vale of the upper Ouse near Cuckfield and Balcombe. This view of typical parkland scenery is obtained from Borde Hill. See p. 202.

GENERAL VIEW OF BAYHAM.

Plate 35 Humphrey Repton's sketch of the farming landscape at Bayham, and his suggested plan for its conversion into parkland. The mansion ultimately built was less ornate than that proposed, but the informal landscaping of the grounds kept closely to the submitted plan. See p. 205.

Plate 36 For nearly four centuries the growth of Lewes was bound up with the Warennes, the feudal magnates who built and repeatedly modified the castle dominating the town. See p. 212.

Plate 37 High Street, Lewes. The Georgian fronts conceal old timber frames. See p. 224.

scape was a change in taste from the geometrical layout of parks and gardens prevailing in western Europe during the seventeenth century in favour of an intimate informality more faithful to nature which was an outcome of the Romantic Movement. Among the greater park landscapes in Sussex four are attributed to Lancelot ('Capability') Brown (1715–83) and nine to Humphrey Repton (1752–1818), and a score or more were designed by lesser, or unknown, specialists. These combine to make some of the finest and most characteristic park and garden scenery in England.

Also important, though these have attracted less attention than they deserve, are the effects in the present scene of the smaller parks about the country seats of the former gentry. Individually, the ornamental plantings in these lesser parks cannot match the marvellous grace and grandeur of the more ambitious settings of the Georgian nobility, but in combination they are sufficiently numerous in several parts of Sussex to bestow on the countryside the illusion of a single, immense, unit of design. Such an impression of a vast landscaped park is still conveyed, for instance, by the scene glimpsed from the Ouse Viaduct (itself a handsome addition to the landscape) which since 1841 has carried the London-to-Brighton railway across the broad and deep Ouse valley. The whole countryside has been imparked at some time or another during the last 600 years, parts of it on more than one occasion. Up to the sixteenth century its deer parks were among the largest and best-known in Sussex—Slaugham, Cuckfield, Bentley, Kenwards and others. During the last two centuries seats of the gentry were built on the valley slopes and the landscape's aesthetic qualities have for generations transcended all other considerations. Despite the increased agricultural and institutional usage since the last war the visual character of the district, with its undivided pastures, free-standing oaks and elms and many groupings of broad-leaved trees, still retains its early-nineteenth-century parkland appearance. An even finer prospect can be obtained from Borde Hill, where the gardens and terraces lead the eye over the surrounding parkland (Plate 34).

The most vivid impressions of conscious design in the Sussex countryside have been recorded by foreign observers, to whom the 'English Style' was a revelation worthy of a sustained rhapsody. Amongst such accounts are the reminiscences of the Comte de la Garde in his book *Brighton*, compiled after a visit to that town in 1834. The flowing succession of pictures (*galerie de tableaux*) which unfolded before his coach on the journey from Brighton to London was composed of woods, lakes, meadows and rocky outcrops, the setting for country retreats (*maisons de plaisance*) enriched by a profusion of azaleas, laurel and rhododendrons, as well as herds of deer. Even the humble cottages beside the Brighton road bedecked their doorways and casements with climbing roses or jasmine and filled their gardens with flowers, and the merest hamlets were as neat and tidy as a Dutch village, though less monotonous. In his account we have evidence of the English traditional taste for gardening and landscaping, and also confirmation, consistent with the previous evidence already discussed, of the marked 'metropolitan' characteristics which the Sussex landscape had acquired by the early nineteenth century.

The landscape architects practised their most artful contrivances on the bare hillsides of the Downs or on the heathy ridges of the Weald. According to present tastes in scenery open landscapes have a certain haunting beauty and quiet serenity, but to Romantics who craved for the "unseen genius of the wood" they held less allure. W. Gilpin in *Observations on the Coasts of Hampshire and Sussex* (1804) regarded the Sussex heaths on the Greensand as scenically 'tiresome' and Chalk he judged to be 'disfiguring'. A. B. Granville's remark in his *Spas of England* (1841) that "nothing can be more dismal looking, barren or discouraging" than the general aspect of the countryside around Brighton suggests that the concept of landscape perfection was still unchanged. Accordingly, the 'naked surface' of the Downs was the greatest challenge to the landscape designer. It had been previously laid down by Walpole that "an open country is but a canvas on which a landscape might be designed", and Humphrey Repton, under whose inspiration English landscaping attained its most sophisticated form, adopted as a cardinal principle that "the horizon should all be wooded".

These principles, amongst others, were applied by the landscape practitioners in Sussex. The planting of clumps of beech to diversify bare chalk slopes was widespread. The circle of trees planted by Charles Goring at Chanctonbury Ring on the crest of the South Downs in 1760 is visible for more than thirty miles across the Weald, making it one of the best-known summits in Sussex. A more ambitious setting to match the grace of a large mansion is that of Stanmer, a seat of the Pelhams, one of the most prominent Whig families of the eighteenth century. The house was built about 1724, early in the Palladian revival, but the beauty of its setting is largely due to informal landscaping undertaken at the initiative of Thomas Pelham II. Several scenic elements at Stanmer illustrate late-eighteenth-century landscape taste. The sense of space, beautifully diversified by great trees, is typical of English parks. Characteristically, the pleasure grounds and gardens are concealed. Fringing the park is a narrow belt of beech, a standard feature of Brown and his followers, but repudiated by Repton as monotonous and unimaginative. Another feature which dates the park to the era of 'Capability' Brown rather than Repton is the pair of entrance lodges, like twin tea-caddies. Repton ridiculed this style as an example of 'childish symmetry'. The house faces the parish church, rebuilt in the style of the Gothic Revival in 1838, for landscape effect, and the village pond, 'improved' by a border of large sarsens from the Downs, enticed deer and cattle to browse on the lawn in front of the windows, so adding interest to the scene. In order to enlarge his park Thomas Pelham II removed some of his tenants to his Wealden estate at Halland, and Stanmer village was entirely rebuilt behind a screen of tall trees. It now takes on the character of an 'estate village' in a neat brick and flint style. The mansion is at present used by the University of Sussex and the park was bought by Brighton Corporation who are attentive to its conservation.

A more elaborate landscaping of the Downs took place at Uppark on the western border of Sussex. The house, built about 1690 in the Dutch style fashionable in William III's reign, was much altered a century later by Repton. The original layout of the gardens, preserved in one of Kip's drawings, was described by the seventeenth-century traveller, Celia Fiennes, who mentioned the "fine gardens, gravel and grass walks . . . with breast walls dividing each from the other . . ." The old terraces and parterres can still be seen under the turf. By the time Repton was employed at Uppark, these rigid geometrical gardens had been superseded by sweeping lawns up to the windows of the house, as is shown in Peiter Tilleman's 'View of Uppark'. Repton further modified the scene by adding a Doric colonnade to the north side of the house. A new drive was built through the beech woods, which he opened up to give more varied prospects. This 'cutting of a woodland to size' was Repton's preferred way of creating a wooded landscape on the Downs. It is in the vicinity of Uppark that the South Downs attain their greatest extent, and landscape architecture its ultimate grandeur. To the eighteenth-century taste Stansted Park was rivalled by few in England. Horace Walpole, whose *Essay in Modern Gardening* did much to influence the landscape taste of the times, regarded it as an archetype of landscape design, recalling "such exact pictures of Claude Lorrain that it is difficult to conceive that he did not paint them from this very spot". This and Goodwood, where the racecourse was laid out in a splendid setting with horizons bounded by sea and woods, still form a charming man-made landscape providing vicarious enjoyment to several thousand visitors yearly.

The face of the Weald was also being transformed by landscaping (Plate 35). One new feature was the deliberate planting of heaths of the High Weald with larch, Scots pine, the Lombardy poplar and other exotic species. One form of this, adopted all over England at the turn of the eighteenth century, was the planting of clumps of conifers over extensive commons and wastes not intended for enclosure, for the dual purpose of ornament and conserving game. The best example of this in Sussex is in Ashdown Forest where Scots pine, planted on commanding hilltops about 1800, has seeded itself naturally on the heath and in abandoned quarries, so perpetuating a distinctive parkland scene. This "clumping of the common with miserable Scotch fir" was deprecated by Repton. Even more censure was focussed on the extensive plantations of conifers in Ashdown and St Leonard's Forests. By Cobbett's day they appear to have been short-lived. The most probable explanation of their extinction is that after acting as 'nurses' to broad-leaved trees the conifers were progressively extracted as the other species matured. Some of the finest landscaping in the Weald was achieved at Sheffield Park, Ashburnham and Petworth. Much of Brown's work at Sheffield Park, where John Baker Holroyd, first Earl of Sheffield, built Sheffield House, a neo-Gothic building, in 1775, has given way to more modern gardens and landscaping, themselves beautiful. Nevertheless, Brown's brilliant use of water is exemplified by the lakes and waterfalls, and the studied chiaroscuro effect that Repton aimed at is maintained by the great variety of trees and shrubs. 'Capability' Brown's work at Ashburnham (Fig. 28) is a good example of the effects of replacing many formal avenues with wilder and more informal woodlands.

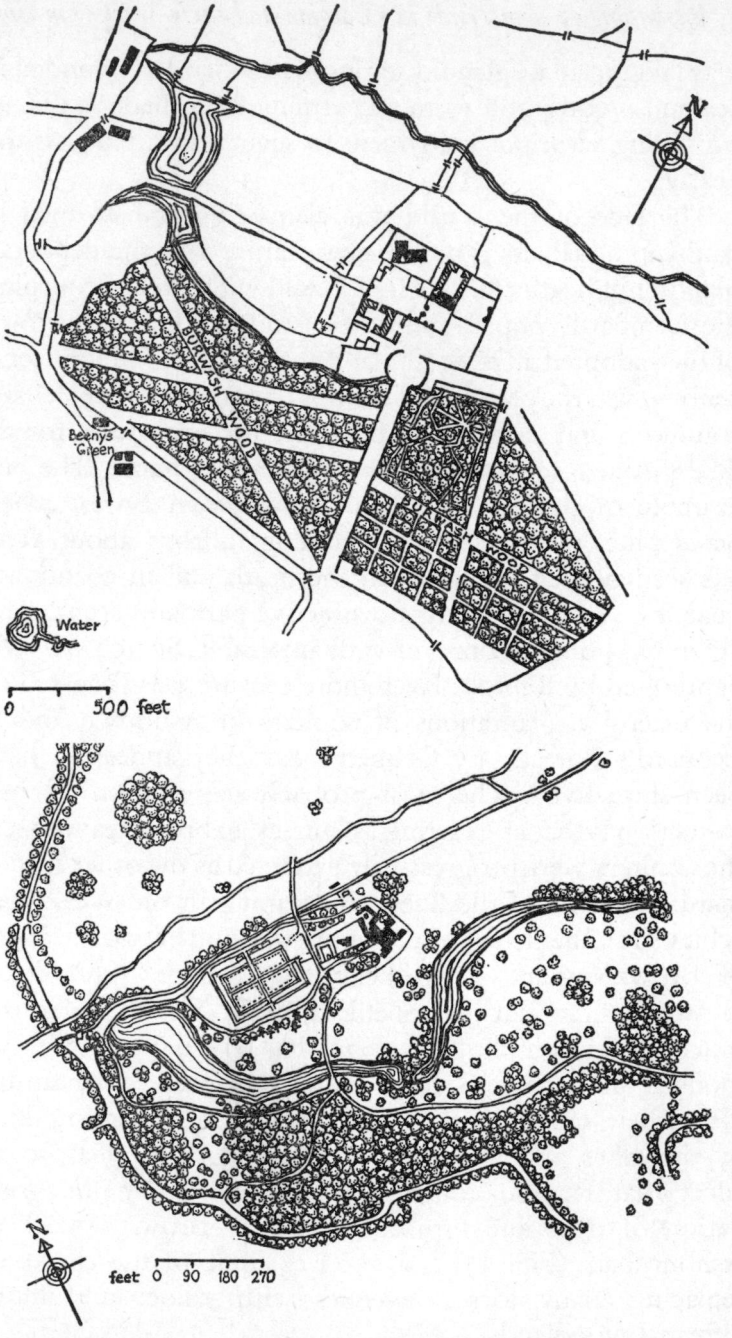

Fig. 28. The formal landscape of Ashburnham Park and Brown's conversion.

As befits its great house, Petworth is the most magnificent and spacious of the Sussex parks. Here Brown extensively remodelled the ground into artificial undulations to give the cherished quality of surprise. A spring was cleverly exploited to make the serpentine lakes and the park boundaries were concealed to give the impression of boundless space. The sentiments in Pope's couplet:

> He gains all ends who pleasingly confounds
> Surprises, varies and conceals the bounds

were nowhere more explicitly put into practice than in Brown's masterpiece at Petworth. Celebrated in oils by Turner, it is now immaculately maintained by the National Trust and those who seek to drive a four-lane by-pass through its middle would for ever desecrate its beauty and tranquillity.

SELECT BIBLIOGRAPHY

Marshall, W. *The Rural Economy of the Southern Counties* (1798), Vol. 2.
Meade-Fetherstonhaugh, M. and Warner, O. *Uppark and its People* (1964).
Repton, H. *The Art of Landscape Gardening* (ed. J. Nolen) (1907).
Stroud, D. *Capability Brown* (1950).
Vine, P. A. L. *London's Lost Route to the Sea* (1965).
Young, Rev. Arthur, *A General View of the Agriculture of the County of Sussex* (1813 edition).

7. Urban landscapes

*The estuary ports. Market and county towns. Resort
towns (1750–1860). Brighton. Other Sussex resorts.*

MUCH OF THE attractiveness and individuality of the older
Sussex towns is derived from their long use of local building
materials which harmonise with the adjacent countryside.
The clunch and flint pervading Steyning, for example, mark
it as a typical downland settlement, whilst the general use
of stone slabs for roofing records the long-continued use of
the river Adur for bulk transport to and from the Weald.
At Petworth the liberal use of local stone has helped to
impart the atmosphere of a town to what is only a small
community; the range of mellow tones from the reddish-
brown Carstone through the yellows and buffs of sandstone
adds a variety to the scene, and blend quite artlessly and
accidentally into a beautiful total effect. The church tower,
with a sandstone base and a rosy-red bricked upper part,
sets the theme for the entire town. At Horsham the
perishability of the timber used in the construction of its
ancient buildings accounts for the fewer surviving old
houses.

The setting of many Sussex towns in relation to the
surrounding countryside also emphasises the intimate
relationship between urban and rural life in the past. A
striking and unusual feature is the hill-top situation of
numerous towns—whether for refuge against the sea or
fortress. Rye and Winchelsea dominate the surrounding
marshes from their hill sites and the glorious location of
Lewes comes into mind, with framed views from its streets

of the landscape below. William Morris considered Lewes to be "set down better than any town I have seen in England".[1] Its visible presence has an aesthetic and spiritual value for neighbouring villages. Arundel, clustered on a steep hillside surmounted by its castle, makes one of the most striking townscapes of all. In a rather different manner the spire of Chichester cathedral, rising high above the low, flat, corn country of the coastal plain provides a unique focus for the landscape between the sea and Downs which would otherwise lack a sense of coherence. The naturalist W. H. Hudson remarked upon this role when he wrote: "this solitary soaring spire has a value above that of any spire in the land".[2] It is fortunate that no modern building has been allowed to destroy the scale of this historic composition.

The harmony fortunately still existing between town and country over much of Sussex is also attributable to the small scale of the old towns. Several of the most historic contain little more than a single street—such as Battle, Hailsham, Robertsbridge and Steyning. Even the two largest old towns of Sussex—Chichester and Lewes—are really only towns in miniature. Their smallness is appropriately matched by the scale of their buildings. Indeed, all the old Sussex towns retain the quality of which Thomas Sharp in *English Panorama* has said: "we in England once showed a natural genius—the genius of creating towns that nearly always have had pleasantness and seemliness; that often have quite a remarkable beauty; that always have maintained a comfortable human scale". At the first census in 1801 the populations of Horsham, Lewes, Midhurst and Steyning were 3200, 4900, 1000 and 1200 respectively, and most other towns had populations of between 1000 and 2000. Even today, Chichester, the largest, does not exceed 20,000 people. The arrested growth of the older towns, now

[1] *Letters* (ed. P. Henderson), p. 155.
[2] W. H. Hudson, *Nature in Downland* (1951 edn.), pp. 235-7.

regarded as an inspired blessing, is largely due to the enormous success of the resorts and the lack of nineteenth-century industrial development in Sussex. With the construction of railways in Sussex connecting London and the new seaside towns, the eclipse of the older towns became complete. They survive as remarkably unspoiled expressions of the pre-railway age and the townscapes record their era of greatest prosperity in the eighteenth century. In few parts of England is it possible still to savour so much Georgian architectural beauty and refinement.

In exploring the origins of Sussex towns few threads lead beyond the Norman Conquest. Existing information suggests that Roman Sussex was devoid of urban settlements apart from Chichester, and that the Saxons raised few towns beyond the stage of very humble beginnings. The most instructive Saxon document relating to urban growth is the 'Burghal Hidage' of the early tenth century which refers to artificially made towns called *burhs*, fortified sites peopled for the defence of Wessex. Four such fortresses are listed under Sussex—Burpham, Chichester, Hastings and Lewes. Amongst the unresolved topographical problems of Chichester is the extent and alignment of the Saxon defences. Possibly the whole perimeter of the Roman wall was strengthened against attack. The other three borough sites were selected because of their natural strength. Burpham's importance was short-lived, its defensive role in the Arun valley being assumed by Arundel after the Conquest. Its unoccupied ramparted enclosure of some twenty-two acres still occupies a bluff overlooking the river Arun.

The most thriving Saxon *burh* was Lewes, owing its importance for centuries to the natural steepness of the promontory site above the river Ouse. Its very name is derived from Old English *hlaew*, a hill. On its west side, the only part not naturally defended, earthworks are still visible along the line later followed by the medieval town walls. A striking characteristic of the old nucleus of Lewes is the regular layout of streets south of the castle. Here, narrow lanes and passages run down the hillside for about a furlong from the east–west axis of the street between the sites of the East and West Gates, some 666 yards apart. As no Roman building has yet been proven in Lewes, this deliberate planning could be the work of the Saxon *burh* builders. The presence of two moneyers in the defended Saxon town of Lewes is another sign of its unusual importance. In 1066 it was the chief town of Sussex, being valued in Domesday Book at £26 per annum compared with Chichester, worth only £15. One other Saxon town deserves mention. This is Steyning which owes its early urban development not to fortifications but to the initiative of the royal house of Wessex, who held the manor.

An important turning-point in Sussex urban development was the Norman Conquest, with its new sources of wealth and creative energy. Towns arose as adjuncts to castles, initially as small settlements outside the castle keep. It is easy to visualise Norman Arundel because its plan has suffered little change since. The steeply descending High Street, widening at the bottom of the hill to accommodate the market, led down to the town quays. A causeway constructed by the monks of Lyminster continued the road southwards. The only other main streets in Arundel, Maltravers and Tarrant Streets, follow the contours of the hill at right-angles to High Street and probably represent early medieval extensions.

While Arundel grew at the foot of the huge motte raised by Roger de Montgomery, William de Warenne was founding some notable buildings in Lewes. He fortified his town with an ovoid bailey, unusually having two mottes. Brack Mount, slightly the lower, is generally considered the older. Warenne, who seems to have been a man of exceptional achievement, and his wife also founded the great priory of St Pancras at Southover, on the southern edge of the town. In the succeeding centuries the fortifications of the castle were constantly renewed by the Warennes. The projecting towers added to the great shell keep remain, and the last of the Warenne line built the strong and graceful barbican in the early fourteenth century. This has the beautifully knapped and squared flintwork, by then traditional in Sussex building. The old castle courtyard is still partly bounded by its high curtain wall, seen to the best advantage from Castle Ditch, an unpaved street remaining in its primitive state. The great keep still dominates the little town as it did when the closely packed houses huddled under its protection (Plate 36).

The estuary ports

A fascinating aspect of urban history in Sussex is the waxing and waning of estuary ports depending on changes in river courses and the advance and retreat of the sea. Although much visual evidence of past maritime activity has been obliterated by wholesale rebuilding following recent industrial and residential development, and the sites of several old seaports have been completely overwhelmed by coastal erosion, there still exist on every arm of the sea abandoned or decaying quays, wharves, jetties, old ship-yards, warehouses and fishing 'shops'. These draw attention to a serious drawback of the Sussex coast, the vulnerability of its low and yielding cliff-line to the damaging effects of severe Channel storms at the moment of high spring tides. Generally speaking, harbour-making in Sussex has been discouragingly difficult. Natural harbours in the Middle Ages there were in plenty; scores of estuaries and creeks existed along the former embayed coast of Sussex, sheltered by headlands, and the surge of high water carried sea-going ships far inland. Yet coastal processes operating throughout historic times have produced the shoreline's present smooth aspect. Headlands have been trimmed back and harbour entrances deflected eastwards by longshore drifting of eroded material. Upper reaches of rivers have silted up owing to the human action of 'inning' the marshes, thereby reducing the volume of water which previously kept entrances unobstructed. Above all, the sea has encroached on the land throughout history. Erosion has been responsible for the coastline's retreat averaging between one and two miles in west Sussex since the Roman period.

These natural processes involved man in a constant struggle with the sea which has been an important element in Sussex town-making. The sites of ports have needed replacement by fresh ones, which required the layout of new streets and the construction of public, commercial and domestic buildings, together forming a new urban landscape. Sussex ports have therefore experienced an exceptionally interesting topographical development. Their 'life-cycle' has often included a short period of intense activity, followed by early decline, and a prolonged period of stagnation, when a rival port, potentially more favourably sited, usurped the older settlement's trade. In this way New Shoreham and New Winchelsea succeeded ports bearing the same name, Newhaven assumed the role of Seaford, and Littlehampton that of Arundel.

The evolution of the Adur ports typifies salient developments occurring on other Sussex inlets. A major port existed on the Adur from Saxon times, if not earlier. Before the Norman Conquest the main harbour was probably St Cuthman's port at Steyning, some six miles upstream. Vessels still passed Bramber bound for Steyning in the early twelfth century but this trade was extinguished soon afterwards by silting of the river and the interference to traffic by the Braose family, a fragment of whose castle survives at Bramber, just downstream. Today the site of this Saxon harbour can only be surmised. G. Mitchell suggested that it lay near the present Steyning vicarage.[3] An alternative site is just north-east of Bramber castle where an accumulation

[3] G. Mitchell, *Sussex County Magazine*, Vol. 21 (1947), p. 127.

of shingle once existed and flood-water reoccupied a wide creek in 1924.

By Domesday, the main harbour on the Adur was at Old Shoreham, an episode leaving no trace on the landscape apart from the unusual size and beauty of its eleventh-century church. Within a generation this port was super-seded by New Shoreham, one of the leading English ports until, in its turn, sand blocked the harbour entrance and the sea half destroyed it in the late fourteenth century. Its zenith of importance was the time when Sussex was acting as a gateway to Norman lands overseas. New Shoreham's founder was probably William de Braose I, lord of Bramber Rape, who died about 1094. Its ordered, rectilinear street pattern suggests a planned town. Henry Cheal, writer of *The Story of Shoreham* (1921), observed that the streets north of High Street are each about a furlong in length and that the town plan was almost exactly duplicated on the south side by 'hards' (public ways to tide-water) directly opposite the other set of streets (Fig. 29). He concluded that the southern half of the town was washed away by the sea before 1401, when Shoreham was reported 'largely destroyed'. Cheal's ingenious conjecture, resulting from carefully unravelling the street plan, is still unproven, but the new technique of infra-red aerial photography may be the means of recovering at last the plan of features buried under river silt.

The impoverishment of New Shoreham by late medieval natural disasters is well known, but an early and unequivocal record seems to have passed unnoticed. This is a report of 1369 that "the old port is blocked"[4]—implying that some new port already existed on the Adur. No evidence has yet come to light to solve this problem, but the most likely successor to New Shoreham was Kingston Buci, mentioned as a port as early as 1234.[5] Since Kingston

---

[4] P.R.O. C.135/312.
[5] P.R.O. *Calendar of Close Rolls*, Henry III, Vol. 2 (1231-4), pp. 556, 563.

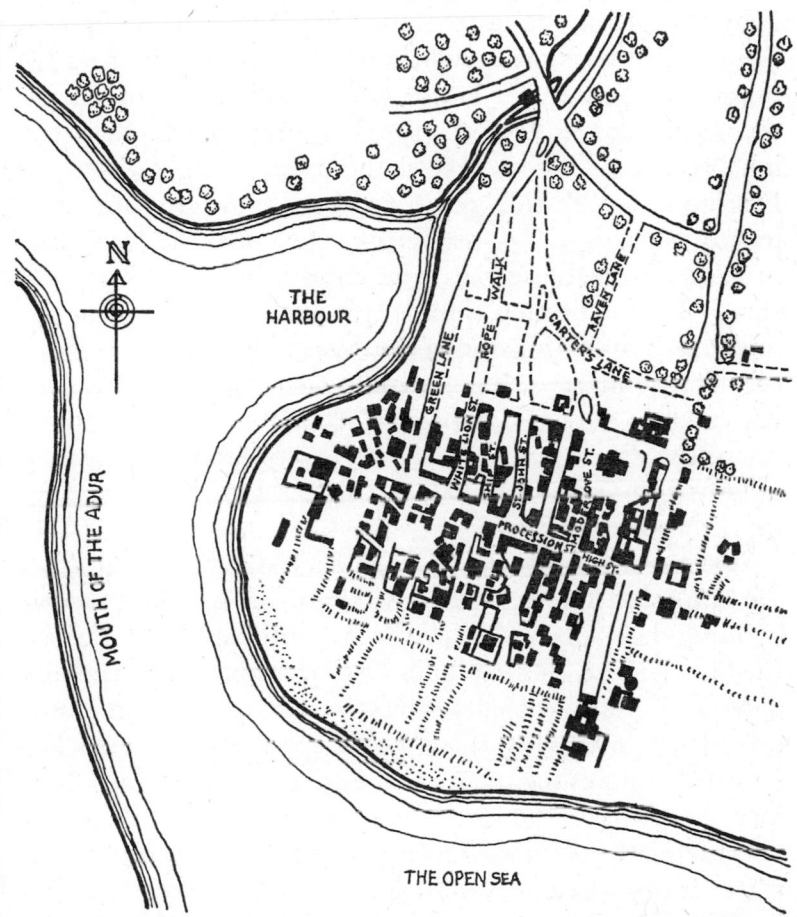

Fig. 29. New Shoreham before the flood disasters of the late Middle Ages.

originally lay on the open coast it is likely that the sheltering shingle spit had already deflected the Adur eastwards.

Whatever mystery surrounds the harbour succeeding New Shoreham, the facts of the town's history are beyond dispute. By the sixteenth century it had fallen into comparative obscurity. Only eighty houses were liable to Hearth Tax in the 1660s and as late as 1801 it mustered less than 800 inhabitants. Its revival reflects the overflowing demands of Brighton as a seaside resort in the eighteenth and nineteenth centuries. To resuscitate the port it was first necessary to stabilise the Adur mouth by an artificial cut through the deflecting shingle spit. An abortive attempt to fix the mouth at Kingston in 1762 was followed by a successful venture in 1818. The canalising of the channel east of Kingston in the 1850s boosted trade still further. This canal has recently been modernised and New Shoreham has grown rapidly into one of the most successful of the smaller English ports.

When one regards the Adur ports today there is little in the landscape to recall their past. Only one medieval secular building has survived—'Marlipins', probably the earliest Customs House—solidly built of Caen stone and tastefully decorated with knapped flints. Churches are the most enduring symbols of these ports' past importance. The unusually interesting one of Old Shoreham has already been mentioned. At Kingston Buci, a humble pre-Conquest village church was greatly enlarged and gracefully elaborated in the thirteenth century—"not at all a village effect", writes Ian Nairn. New Shoreham church is a splendid building, the noblest of the Sussex parish churches. Since its endowment by William de Braose I, it has been the church 'of the port' (*de haura*). Succeeding Braoses lavished wealth upon it and although the nave fell into ruin in the seventeenth century (by which time Shoreham was in abject decay) the fine Norman tower and beautiful choir, both completed at the height of Shoreham's importance, remain as masterpieces of medieval art. This is the church which inspired Swinburne to write, admittedly with more feeling than accuracy, "... Strong as time ... stands the shrine that has seen decline eight hundred waxing and waning years ..." These three remarkable churches exist within as little as one square mile. Truly they are a striking legacy of the Adur's brief importance as chief gateway between the two parts of the Anglo-Norman realm.

Ever since the fifteenth century the Adur's main trade has been conducted from numerous subsidiary creeks east of Shoreham, along the river's deflected outlet, at Aldrington, Fishersgate, Southwick and Kingston. A late-eighteenth-century traveller, William Gilpin, noted that "Southwick, Shoreham and other towns appeared lying at our feet in creeks or winding bays, adorned each with its little harbour and coasting vessels".[6] This picturesque scene was previously a source of inspiration to countless artists but during our own times continuous industrial development has taken root along the eastern arm of the Adur. The ancient creeks have been filled in and the shingle bar firmly stabilised. Yet to a surprising extent old buildings still commingle with new, despite large transit sheds and power stations, making it still possible to reconstruct the scene as in Gilpin's day (1774). The oldest port buildings on the Adur form a line of cobble-built, single-storeyed warehouses, remaining on the extreme eastern arm of the river. They were probably built before the river mouth was firmly secured at Kingston. From this point westwards, clusters of old buildings can be found at ancient ship-building and trading sites. One such group overlooks the modern oil terminal at Fishersgate and at Southwick a fine waterside exists between the Schooner Inn and the Old Town Hall. Another eighteenth-century group of warehouses survives near the lighthouse at Kingston.

[6] W. Gilpin, *Observations on the Coasts of Hampshire, Sussex and Kent, 1774* (1804), p. 42.

The shores of Rye Bay provide on the ground other rewarding studies of decayed estuary ports. Old Winchelsea disappeared in the late-thirteenth-century Channel storms. Its successor was stranded economically by silting in the later Middle Ages. This replacement of Old Winchelsea occupies a special place in the history of English towns. New Winchelsea was founded by Edward I in 1288, the most ambitious of the planned towns he created, modelled on the bastides of Gascony. New Winchelsea, in its own decline, was aptly described by Defoe as a "skeleton of an ancient city rather than a real town". This limited building enabled the topography of its fossilised structure to receive careful and expert observation, together with the voluminous relevant documents. Of great interest and importance is the record of a commission set up by Edward I "to plan and give directions for the necessary streets and lanes, for places suitable for a market and two churches". As Professor T. F. Tout has observed in his *Medieval Town Planning* (1917), "in these minute directions we have the most detailed evidence of conscious town-planning by royal authority that the age was to witness".

The first Winchelsea lay in a very exposed site in Rye Bay, about three miles south-east of the present town. In 1287 a severe storm finally rendered the old port uninhabitable. The entire population was transferred to a new site prepared some years earlier, in readiness for the anticipated disaster. New Winchelsea was laid out on a hill-top promontory at Iham above the river Brede. A chequerboard of five long north–south streets intersected at right-angles by eight other streets divided the town into thirty-nine *insulae* (rectangular-shaped plots). This geometrical layout, fashionable at the time, is still basically unmodified, and traceable even under the grass-grown parts of the town (Fig. 30). New Winchelsea was no ordinary town. Its large size (about 150 acres), the scale and magnificence of

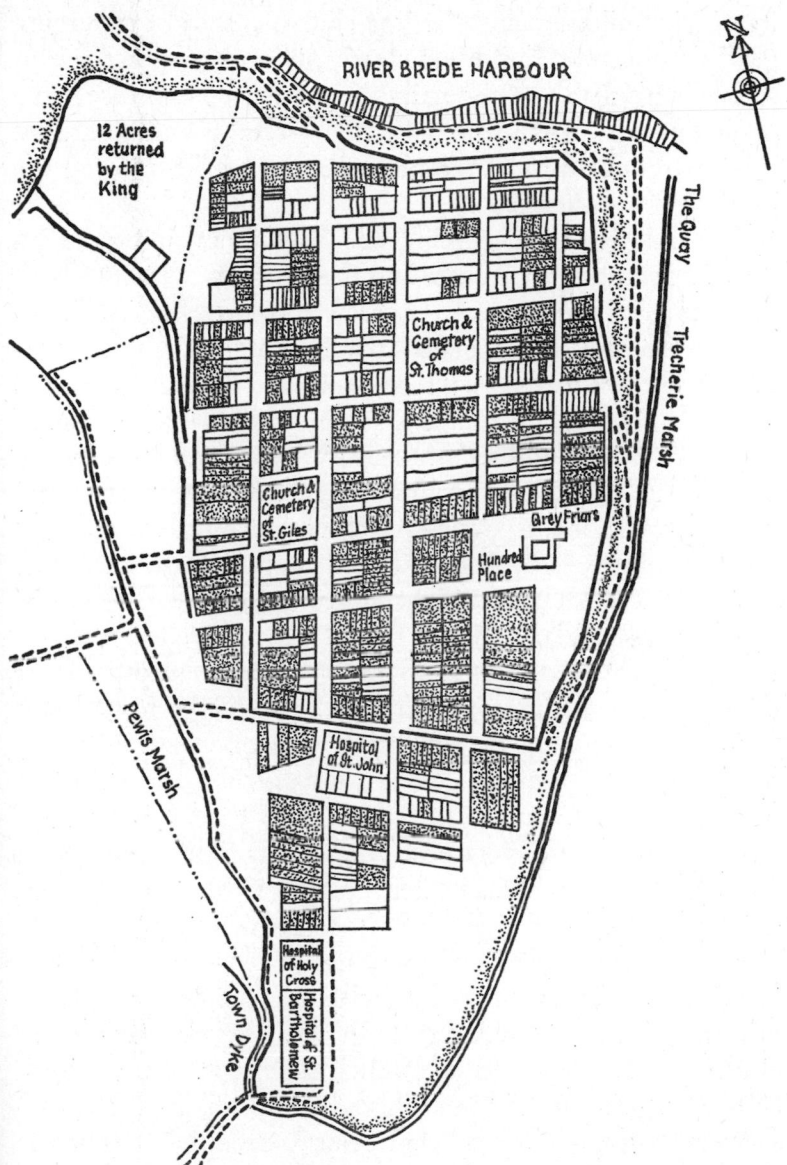

Fig. 30. New Winchelsea: a medieval new town.

its public buildings and the fine craftsmanship of surviving parts of domestic buildings clearly show that it was meant to be an English town worthy of its function expressed in a contemporary document as a "key, refuge and guard of these parts against the tempestuousness of the sea and the insults of our enemies".

The ambitious undertaking was, in fact, never completed. Impoverishment by plagues and French raids, together with the silting of its harbour, brought about decline. By 1575 there were only about sixty inhabited houses, although in 1292 a rent roll had shown tenements held by as many as 700 persons. The present buildings at New Winchelsea, mainly seventeenth- and eighteenth-century, are confined to twelve of the thirty-nine *insulae*. A plot of 2½ acres in the town centre was reserved for the parish church of which little more than the chancel was built. If it had been completed on this scale, it would have been one of the largest and most magnificent churches in England. The Franciscans received a grant to build in New Winchelsea, and the ruined chancel of their church also remains, together with three of the town gates and fragments of the original town walls. Beneath the town houses the remarkable "costlie vaults arched and set forth with pillars of Caen stone, as meant to have houses built over them mete for famous merchants" described in a sixteenth-century survey[7] still exist. These vaults were doubtless used for the wine trade, which contemporary documents in Bordeaux show to have been one of the main activities of fourteenth-century New Winchelsea. Their beautiful craftsmanship equals that of the rich tracery in church architecture and is another indication of the wealth of the town before the sea worked its doom.

Rye, a town of unparalleled beauty, occupies a dramatic site on a small hilltop rising above surrounding marshes. Its name is derived from the Old English *eg*, an island, indicating that in early times Rye was frequently cut off by the

7 P.R.O. S.P. 12/75, f. 70.

sea. Even in the early nineteenth century the passage along the causeway towards Winchelsea and London could be dangerous in stormy weather. Turner in one of his sketches admirably captures such a stirring scene. Rye's comparative isolation from the land and its centuries-old connection with the sea has contributed to its unique atmosphere, more reminiscent of a north European port than a Sussex market town. The general aspect of the town with its irregularly built streets and alleys, many still cobbled, containing a delightful medley of closely-piled red-roofed houses surmounted by a majestic parish church makes it one of the most splendid of the old English seaports. Esther Meynell has said that Rye "may be seen, complete and perfect, like a vignette in some fourteenth-century Book of Hours".[8] Although this statement is not historically accurate, little medieval fabric being visible in the present townscape, the impression is still retained of a medieval town because little change has occurred in the cramped nature of the site for 500 years.

Rye first appears in documents when it was already a thriving port. The date of its origin remains a matter for speculation. W. Page has plausibly suggested that the unnamed 'new borough' with sixty-four burgesses recorded in Domesday Book under the manor of *Rameslie*, of which Rye formed a part, can be identified with Rye.[9] Its important defensive role is sufficiently recalled by extensive remains of fortifications. The oldest fragment is the Ypres Tower, the keep of a thirteenth-century castle. The town walls and gates were built at the outbreak of the Hundred Years War, made necessary by the sea's destruction of part of the port and repeated French raids. The Land Gate still survives and behind Cinque Ports Street and along Conduit Hill are good stretches of the town walls.

Whilst Old Winchelsea remained a port it always appears

---

[8] E. Maynell, *Sussex County Magazine*, Vol. 8 (1934), p. 132.

[9] W. Page, V.C.H. *Sussex*, Vol. 9 (1937), p. 49.

to have been larger and more prosperous than Rye. As Winchelsea declined in the fourteenth century so Rye attained its zenith and, strongly protected by its new walls, remained a powerful trading and fishing community into Elizabeth I's reign. Iron, wool and foodstuffs to London were then the main commodities exported by Rye and her imports were mainly coal and grain. By this time the retreat of the sea, aggravated by extensive inning of the bordering marshes, brought about a marked decline in the town's fortunes. Camden noticed at the end of Elizabeth's reign that the town "beginneth to complain that the sea abandoneth it" and Celia Fiennes, a century later, reported that Rye harbour was choked with sand. Thereafter Rye subsided into a minor local role as a market town. It is a place of white weather-boarded, tile-hung or timber-framed houses, many with handsome Georgian fronts, and the whole hill over which Rye has grown takes on the character of an historic monument.

Market and county towns

Although the dissolution of its priory in 1537 was a blow to *Lewes* it increasingly acquired the functions of a regional capital where folk from Down and Weald did their marketing and legal business (Fig. 31). Ogilby's *Britannia* (1675) reported that Lewes "was esteemed the best borough town of the county" and "chiefly composed of gentlemen's seats joining one to another with the gardens adjoining". A Poll Book of 1837 giving details of occupation and residence of voters described no less than 52 of the 482 inhabitants on the voting register as 'gentleman' (most of whom resided in High Street). In addition many were professional people, surgeons, attorneys, land agents, bankers and brokers, as well as shopkeepers and others.

Lewes still gives the impression of a gracious and comfortable Georgian town. Few façades older than the early

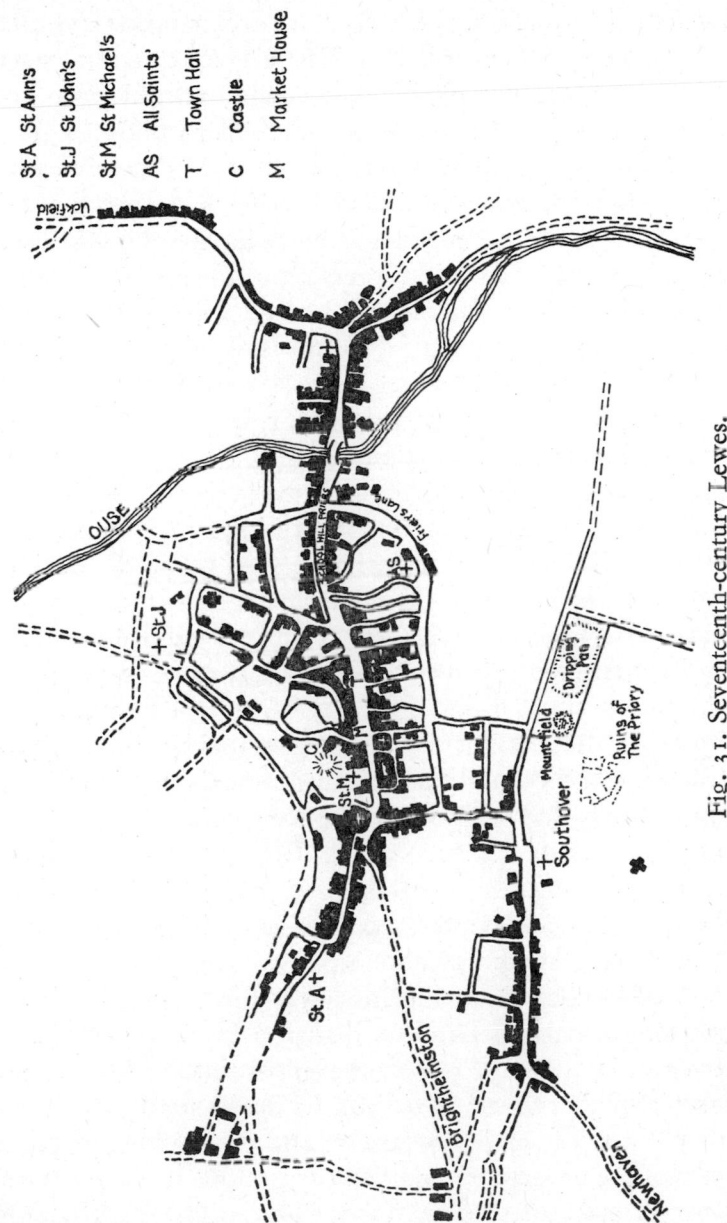

Fig. 31. Seventeenth-century Lewes.

St A — St Ann's
St J — St John's
St M — St Michael's
AS — All Saints'
T — Town Hall
C — Castle
M — Market House

eighteenth century survive. Many older houses were demolished to make way for classical architecture favoured by the eighteenth century. Thus Castle Place in High Street, the home of Gideon Mantell, the celebrated physician and geologist, occupied a site cleared of smaller buildings. This was the work of Amon Wilds who was later to build in Brighton. In general, however, the town was being refronted rather than rebuilt in the eighteenth and early nineteenth centuries. Most of the High Street is of great antiquity; Elizabethan or even earlier structures are hidden behind the Georgian façades (Plate 37). A typical example is Barbican House, owned by the Sussex Archaeological Society. This presents to the High Street a handsome Georgian front concealing a sixteenth-century framed building with an original stone fireplace, bearing the date 1579. Some larger houses underwent more than one alteration. The residence of the Shelleys, now Shelleys Hotel, has an entrance front retaining much of its Elizabethan character but its garden front was "newly built in the modern manner with bricks" in 1763 and this in turn was 'new-fronted' by Amon Wilds in 1812.[10] Some of the rapid fluctuations in architectural taste at Brighton were adopted by the rebuilders of Lewes, such as the use of black mathematical tiles, and the ubiquitous shallow bow fronts, so popular in Brighton before the Regency.

Lewes owes its appearance mainly to the activities of its wealthier citizens. By contrast, *Petworth* and *Arundel* can appropriately still be termed 'feudal' towns since their layout is still strongly influenced by the residence of a family descended from the medieval lord. Set in a frame embracing a palatial Baroque mansion in an ancient park, Petworth is unquestionably the most interesting of the county's smaller towns (Plate 38). Its urban status originated with the rise of the Percy family, and the narrow, tortuous streets of the urban core grew up contiguous to the medieval manor house, fortified in 1309. The task of providing

[10] S.A.T. DN. 184.

services to this stronghold greatly increased in importance when the Northumberlands took up permanent residence in Petworth from the sixteenth century. By this time Petworth had a reputation as a cloth town. It also drew much of its wealth from local land-owners who occupied the largest houses during the winter months, returning to their country homes when they could travel around their estates.

Even today Petworth is overshadowed by its feudal past and its great house, unusually built on the very edge of the town, and dominating the huddle of smaller houses tightly packed around it. The town streets wriggle around the towering walls of the park into the old market place occupying the centre of the town. At the corner of High Street and Golden Square is one of the many surprises belonging to the topography of Petworth. Disguised behind a modern brick façade is a half-timbered house of great antiquity, probably the town house of the Mitfords, who, with the Peacheys and the Dawtreys, had settled in the town by the sixteenth century. The interior of this house strongly suggests a 'hall' house with solar, recessed hall and kitchen. A fine early-sixteenth-century wall-painting was recently discovered beneath match-boarding. The building has undergone several alterations during the last three centuries, and shows how the exterior of the present Petworth houses can mislead the historical researcher. It seems certain that town houses owned by local country squires were in existence here well before the close of the sixteenth century, a social development about which little is yet known in Sussex. Petworth still possesses, to an unusual degree, fine specimens of sixteenth- and seventeenth-century gentlemen's houses.[11] Denman's in East Street, now a shop but originally a fine residence, as the carriage-way and yard behind indicate, has a brick-nogged close-studded frame with an overhang. Opposite the church is the town house of

[11] R. T. Mason, 'Some Buildings of Petworth', *Suss. Arch. Colls.*, Vol. 101 (1963), pp. 14–19.

theDawtreys, a family associated with Petworth for centuries. Although no longer a private residence its gabled and mullioned appearance conveys an impression of the Jacobean gentry's wealth and taste.[12]

The small walled city of *Chichester* presents the richest urban scene in Sussex (Fig. 32). The physical change in the fabric of its central nucleus has been so slight since the early nineteenth century that the town has retained much of its Georgian character. It is still possible to enjoy some of the features of a distinguished eighteenth-century townscape where the essence of the past, far from being an encumbrance, goes towards the enrichment of a living city. The special contribution of Chichester to the English urban heritage was first explicitly recognised in 1949 by Thomas Sharp who called Chichester the 'Georgian City' and described it as "the last un-spoiled example now remaining in England of a naturally grown, as distinct from a deliberately planned Renaissance town".[13] Since then the quality of the townscape of Chichester, with that of Rye, has been recognised to be of national importance and the conservation of what is left of the Georgian endowment has become part of government policy.

Although the dominant and all-pervading atmosphere of Chichester derives from its 'Golden Age' in the century following 1725, buildings from other periods, notably Roman and medieval, blend into its landscape. The encircling wall originally defining the town's jurisdiction, and enclosing the entire city until recent times, is substantially Roman. The initial Roman defence consisted of an earthen bank and ditch constructed in the second century A.D. A wall was built during the first half of the third century and numerous bastions were added in the late fourth century. The town walls are still largely intact and have been strengthened and refaced several times, especially

[12] Lady Maxse, *Petworth in Ancient Times* (1952), pp. 10–16.
[13] Thomas Sharp, *Georgian City* (1949).

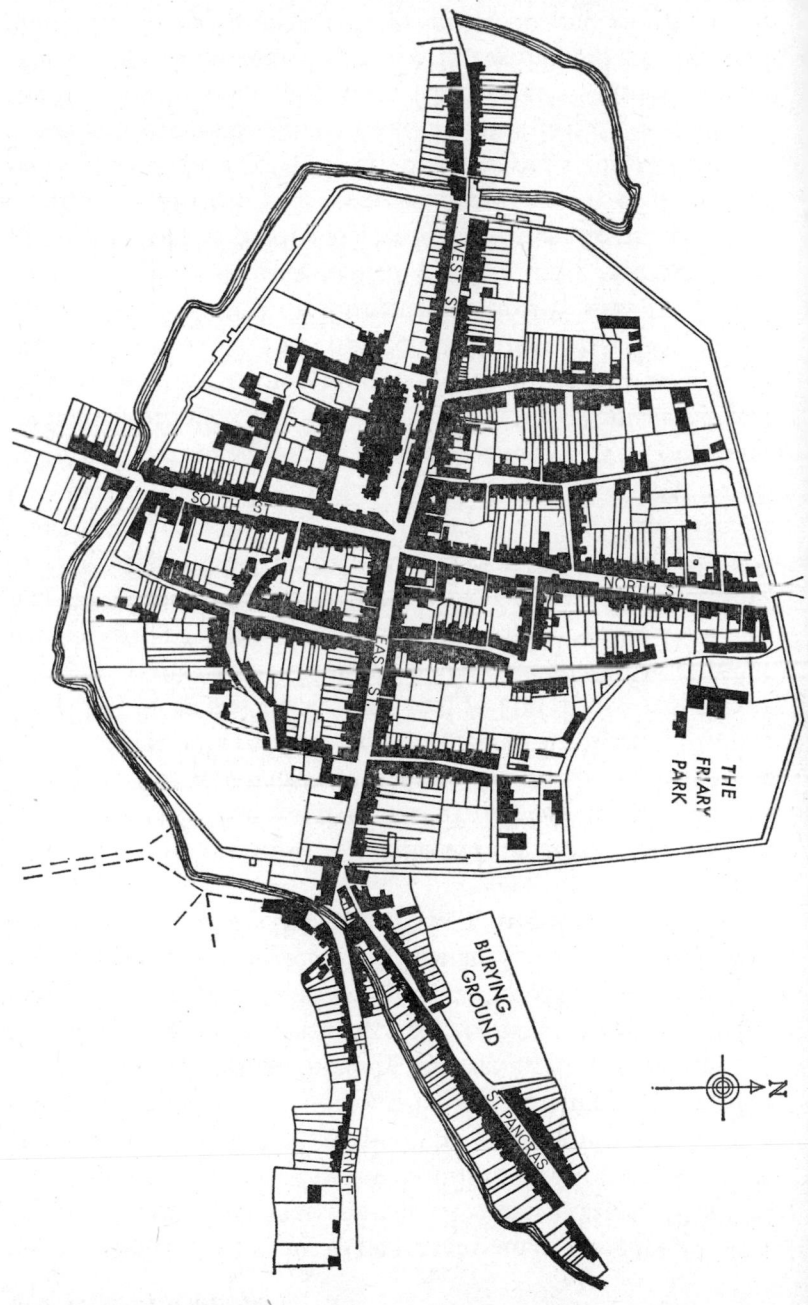

Fig. 32. Georgian Chichester.

during the Middle Ages. The street plan of Chichester is an equally striking legacy of the Roman period. 'Rescue' excavations carried out as new building development occurs are gradually confirming this. The assumption for a long time that present main streets making a simple cruciform pattern follow approximately the same alignments as the Roman streets has been proved correct. However, there seems to be little correspondence between the present minor streets and those of the Roman grid, which suggests a long period of decline before recolonisation in the Saxon period.

Between the end of Roman rule and the Norman Conquest the history of Chichester is obscure. It became a *burh* and the main defences were probably in the north-east quadrant of the town, where a motte was erected in Norman times, which still exists in Priory Park. The most important decision in the early Middle Ages that still affects the present townscape was the removal of the South Saxon see from Selsey to Chichester about 1075. This resulted in the building of the cathedral at the turn of the eleventh century in the south-west quadrant of the town. The built-up area of Chichester seems then to have extended over only the two eastern quadrants; the north-west enclave was occupied by fields until well into the modern period. The ecclesiastical quarter south of the cathedral contains many medieval buildings, notably the fourteenth-century gateway of the Bishop's Palace and the fifteenth-century houses in Vicar's Close. In its spacious walled gardens and narrow lanes something of the medieval scene permeates the present.

Another conspicuous medieval characteristic of the urban scene that has not completely disappeared from Chichester is the abruptness by which building ends at the city walls on the west and south of the town. Chichester's southern aspect where the ecclesiastical enclave is terminated at the wall abutting on to open meadows must be one of the most enduring in Sussex. An additional development of the early Middle Ages, possibly still earlier, which has left a permanent sign on the Chichester layout, is the separate jurisdiction vested in the Archbishop of Canterbury in the south-east quadrant. Much of this sector lay in the Archbishop's Palatinate (hence the local name of Pallant) which functioned as a miniature town within the city. It modelled itself on the larger city to the extent of having its own cruciform street plan and a cross at the centre. The north-east quadrant, the only other part of the medieval city, had a function, and presumably an outward appearance, distinctly its own. It was the burgesses' sector, doubtless the core of the Saxon *burh*. At its south-west corner, in the town centre, was the market place. Here in 1501 Bishop Story built the city cross, an open arcaded octagon in Caen stone. At that time the market place had not suffered the encroachment that has followed over the past three centuries. In recent times attempts have been made to restore the old setting of the cross. An opportunity has just been lost; a new building on the corner of South Street, now erected on the site of an older one, has obscured the view of the cathedral. Yet another medieval characteristic remaining in Chichester is the large number of gardens and other open spaces within the walls. John Norden's map of Chichester, dated 1575, the earliest town plan of the city, is the most valuable witness of the city's early shape. Fields took up the north-west quadrant and large gardens existed on the fringe of the north-east and south-east quarters, the sites of former friaries. These have not entirely disappeared even today. The medieval layout has thus survived in modern Chichester to a remarkable degree.

The present buildings of Chichester are almost wholly Georgian and reflect its rising prosperity throughout the eighteenth and early nineteenth centuries. This had its roots in the progressive agriculture which, according to Hay, the contemporary historian, had increased grain production threefold. For long a market for corn and cattle, Chichester now increased in importance as a milling and shipping centre. R. Blome reported in *Britannia* (1673) that the Chichester haven, the town's outlet to the sea, was choked; but by Defoe's time (1724–6) "some money'd men of Chichester, Emsworth and other places adjacent" had built large granaries near the Crook and sent milled corn to London. The construction of the Chichester Canal, opened in 1823, also brought additional trade.

The eighteenth-century transformation of Chichester was exceeded only by the Roman town building in the first and second centuries A.D. A wealth of gracious fronts and interior improvements remains, illustrating the comforts and civilisation of Georgian society. The quality of the visual surroundings is unusually high for a small cathedral city and country town. This is particularly true in the Pallant which was transformed from a nondescript district of malt-houses and small cottages into a wealthy residential district. Later, in the nineteenth century, it evolved into the town's professional quarter. The vitality of eighteenth-century Chichester is also indicated by the numerous public buildings erected—the Council House (1731), Assembly Rooms (1783), the Market House (1807) and the Theatre (1791) are examples. Nevertheless, the importance of the Georgian heritage in Chichester is not solely due to its sheer architectural quality, valuable though this is. As Sharp has observed, another legacy of the past is the organisation of the town into separate precincts with a character and function each its own. As we have seen, this process began in medieval times and continued with the rebuilding of the Pallant in the eighteenth century. This segregation of Chichester's activities enshrines one of the cardinal principles of modern town planning. The most conspicuous benefit of this historical layout to Chichester is the exclusion of all but local traffic from the precincts, as opposed to the four main streets and ring roads of the town. Even in mid-morning one can walk through them free from the normal noise and danger of moving vehicles. When the scheme to exclude motor traffic from parts of Chichester is realised this unusually agreeable city will recover even more of its Georgian charm and offer civilised surroundings equalled by very few towns in England.

Resort towns (1750–1860)

The social movement of sea-bathing for health which became fashionable amongst the wealthy in the second half of the eighteenth century greatly modified the Sussex landscape. Some effects on the countryside of the ever-increasing throng of visitors have already been discussed. Reference has also been made to the rejuvenating influence of the cult of sea-bathing on the old market towns of Sussex. Above all, from slow yet perceptible beginnings in the 1750s, the new fashion created a fresh kind of urban development engulfing with remarkable rapidity long stretches of the seventy miles of Sussex coastline. The nobility and gentry, consciously disposed to gaiety and leisure even during the Napoleonic Wars, found the impetus irresistible. The movement quickly attracted the operations of adventurers who studded the coast with microcosms of London rather than Sussex towns. These metropolitan pleasure adjuncts bore the same kind of relationship to London as Versailles did to eighteenth-century Paris. Brighton became the very acme of the English bathing resort and in presenting "mile after mile, its gay and fantastic front to the sea" entered upon an entirely new lease of life. As A. L. Wigan, a specialist in the 'water-cure' grandiloquently reported in his *Brighton and its three climates* (1843), it had become the "great sanitarium [*sic*] of the largest and wealthiest city in the world". Its rapid growth has a parallel only in the history of some northern industrial towns.

The fashionable rush to the Sussex coast in the summer months was started by Dr Richard Russell's influential book on the use of sea-water in curing glandular diseases and by the 'discovery' of Dr Relhan, Russell's successor in Brighton, of the purity of sea-air.[14] Such is the force of social convention that the old idea that coastal air was 'aiguish' to strangers was summarily abandoned in the light of new medical approbation. The swing of fashion seeking cures at inland spas to the search for health at coastal resorts could hardly have been timed more favourably for Sussex developers. The only towns sited directly on the coast were the old fishing ports of Hastings and Brighton. Hastings had sadly decayed from its prosperity as a Cinque Port and consisted of a huddle of tall, black weather-boarded houses and drying sheds disposed along irregular, narrow streets. Brighton was also in eclipse. Its heyday had been in the sixteenth and seventeenth centuries when it participated in the Yarmouth herring fishery. This trade had declined and in addition severe coastal erosion had destroyed many fish sheds and houses below the cliffs but by the standards of the time it was a large settlement. The poll tax returns for 1377 show that Brighton had more houses than Lewes, the county town of Sussex. It may also have been larger in the seventeenth century, but most of the houses were then mere cottages and hovels and its trade apart from fish was negligible. "A pretty large, populous, old-built town", as an eighteenth-century observer described it, is probably the most accurate description. The nuclei of other resorts, including Eastbourne, Bognor and Worthing, were no more than villages or clusters of fishermen's cottages. Hove was reduced to a dozen dwellings in 1792 by the erosion which was steadily devouring the Sussex coastline. To each of these decaying settlements the influx of wealthy visitors amounted to a resuscitation.

At the turn of the eighteenth century it seemed to many

[14] Dr Russell's book was translated from the Latin in 1753 under the title of *A Dissertation Concerning the use of Sea-Water in Diseases of the Glands*; A. Relhan, *A Short History of Brighthelmston* (1761).

Plate 38 To an unusual degree the layout and small size of Petworth reveals the close link which existed between a great house and its park and the services provided by townspeople. The large number of former gentlemen's houses and the medieval lynchets running across part of the town fields are visible. See p. 123.

Plate 39 This Regency-style terrace at Brighton embodies some of the dash of jollity, extravagance and whimsy characteristic of the period. The glistening yellow stucco is still traditional and the exquisite wrought ironwork has been carefully preserved. See p. 235.

Plate 40 Typical of the smaller lodging houses built in Brighton for servants and tradespeople *c.* 1790 are these dwellings in Charles Street. The whole district sloping down to the east side of the Steine was laid out in parallel streets and uniformly filled with similar narrow-fronted houses with the shallow-bayed windows fashionable before the Napoleonic Wars. See p. 239.

Plate 41 When Ambrose Terrace, Worthing, was built, *c.* 1820, its occupiers enjoyed a view of the sea over lawns and fields gradually built over from the 1870s. See p. 245.

Plate 42 Late Victorian taste is responsible for these Italianate apartments in the wide carriageway of Grand Avenue, Hove. The cumbrous, austere ironwork of the balconies in comparison with that in Plate 39 is striking. See p. 254.

Plate 43 This late-eighteenth-century print shows the Seahouses, the earliest, and for long the only, seaside buildings at Eastbourne. One of the houses has survived with little alteration as part of Marine Parade. See p. 256.

observers that the sea-bathing mania was becoming all pervading and that eventually "... every paltry village on the Sussex coast that has a convenient beach will rise to a considerable town." Fortunately, this prophecy was not fully realised. Nevertheless, any developer could provide a few bathing machines and open up a lodging house or two. Unembarrassed by scruple, many advertised their bathing stations in exalted and often inaccurate terms. At Shoreham the inns were enlarged in expectation of visitors and the bathing was advertised as "convenient ... and private".[15] 'Private' it possibly was, but 'convenient' it could never have been because the medical ritual involved a river crossing by ferry! Several other bathing stations such as Goring, East Wittering and Selsey failed to flourish for various reasons. At Lancing an enterprising proprietor provided well-publicised bathing machines but even twenty years later it had "no hotel, boarding house, library or public rooms of any description". The proximity of Worthing was probably the cause of Lancing's failure to establish itself as a resort. Another notable failure was Seaford. This decayed port rapidly acquired all the trappings of a resort. By 1798 it provided as good a range of facilities as the larger watering-places—hot and cold baths, assemblies, lodging houses and even a small 'wilderness' for the recreation of its visitors.[16] Yet it was plainly an over-development, and the temporary decline in bathing which followed the resumption of normal traffic with the continent after 1815 killed Seaford's ambitions. Its present townscape is largely Victorian and Edwardian and its rebirth was due to the growing numbers of retired people settling in the town later in the nineteenth century.

The development of Sussex resorts as an urban form during late Georgian and Regency times falls into three fairly well defined stages, each leaving its own distinct

[15] *Sussex Weekly Advertiser*, 7th May 1792.
[16] *Sussex Weekly Advertiser*, 1st December 1798.

imprint on the present scene. The townscapes of the more successful resorts, notably Brighton and Hastings, bear traces of each sequence and serve as a standard of comparison against which the progress of competitors can be measured. In the embryonic stage of growth speculators raised short rows of lodgings facing away from the sea, wherever there was a suitable beach and level ground. The style of houses most convenient for a season's letting to the nobility and gentry was the tall, narrow terrace house, generally four or five storeys high, with bow windows to take advantage of the sun and provide a view of the social scene below. The interior of such early lodging houses was very plain; the façades were generally undistinguished and the whole building usually of a flimsy construction. Libraries, assembly rooms, a promenade and the other recreational facilities were provided in imitation of Bath and other inland spas. All these amenities and other buildings were laid out without conscious plan. It was said of Brighton in 1778 that "this town is built in spots, in patches, and from want of regularity does not appear to advantage; every man seems to have done what appeared right in his own eyes".[17] This rudimentary form of a resort figures in Victorian literature. It is whimsically immortalised by Alice's impression of a sea-bathing place in Lewis Carroll's *Alice in Wonderland* (1862). As we shall see, its traces can also be discerned in the present resorts' town plans.

The next stage of urban growth is marked by the creation of terraces, squares and crescents as single architectural compositions by one architect and landlord, in the manner of Bath. The majority fronted the sea and contained graceful, well-proportioned buildings, reflecting the more successful resorts' rising taste and greater assurance. Brighton attained this stage when the Royal Crescent was built in 1798. Hastings and Worthing did not reach it for another twenty years and Eastbourne's growth was arrested at the first

[17] C. Fleet, *A Handbook of Brighton* (1854).

stage for half a century. Seaford never evolved from the initial stage at all.

A further phase was the more comprehensive development represented by the systematic planning of large estates on virgin ground to create integrated communities in the style of Nash's Regent's Park development. Brighton and Hastings entered this phase in the 1820s but Worthing, Bognor and Littlehampton achieved little in this direction.

The elegance and beauty of late Georgian and 'Regency' architecture has much enhanced the appearance of the Sussex resorts. Although Greek inspiration and the cult of the picturesque prevailed throughout the period of early resort development, there were many variations on classical themes brought about by the mercurial response to swiftly changing architectural fashions, affecting both the basic building style and also such embellishments as ironwork and canopies. The Sussex seaside towns were enriched by two main trends in taste; the more austere tradition predominant before 1815 when simple designs were in favour, and the more dramatic, audacious style of Nash which has left such a renowned legacy all along the Sussex coast. Overlaid on these national trends, the gaiety of seaside towns was receptive to designs with a dash of jollity, extravagance, whimsy and fantasy (Plate 39). The Royal Pavilion at Brighton, Nash's sensational Indo-Chinese domed palace, is the extreme embodiment of these qualities. A Victorian observer severely remarked that its ornamentation was "more appropriate to a tea garden than a royal palace". Fewer people are in agreement with this view today but none will deny that the building could have been erected anywhere but at a seaside resort.

Brighton

The three essential conditions for a resort's success—accessibility, approval of the medical profession, and royal patronage—each found their ultimate realisation in Brighton. As London's nearest point on the south coast it had an immense advantage over its rivals. By the 1820s, when transport by horse-drawn carriage had reached perfection, the fastest coaches covered the fifty-one miles by the direct route to London in less than five hours; private carriages were faster still. It was even possible, as Cobbett noted, for "dark, dirty-faced, half-whiskered tax-eaters" to commute from Brighton to London in early morning and return the same day in time for dinner. During its early growth Brighton was also one of the principal packet ports of the United Kingdom, having a regular service to Dieppe and Paris. This attracted many French patrons, particularly during the Revolution. Brighton was also fortunate in a long line of articulate physicians who by book and pamphlet extolled the varying properties of its sea-water and air—Russell, Relhan, Awsiter, Gibney, Struve, Wigan and Kebbell. Above all, Brighton owed most to its presiding genius, the Prince Regent, who hardly missed a season's residence there between 1783 and 1826, by which time he had succeeded to the throne as George IV. The Prince did not create the gay and extravagant mood of Brighton but he vigorously sustained it and by means of his patronage of the arts can justly be said to have refined it. Under the Regent, Brighton acquired a European reputation and some of the most charming and extraordinary architecture in the kingdom.

The old Town of Brighton was a rectangle bounded by the sea and by East, North and West Streets (Fig. 33). Its narrow, winding streets and the tangle of alleys called The Lanes bring houses and shops closely together into a compact, cramped layout. Its street pattern is probably of medieval origin, but few decades escaped rebuilding when the Old Town was engulfed and transformed by Brighton's seaside development. Nevertheless, the modest proportions of the buildings and pleasant blend of brick, flint and cobble still breathe continuity with the closely grouped community which originally lived by fishing. With the demolition of a somewhat similar urban plan at Yarmouth, Old Town is a precious urban inheritance forming a splendid 'period piece' of late Georgian townscape. A few dwellings escaped conversion with little change and are still recognisable as old fishermen's cottages.

This varied urban scene, the result of centuries of haphazard growth and change, contrasts sharply with the closely ordered unity of building design which developed in the idiom of the day around the Steine between about 1780 and 1800. The Steine was originally the town common where fishermen drew up their boats and dried their nets. The seaside developers transformed it into an elegant promenade that remained the hub of Brighton's social life until the beauty of the sea and beach came to be appreciated in the 1820s. The buildings overlooking this fashionable space still make a fine sustained townscape despite the intrusion of offices and shops into former lodging houses and mansions. The set-piece of this development was the Royal Pavilion itself, built (and constantly rebuilt) on a farm site by the Prince Regent. The Steine's building development is evidently the result of conscious planning by the Town Commissioners, although no documents survive to record the processes of this decision-making. Even though building materials and frontal elevations were left to the choice of individual builders, overall control was clearly kept on the quality and size of dwellings. The result is an attractive continuity of tall, narrow buildings, rather continental in appearance, lining the east side of the Steine. These possess 'unity in variety', an attractive feature of the Late Georgian townscape. Charles Street, with its narrow-fronted houses, is the best preserved of the early side streets.

By the 1790s Brighton was famous all over England as a watering-place but the town remained small and its buildings unambitious. The next forty years saw its most important

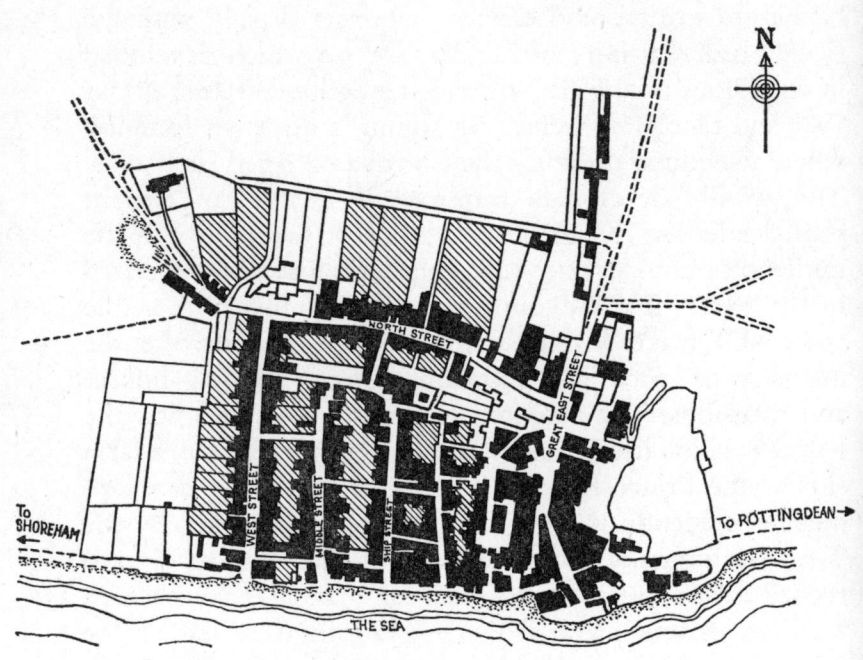

Fig. 33. Old Brighton.

phase of development. Under the continued patronage of the Prince Regent, afterwards George IV, and William IV, Brighton enjoyed a growing popularity causing an extraordinary expansion of the town. The streets and buildings constructed at this time tell their own story. The main development was along the sea front, hitherto unexploited, where a spacious esplanade was laid out and terraces, squares and crescents made a dignified chain of building over a distance of more than three miles, each more majestic than the last. The processional magnificence of these stately groups of classically designed dwellings of traditional yellow stucco still constitutes the chief glory of the Brighton scene. It reflects the self-assurance of a bathing-place which by the 1830s had outstripped all its rivals and had become the acknowledged successor of Bath itself, until then the principal British resort. Such was the influence of its patronage that it overcame the shortcomings of its steeply shelving shingle beach and the bare Downs around it, usually regarded by contemporaries with distaste.

With the aid of town plans and the Land Tax returns the evergrowing number of streets and terraces can be dated with fair accuracy. Most of the early construction was on the East Cliff, east of the Steine, where the building of lodgings around a small square called the New Steine from 1793 was the first sign that the beauty of the sea had come to be appreciated in Brighton (Plate 40). Yet not until 1798, when Royal Crescent was begun, did the first group of houses actually face the sea and make a single composition. In the 1810s building continued on the East Cliff, but the main developments were Bedford and Regency Squares on the West Cliff. During the 1820s the demand became intense for larger, gracefully designed houses for residence as well as for letting. Most of the finest buildings in the town date from this decade or shortly afterwards

The zenith of achievement in this period was the systematic planning and development of the large estates known as

Kemp Town and Brunswick Town. In their magnificent layout and well-balanced composition they serve as an excellent example of the survival of Regency architectural inspiration in the present urban scene. They are imitations by Brighton's resident architects, Charles Busby and the two Wilds, father and son, of Nash's town-planning schemes for London's West End. Both were intended to be self-contained communities, as was Regent's Park, with open spaces, housing of varying quality and size for each social class, resident or employed on the estate, and such facilities as churches and markets. At Kemp Town, named after Thomas Read Kemp, who financed the great enterprise, palatial houses unmatched by earlier building in Brighton were laid out on three sides of Sussex Square which opened out to the sea to form the vast span of Lewes Crescent and its flanking wings of Chichester and Arundel Terraces (Fig. 34). Like all building of the period the façades were built as 'apron architecture' concealing mere shells which were later fitted out by interior designers to the specifications of purchasers. Kemp's funds ran out before the smaller squares and more modest houses could be built. The estate was never finished, but among its most interesting features are the private esplanades constructed in the cliff face, leading into the promenade below.

Brunswick Town lacks the enormous scale of Kemp Town but is a more complete specimen of early estate planning. It comprises Brunswick Square and Terrace, the latter providing the most sumptuous lodgings in the town. In the adjacent Waterloo Street lesser houses and the town church were built. Between Upper and Lower Market Streets, built for the estate employers, is an old covered market-house which obviated the need for shops. The whole town is remarkably well preserved and, apart from the later spread of shops in the side streets, and garages occupying mews, it has changed little. The original inspiration of the 'Regency' style at last faltered in Brighton

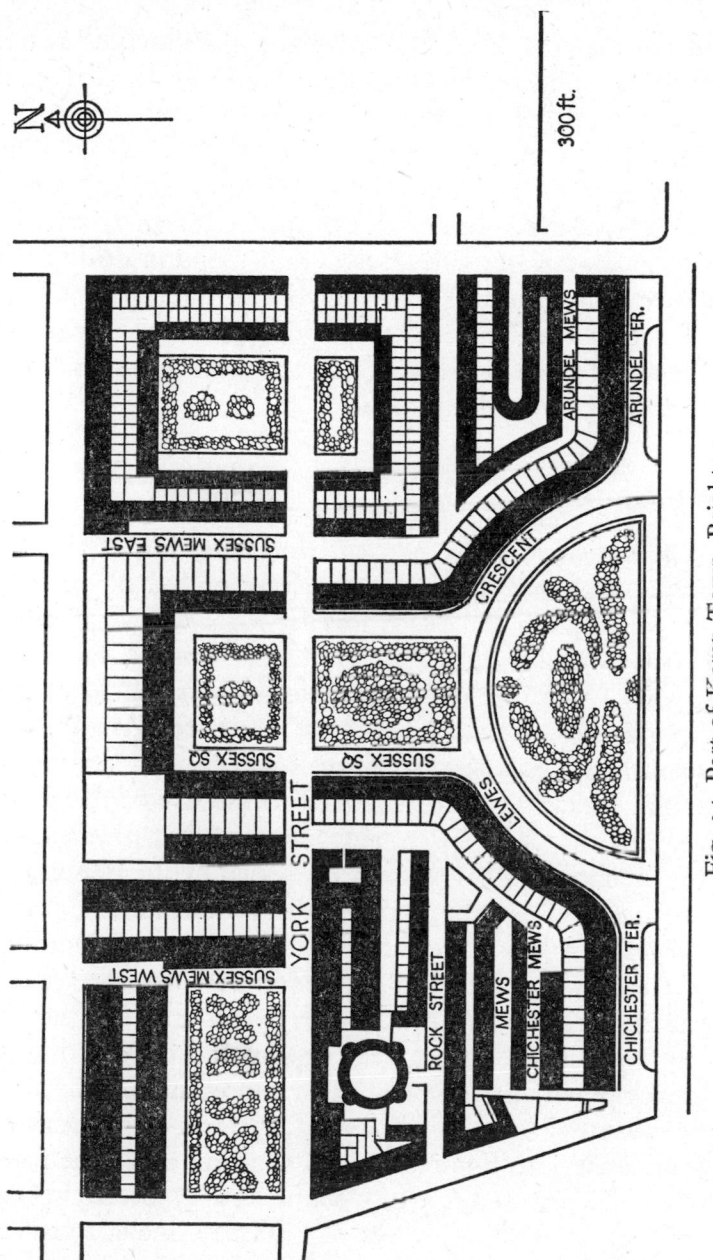

Fig. 34. Part of Kemp Town, Brighton.

about the 1840s at Adelaide Crescent and Palmeira Square. Only the ten houses in the south-east part of the Crescent were the work of Decimus Burton, the architect of St Leonard's, and these were completed about 1834. The Crescent was finished in a simpler style of the 1850s and Palmeira Square was built still later in the Italianate style so popular in Bayswater and elsewhere in London during the mid-Victorian period. The originality of the layout of the whole scene, with its memorable double curve imparting grandeur and grace, is, however, in the best traditions of the 1830s when Burton designed it.

Other Sussex resorts

Worthing's townscape is particularly interesting because it records both rapid growth and a long period of arrested development from the 1820s leaving it for several decades with sporadically dispersed buildings amidst farmland (Fig. 35). Worthing exemplifies in an extreme form the amorphous town plan typical of early resorts. It was consciously designed as a small-scale and cheaper version of Brighton. Imitation even extended to the use of the name 'steyne' for the open space laid out as its first promenade. Just as the mood of Brighton is expressed by the bravura of its architecture, so the quieter disposition of the early patrons of Worthing is reflected in its more austere building style. The first signs of a building boom at Worthing are not detectable until the late 1780s—forty years after Brighton's rise to fame. There is no clear explanation of Worthing's late development as a resort, but an important contributory factor was the severity of coastal erosion—a source of constant anxiety to owners of land abutting on to the foreshore until alleviated by groynes in the 1790s. By 1812, boosted by the publicity value of Princess Amelia's visit in 1798 and that of other royal patronage, Worthing offered all the facilities of the complete resort. Its continual develop-

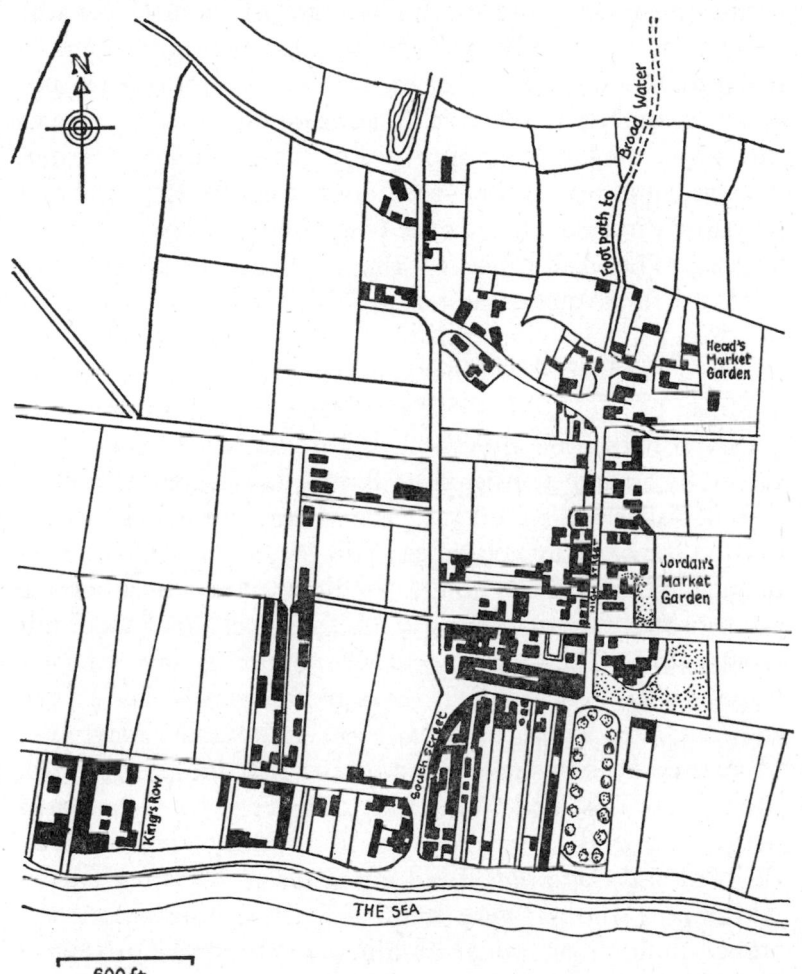

600 ft.

Fig. 35. Early Worthing.

ment in the manner of Brighton seemed assured, but soon its popularity sharply declined. The fall in the number of bathing visitors to the south coast from 1815 after the war was felt more severely at Worthing than at Brighton which had the advantage of greater accessibility and the momentum of an enormous reputation. The deadliest blow of all was the loss of the universal approval of the medical profession. A contemporary writer attributes this to the 'illiberal hostility' directed towards the town by rivals envious of its success. The real cause of the trouble appears to have been the inadequate sanitation which was aggravated by Worthing's low-lying position. This problem was not resolved until the mid-nineteenth century.

Most of the old fishing village of Worthing has survived with little alteration. Before its development as a resort, Worthing consisted of farms and a separate collection of fishermen's cottages. The village, on to which was grafted the watering-place, can still be identified by a series of ancient flint-walled cottages in High Street, which became the thoroughfare of the resort until Chapel Road was built about 1810. The first speculative building was concentrated on land enclosed earlier near Warwick Villa. In 1789 the inn was enlarged and soon afterwards Nos. 1–7 Montague Place were erected as the first lodging houses. Montpelier Row and Great and Little Terraces also existed before the end of the eighteenth century and by 1805 Bedford and Copping's Road and Warwick Street (originally without its shops) were built. All these houses lack the embellishments of similar buildings in Brighton. In 1807–8 the Steyne Hotel and several lodging houses on the west side of the Steyne were built, of local cream-coloured brick. The Steyne itself was laid out as a simple, little, open space. It soon lost its focal importance to an esplanade, and with the random building over the old west common field (enclosed in 1810) and later building, became increasingly left on the outskirts of the town. To this day, Worthing lacks a recognisable focus. The most notable buildings, erected in the 1820s and 1830s, were the colonnaded Liverpool Place, comprising the finest town-houses in Worthing, and Park Crescent, with thirteen villas in their own landscaped grounds. Although of architectural distinction they are outclassed by the quality and number of contemporary developments in Brighton. The fall in its popularity has left Worthing with a haphazard collection of buildings over the last two centuries, some put hopelessly out of scale by later construction, and finely treated elevations have been obscured by subsequent building. The open spaces were merely gaps which were filled in later. A good example of the defects of this lack of building control in Worthing is provided by Ambrose Terrace, a row of delightfully balconied houses originally looking out upon the sea but later hidden by mid-Victorian building in the intervening space (Plate 41).

Bognor was the earliest English resort to be promoted by one man. It was the creation of Sir Richard Hotham, 'the London hatter' as Dr Johnson scornfully called him, who, after restoration to health there in 1784, embarked on building a select resort originally named Hothampton. He deliberately designed the resort to cater for those desiring seclusion with the same luxury and refinement as at Brighton. He obtained the requisite royal patronage and a clientèle of English aristocrats and French émigrés and housed them in distinguished villas and crescents. He acquired 1600 acres but never planned his resort as a whole. His showpiece was Hothampton Crescent (now occupied by a College of Education) of which the central residence called the Dome has been described as "the best example of late eighteenth-century work in any seaside town in Sussex". Rock Gardens Crescent (1804), Waterloo Square (from 1811) and West Side (about 1820) followed after Hotham's death but Worthing, before suffering eclipse in turn, increasingly gained ascendancy over it and little additional building took place in Bognor after the 1820s.

Hastings' transformation from a fishing port and small market town was slow. Despite the efforts of John Collier, one of its most notable pioneers, it was 'little frequented' in the 1760s. The first library at Hastings was not established until 1788 and even in 1804 the town comprised little more than two streets, High Street and All Saints Street, divided by a little stream called the Bourne, adjudged "exceeding good for all culinary purposes". Hastings' real prosperity is not evident until the early nineteenth century when under the influence of the Romantic Movement the delightful cliffs, coves and wooded scenery as well as the mildness of its air were appreciated. It then developed rows of the customary lodging houses and equipped itself with an esplanade in 1812. Pelham Place provided accommodation for more elegant residents. Its growing popularity amongst London stockbrokers in the 1820s led James Burton to purchase land to the west for an entirely new town which had the same relationship to Hastings as Kemp Town to Brighton.

Burton was a great London builder and the father of Decimus Burton the celebrated architect who designed part of Regent's Park. Their work at New Hastings, or St Leonard's as it afterwards became known, has a noble sense of design lacking at other Hastings creations. Commenced in 1828, the town grew rapidly. The Marina is a palatial row of houses of which the Victoria Hotel is the centrepiece; only the crescents of Bath and Brighton rival it. Italianate villas on the hillside overlooking the town and beaches provided more rural alternatives to colonnaded terraced houses, and elegant boundary arches (since removed) added dignity and grace to the scene. Warrior Square, the centre of the whole composition, was laid out early but not built until 1853–64. So yet another health resort was added to the string of bathing places along the Sussex coast.

SELECT BIBLIOGRAPHY

Beresford, M. *New Towns of the Middle Ages* (1967).
Dale, A. *A History and Architecture of Brighton* (1950).
Dale, A. *Fashionable Brighton, 1820–1860* (1947).
Gilbert, E. W. *Brighton, Old Ocean's Bauble* (1954).
Granville, A. G. *Spas of England* Vol. 2: *The Midlands and South* (1841, reprint 1971).
Musgrave, C. *Life in Brighton* (1970).
Salzman, L. F. *Hastings* (1921).
Sharp, T. *Town and Townscape* (1968).
Smail, H. *The Worthing Map Story* (1949).

8. The living landscape (1860–1974)

Later Victorian and Edwardian development (1860–1914).
Changes between the wars. The post-war scene

UNTIL THE MID-NINETEENTH century, man and nature in Sussex maintained a harmonious relationship. Also, man's imprint was guided by a fashion in building and landscape design which is still regarded as enhancing the appearance of the present scene. Undisturbed by the Industrial Revolution, the 'improved' Sussex landscape of refaced small towns and villages set amidst grandly timbered parks matured to its culminating point of perfection about 1860. Ever since then Sussex has been tremulous with accelerating change which has left a far-reaching visual impact, often damaging to the landscape. From mid-Victorian times the seaside resorts, previously the habitat of wealthy rentiers, increasingly attracted the rapidly expanding middle class, using the extended range of travel made possible by railways. The stream of day-trippers pouring down from Brighton station to the sea, the people flocking to the mild and sunny coast to retire, and the swelling numbers who elect to live in Sussex and work in London, illustrate the changing social background which has been constantly modifying the face of Sussex. In short, Sussex was increasingly drawn into the huge urban region that is London. The Sussex coast is now the most developed part of the English coastline and the proliferation of dormitories and suburbanised villages have provided the county with an early taste of the problems brought by rapid urbanisation.

This unplanned urban growth remorselessly covered much of Sussex when standards of taste in building between the two World Wars had never stood lower. It produced a dramatic ugliness which has visually degraded the landscape. "A venturesome people," wrote Dr Joad in a mood of cynicism imparted by the drabness condoned around Newhaven, "might even have sought to embellish the beauty of nature with the works of man."[1] Instead, Sussex will always recall places where bungalow buildings of the worst type were ranked along the cliffs and radially on the country roads leading from the resorts. Since 1945 the demands on many Sussex open spaces have become even more intense. The very survival of much landscape of unrivalled beauty is at risk because of the heavy toll of land for outdoor recreation, wider roads, bigger airports, schools and hospitals, as well as taller hotels and office blocks. Fortunately, Hilaire Belloc's remark that "the love of England has in it the love of landscape, as has the love of no other country" still holds true and the widespread public concern at the present changes may prevent the worst excesses.

Later Victorian and Edwardian development (1860–1914)

The expansion of London into Sussex was still undreamt of at the beginning of Victoria's reign. By 1901 urbanisation was rapidly engulfing much of the coastal plain and edges of the downland. The making of a greater Brighton was one of the chief developments of Victorian Sussex. Although the Court deserted it in 1841 and fashionable patronage declined, the popularity of Brighton amongst the nineteenth-century middle class was unbounded and persistent. "Few places gave so much pleasure as Brighton," writes Sir John Betjeman in *Victorian and Edwardian Brighton*. Its continued success finds a vivid expression in King's

[1] C. E. M. Joad, *The Untutored Townsman's Invasion of the Country* (1946), p. 35.

Parade. Here a row of palatial hotels arose in the last quarter of the nineteenth century and the traffic of private carriages equalled the busiest parts of London's West End. The outstanding attraction of the 'London set' in Brighton was the Metropole Hotel which, at the height of its fashion in Edwardian times, served as many as 800 lunches in a single day and handled 150 of the new motor cars an hour. The rest of Brighton succumbed to what M. Barton and Osbert Sitwell in *Brighton* have termed "Victorian elephantiasis". Houses supplied with water by the town's water company increased from 7000 in 1854 to 23,000 in 1876 and doubled again by 1901. The uncompromising Victorian residences in the Seven Dials area, the rows of artisans' cottages behind the railway station and in Kemp Town, as well as the tongues of villadom extending along the London and Lewes roads, represent some of the rapid growth of this period.

The Victorian townscape of Brighton is worthy of more detailed attention but its westward growth, virtually a new creation, is even more illustrative of nineteenth-century civic design. Formerly, the plain west of Brighton was a chequerboard of heavily-timbered hedges, market gardens and orchards, threaded by narrow lanes overhung with elms. As the suburban frontier of Brighton pushed westwards, the countryside gave way to wharves, factories and houses submerging the old agricultural villages. A little of the former rural landscape still persists at Kingston Buci where the Gorringe estate did not come on the building market until after the Second World War. Along the Adur Ship Canal, however, and the branch of the railway constructed to New Shoreham in 1840, working-class and other smaller houses were raised. By 1945 much of this building had become obsolete. Recent urban renewal has removed most of the blight, especially at Southwick where a new town centre has been built behind the old ribbon development.

The outstanding new development of the late nineteenth

century was the creation of *Hove* which grew from a fishing village with a population of 100 in 1800, to 18,000 in 1881 and to nearly 30,000 in 1901. The layout of Hove differed from that of any earlier town in Sussex. Unlike the compactly clustered medieval towns, or the formalised terraced Regency estates, Hove is a place of detached and semi-detached villas, ranged street upon street, geometrically laid out in spacious gardens in the manner of St John's Wood, Bayswater or Belgravia. The town was not consciously created as a single entity, but grew piecemeal as the jigsaw of landed estates came on the market. It still retains the character of an agglomeration of estates which lacked overall control over private effort. The resulting composition has no central focus such as a group of public buildings and many of its amenities have always been provided by Brighton. "The western independent suburb of Brighton", as the town was called in 1880, is an accurate description of Hove to this day.

Until the 1850s the original fishing village of Hove lay more than a mile to the west of Brunswick Town, which although physically in the parish of Hove was known as West Brighton and separately administered by its own commissioners. Hove as a town with an identity of its own is the product of two generations of building in the second half of the nineteenth century. From the outset it was conceived as a residential town rather than a health resort. It attracted residents who turned up their refined noses at the 'lodging, letting and shop-keeping' community of Brighton. A 'good middle class tone' was set by the rectilinear pattern of spacious avenues (the most majestic not named but numbered in the American fashion) and by large and thoroughly Gothicised churches—one of the most conspicuous marks of Victorian estate development. Wage-earners' dwellings, shops and mews were segregated from the fashionable residences. Proudly it spoke of its massive sea defences, protecting a site formerly flooded by every tide, and its sewers, accounted 'the most perfect in the kingdom'.

Three individuals, Goldsmid, Gallard and Stanford, each of whom developed a single estate, were more than anyone else the creators of Hove (Fig. 36). Their combined work spans a time when the pendulum of fashion in architecture swung faster than in previous centuries. To walk the streets of Hove today is to pass successively through a sequence of architectural styles which illustrate the changing architectural doctrines and social background of their age. Goldsmid, the first Victorian builder of Hove, completed the Adelaide Crescent estate which was left unfinished for over twenty years after Burton's beginning. Goldsmid's work is faithful to the classical concept of the original, and his palatial houses mark no fundamental departure in design. A complete break with the past was Cliftonville, an estate developed mainly by the local brewer, Gallard, in the 1850s. This estate was intended for the well-to-do who nevertheless had smaller means than residents of the sea-front terraces of Brighton. The terrace form of building was eschewed and villas line streets reckoned broad at the time, though they do not match those laid out later, nor have the rigid rectilinearity popular in late Victorian times. St Aubyn's Villas, the main street, was designed with the vista of Hove parish church at its northern end. Church Road, the chief shopping street, formed a social boundary, smaller houses being built north of this road. The meanest dwellings of all were built in George Street, and the names of the occupants were withheld from street directories until the street was refaced with shop fronts some twenty years later.

Cliftonville was an enormous success. Houses multiplied and in a decade its population numbered more than 3000. The growth of Cliftonville was separated from Adelaide Crescent by a tract of undeveloped land. This was filled by the West Brighton Estate Company on land owned by

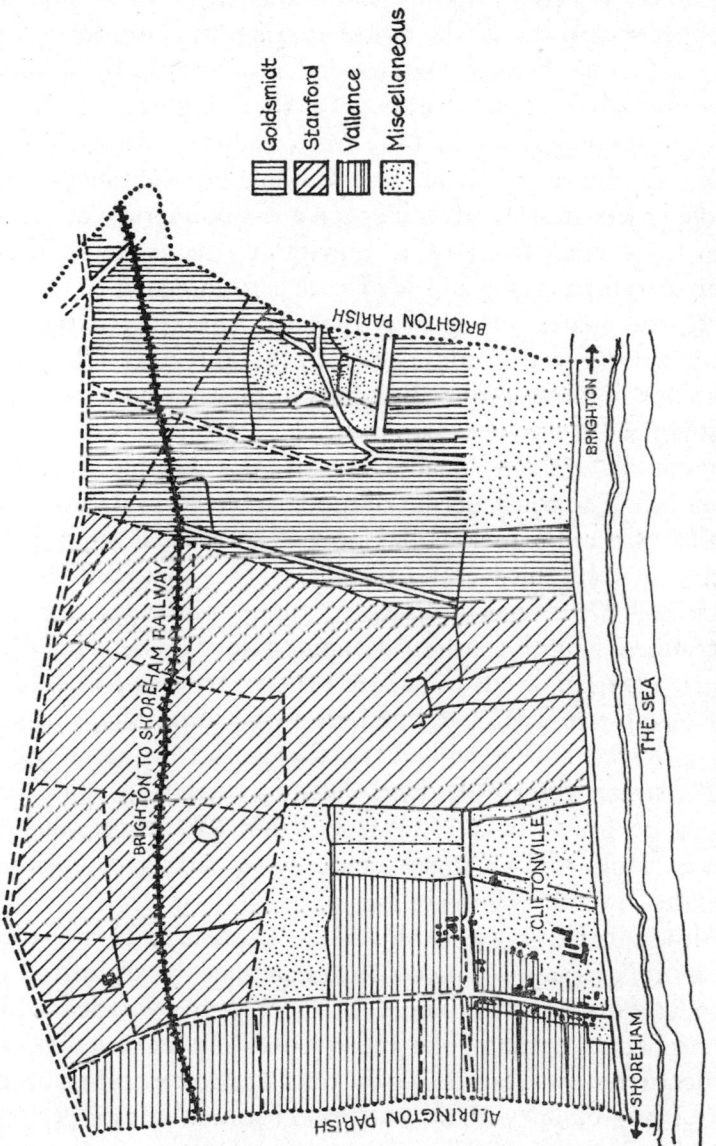

Fig. 36. Hove: private estates on the eve of urban development.

Thomas Stanford, lord of the manor of Preston. It was to be a showpiece of dignity and opulence. Its most impressive characteristic is the wide carriageway bordered by lawns. Grand Avenue was carried northwards by a wide thoroughfare which swept over the Stanford lands to Preston, giving Hove its only main route in that direction avoiding central Brighton. The buildings of the estate were erected piecemeal by several speculative builders over more than forty years from 1871. Inevitably, the estate suffered from a stylistic chaos and is organically unrelated to earlier developed parts of Hove. Broadly speaking, building advanced westwards and a walk in this direction follows a sequence of terraced developments in First Avenue through heavy-handed, yellow stock-brick Italianate villas, to exuberantly gabled residences of the Gothic Revival (Plate 42). The construction of modern blocks of flats on the rubble of these mansions has now disintegrated what little sense of continuity and orderliness the Victorian estate possessed. Dale's recent discovery of an unexecuted plan by Barry for a magnificent self-contained development for this site in 1825 heightens the sense of loss. By 1900, when the Vallance estate was developed west of Cliftonville, smaller two-storeyed houses with just sufficient garden space for a tennis court were in demand. Houses of this specification are to be found in Westbourne Villas and neighbouring streets. Horse-drawn buses made these further extensions feasible.

Although Hove was designed as "a place of fashionable residence", its supporting colony of artisans was estimated at 5000 as early as 1881. These workers were provided with homes which sprang 'like mushrooms' in the north-west corner of the town, bordering the railway. Here in 1881 streets were being built "with amazing and formidable rapidity"—narrow, ill-lit and badly maintained. Within a few years some houses had become "as bad as some of the slums of London". The worst area, in the vicinity of Conway Street,

has recently been demolished and newly constructed blocks
of flats have replaced the former urban squalor.

Another massive monument of Victorian town-building
is *Eastbourne*. For all its early promise as a resort, the favourable publicity gained by royal patronage in 1780, and
splendid natural advantages of scenery and climate, the
town remained in the shadows until the 1860s. The causes of
its failure to grow after the same fashion as Brighton,
Worthing or Hastings remain speculative. R. Cooper who
published his *Reminiscences of Eastbourne* in 1903 attributed
the lack of building in the early nineteenth century to the
aversion of the Cavendishes, the leading land-owners, to
change. He illustrated this resistance by the Burtons'
failure to purchase land in Eastbourne for speculative
development before they turned to their successful venture
at St Leonard's. These statements remain unverified, but
they have the ring of plausibility. Most of the site of present
Eastbourne formed the estate of Compton Place, a stately
mansion which was the home of the Cavendishes for much
of the year. They would therefore have resisted any change
likely to compromise the attraction of their country retreat.
After 1858 a conjunction of events put an end to these
restrictions. In that year the Cavendish estate at Eastbourne
was inherited by the seventh Duke of Devonshire. By this
time Compton Place was in a poor state of repair and was not
required as a permanent residence. Moreover, the railway
had reached Eastbourne in 1849 and George Cavendish,
Earl of Burlington, had already initiated some modest
building in the town. Eastbourne, having long awaited a
promoter, found him in the seventh Duke, who committed
part of his vast fortune in an ecstasy of building of such
taste and quality that Eastbourne became known as the
'Empress of Watering Places' in the 1880s.

The dimensions of change were so great that there is
little visual record of the earlier stages of Eastbourne's
growth. These are not, however, without interest or

importance. The oldest seaside buildings, a row of lodging houses called the Seahouses, were built on the site of Marine Parade in the eighteenth century. No. 6 has survived with little alteration. As early as 1743 the Seahouses had a clientèle of visitors, seeking relaxation, it would seem, by fishing, rather than by sea-bathing, "on account of the agreeableness of the situation there and the good entertainment . . . "[2] (Plate 43). Little further development than this seaside terrace occurred in Eastbourne until Terminus Road was laid out in 1850 from the railway station. The narrowness of this street was acceptable by contemporary standards, and this and neighbouring streets were lined with lodging houses. Most have since been encroached upon by shops but the upper storeys have the plain low-fronted façades of similar houses in early Brighton. More of Lord George Cavendish's work can be found in Grand Parade which bears the classical influence of Decimus Burton, the builder of St Leonard's.

These and similar projects in the relatively small space between the railway station and the sea were only an earnest of the much bigger projects of the seventh Duke of Devonshire, who was mainly responsible for the fabric of modern Eastbourne. The town was conceived in the grandest manner and, intentionally or not, outrivalled all but the very best of Brighton. As a single sustained piece of town-building it is unmatched in Sussex and only the larger development at Bournemouth, which strongly influenced the civic design of Eastbourne, is at all comparable. It was the Duke's achievement to convert a "straggling series of hamlets into a handsome well-laid-out town with miles of streets ornamented by noble terraces and princely mansions". There is stamped over the townscape a greater singleness of purpose than at Hove, the explanation being the less divided ownership in Eastbourne. There were only two

[2] Rev. J. Milles, *An Account of a Tour in Hampshire and Sussex* (1743), B.M. Add. MS. 15776, f. 213.

major estates, covering 6000 acres, of which the larger was the Devonshires'. Its access to beautiful cliffs and rising ground diversified by coombes also gave it greater potential. In this spacious setting the Duke fashioned the parades and promenades, tier upon tier, and laid out wide tree-lined avenues like boulevards, for 'fashionable' Gothic villas with gabled frontages and red-tiled roofs. The informal street layout, which is related to, but not dictated by, the contours of the ground, the wide brick-set pavements, large gardens and open spaces, made it a veritable Garden City. The estate was a burst of development which was hardly begun in 1877 yet almost completed a decade later when some 1500 houses had been finished.[3] The townscape has a pleasing urban form and is a model of early planning which in the opinion of Christopher Hussey should be recognised by town-planners as a masterpiece of its genre.[4] A century later it is still remarkably intact but its streets now echo to the clatter of cement-making machines laying new foundations on the site of the old.

The other large estate in Eastbourne, owned by the Gilberts, at Upperton, north-east of the railway station, is composed of medium-sized and small villas. It was also built in the great late Victorian wave of Sussex coastal building and is a neat and orderly development, laid out around main and subsidiary squares. Although lacking the distinction of the Devonshire estate, its general character is superior to most contemporary Sussex building. To Eastbourne's vigorous growth is owed the single-track railway between Eastbourne and Tunbridge Wells which was opened by the London, Brighton and South Coast Railway in 1881, and closed recently. The Duke of Devonshire regarded it as an integral part of his town-building scheme and it was widely believed that he was prepared to make the line himself if a company had not been induced to undertake it.

[3] *The Builder*, 1st October and 12th November 1881.
[4] *Country Life*, 19th February 1935, p. 137.

Yet another new Victorian urban development was *Crowborough*, which originated as a health and holiday resort, the last of its kind to be promoted in Sussex. Just as Brighton's growth was initiated by the influential book of Dr Richard Russell, so did the persistent meteorological studies of the physician Dr C. L. Prince lay the foundation of Crowborough.[5] Prince, who resided in Crowborough from 1872, realised its potential, at more than 800 feet above sea level, as a health resort. Extensive tracts of land were laid out for this purpose bordering Ashdown Forest by the principal land-owner, Lord Abergavenny. Crowborough still retains much of its Victorian character as a town of detached villas.

Although most Victorian and Edwardian urban growth in Sussex was concentrated on the coast, the suburbanising influence of Brighton also extended northwards into the Weald. Burgess Hill and Haywards Heath both began as 'urban villages' on commons enclosed by Parliamentary Act. They owe their existence primarily to the increased range of movement provided by the London and Brighton railway. In the mid-Victorian period many residents of these settlements commuted to Brighton, but as faster and more frequent train services developed, London came within daily reach. Only in recent years have both places attracted industry and office employment. *Burgess Hill* began in 1828 when all the commons and wastes in the manor of Keymer were enclosed.[6] The cost of obtaining the Enclosure Act and the legal and other expenses involved were defrayed by the sale of about 200 acres of St John's and Valebridge commons to speculators. Villas sprang up on these former commons along the turnpike between Cuckfield and Brighton. Settlement became more rapid when the Brighton railway passed through its station, opened in 1841.

[5] C. L. Prince, *Crowborough Hill* (1898).

[6] P. F. Brandon, 'The Enclosure of the Keymer Commons', *Sussex Notes and Queries*, Vol. 15 (1960), pp. 181–6.

Haywards Heath was a similar suburban dormitory, or 'town of the London sort', in Hilaire Belloc's phrase, which originally grew up around a lonely railway station to serve Cuckfield in 1841. Residents still speak of the town affectionately as 'The Heath', although the common has been enclosed since 1862 and virtually obliterated by subsequent urban growth. From Lewes the Rev. Lower in his *Compendious History of Sussex* could write approvingly of Haywards Heath in 1870 as "the abode of civilisation, many villas and pleasure residences having sprung up almost by magic". At Lindfield, a neighbouring place with its own fairs and markets, the impression of the upstart Brighton suburb in 1898 was, not unnaturally, distinctly less warm: it was likened to "a congeries of stucco villas and builders' lots, nursery grounds and brick yards fenced with corrugated iron and barbed wire . . . round about a dreary wooden pile of buildings perched high on a red clay embankment . . ."[7]

Meanwhile, the Wealden countryside generally became steadily more metropolitan in character. One of the least welcome signs of London from the late nineteenth century was smoke-laden sky emanating from its "stupendous volcano with a million fumaroles" which brought the smells of the Brompton Road and the tang of soot and sulphur to Wealden villages.[8] Less overtly, the houses of the old-established gentry, yeomen and former ironmasters passed gradually into the hands of city financiers. John Halsham's *Idlehurst*, a valuable sketch of social and landscape change in mid-Sussex during late Victorian times, brings out the entirely different attitudes and ways of life of the old village families and the wealthy Cockney newcomers. He tells of a "Mrs. Latimer of Blackhatch", a thinly disguised real person, who "for inscrutable reasons" built a flamboyant

[7] J. Halsham, *Idlehurst: A Journal kept on the Country* (1898), p. 220.
[8] J. Halsham, *op. cit.*, pp. 15–18.

mansion surmounting a lonely hill "all red gables and chimneys . . . with sweeps of bare gravel drive and groves of eighteen inch laurustinus and arbor-vitae . . ." "Now of course," remarked this lady, "we had to make all the garden out of fields . . . we really beat you in the view . . . it only wants a few more really good houses on the best sites to be really perfect . . ."[9]

Mrs Latimer and the other villa-owners had a profound effect on the face of the Sussex Weald. Halsham says that the hill-top villa became "a sign to half the county". The most thoroughly refaced part of Sussex was the western High Weald, between Horsham and East Grinstead, a district with fine views and natural rock outcrops, relatively cheap land (mostly bare heath and scrub) and conveniently accessible to London by rail and road. Here the newcomers colonised great stretches of Sussex countryside, gothicising their county homes in the manner of medieval French chateaux and fourteenth-century English manor houses, or building a neo-Tudor or Georgian mansion. The possession of country houses or landed estates conferred on them both social status and political power. For two generations the villas were lively with laughter and song and the neighbourhoods prosperous, as the many trim little cottages and lodges, the well-constructed farm buildings and the carefully tended by-ways still tell us. By 1939 the villa-building era had ended and it became the anachronistic survival of what Osbert Sitwell has called "the sunset hour of one of the periodic calms in history". The roofless shell, windowless mullions and chapel-like doorways of Nymans, an elaborately built house in the style of a late medieval manor house, its walls corbelled and battlements still covered by wistaria, roses and magnolia, form one of the melancholy memorials of this influence that bore down upon the Sussex landscape before the Second World War (Plate 44).

[9] J. Halsham, *op cit.*, pp. 187–8.

Although many regretted the infiltration of the new gentry, Sussex takes justifiable pride in the splendid gardens created by her wealthy immigrant families. The newcomers acquired the taste for planting, long characteristic of the Sussex county gentleman, and the vista, pinetum, arboretum and 'wild garden' began to modify the surface of entire parishes, such as Upper Beeding, Ardingly, Horsted Keynes and West Hoathly, into one continuous garden. These gardens, now in their maturity, have an important place in the history of landscape design. They were inspired by the romantic naturalism movement, led by William Robinson, the celebrated lifelong Sussex gardener of Gravetye in West Hoathly, and Gertrude Jekyll of Munstead in Surrey. In them informal planting was practised, against a background of rock outcrop, parkland and wood, as a reaction against the severely formal 'bedding-out' customary in the early and mid-Victorian garden. Robinson's circle included Messel of Nymans, Loder of Leonardslee and Stephenson Clarke of Borde Hill, all enthusiastic owners of now famous gardens between Haywards Heath and Horsham. Other outstanding gardens in the same district are Gerald Loder's at Wakehurst Place (Plate 45) and Soames's at Sheffield Park. These earliest of modern gardens are particularly famous for such exotic conifers as the stately Wellingtonia Redwood, the lofty Hemlock and Douglas Fir, the Monkey Puzzle and Magnolia (both then still regarded as sensational) and a great number of hardy evergreens, especially rhododendron. Enjoying these gardens today one can still sense something of the excitement with which Sussex gardeners discussed and exchanged newly discovered seed from the temperate regions of the Caucasus, the Himalayas, western and central China, Japan and Tasmania. Long after the last villa has tumbled to ruin or been converted to flats the great plantings of such majestic conifers as the Calabrian Pine, Norwegian Spruce and Noble Fir, which crown every hill and make landmarks for miles around, will serve as a reminder of a vanished way of life and a major contribution to the art of landscape.

Changes between the wars

For all its faults, the Gothic Revival which so changed the face of Sussex, imparted a sense of grace and urbanity to the hereditary landscape and the lavishly ornamented buildings remaining to us are becoming better appreciated with the passage of time. By contrast, the activities of speculative building syndicates in Sussex between the two World Wars fell sadly short of previous standards and the universal adverse judgement of more than forty years seems irrevocable. Sporadic estate development on cheap land produced the endless scatter of houses forming neither town nor country, which Lord Holford has called "a kind of urban desert". Such indiscriminate estate development threatened the entire Sussex shoreline at a time when the general public seemed blind to the loss of one of the most beautiful coastal regions in western Europe and local authorities had ineffective powers of planning control. Bungalows were built by the hundred, the unhappiest form the town has yet taken in Sussex. The term 'bungalow town' was originally applied to the shack and shanty building on the quieter coastal stretches, an aspect of the unplanned growth permeating the whole area from Camber Sands to the Witterings before the First World War. Weekend residents from the 1890s erected any building that took their fancy, from disused railway carriages and tramcars to the more sophisticated structures resembling verandahed dwellings adopted by the English in India. Most of these unsightly buildings were demolished at the beginning of the Second World War when the beaches were protected against enemy invasion, but some of the larger and better constructed ones can still be identified, as at Shoreham, where the 'bungalow town' on the shingle bar in the 1930s supported a population almost as large as that of the old town itself.

The beginnings of the ribbon dispersal of bungalow building along cliffs and main highways can be traced to the years just before the First World War. By 1900 the menace of cheap corn, meat and wool from the plains of Dakota and the Australian Riviera had become a reality and downland farming became so unprofitable that some land-owners gave up the unrewarding struggle and sold parcels of downland to property companies. Warren Farm at Telscombe Cliffs, between Rottingdean and Newhaven, was sold by the Earl of Chichester to the Cavendish Estate Company who had raised a few buildings on the site before 1914. A similar venture had begun at Poverty Bottom in the Ouse Valley, but the compulsory land requisition for wartime agriculture deferred development for another decade. On the outskirts of Brighton, at Woodingdean, a rash of temporary dwellings and shacks had appeared before the First World War which multiplied afterwards. It is significant that much of the downland that had become semi-derelict farming land was rabbit warren before its reclamation for arable during the Napoleonic Wars.

The First World War and the subsequent shortage of building materials purchased a temporary reprieve for the Sussex coastline, but by the mid-1920s the spate of unregulated building inspired local and national concern. Until the early 1920s the downland sites remained remote from towns and railway stations; their development now increased owing to provision of bus services, widening general use of the motor car and the changing social conditions produced by the war. C. W. Neville, the promoter of Peacehaven, has left a vivid account of the flinty, rutted track which passed for the highway along the cliffs between Brighton and Newhaven as late as 1914.[10] By the

[10] C. W. Neville, *Peacehaven Post*, Vol. 1 (1921) and *Downland Review*, Vol. 1, Nos. 1–3 (1959).

mid-1920s such roads had been greatly improved and the war veterans who wished to build themselves little houses on the coast were remorselessly plied with propaganda by the property companies.

During the critical period between 1925 and 1936 the Sussex coast and the unspoiled scenery of the Downs were severely threatened. Speculators did infinite damage to large stretches of the shrinking countryside and the Downs were threatened by submergence under a sprawl of building. Fortunately, the despoliation was brought increasingly under control in the years before the Second World War. The credit for this does not primarily lie with the national government, for all its sympathy and concern. Not until the passing of the Town and Country Planning Act of 1947 did local authorities gain planning powers which would have prevented the earlier destruction. Before this, and the awakening of a public conscience to the desecration of open spaces, the initiative rested with public-spirited land-owners, enlightened public authorities, conservation societies and individuals with sufficient foresight and imagination to strive to maintain the beauty of rural Sussex.

Despite their concerted action Sussex was the victim of much clutter and sprawl, as the landscape readily bears witness. Yet the achievements of voluntary co-operation and restraint during those years were very great. Many land-owners willingly made agreements with local authorities not to release land for building and several town corporations purchased land in their vicinity to forestall its disorderly development. By 1936 local authorities, broadly speaking, had accepted the 200-foot contour line as the upper limit of permissible building on the Downs. All this was achieved by persuasion and discussion among the many interested parties and not by government direction. An incalculable debt is also owed to preservation societies such as the Council for the Preservation of Rural England and

Plate 44 Nymans, the home of the renowned Sussex gardener, Colonel Messel, was one of the last gothicised villas to be built in Sussex. Now gutted and left as a shell, its architectural detail included such medieval features as finials, achievement of arms, corbelled walls, crockets, gargoyles and a gazebo. The overall effect was the imitation of a house like Cowdray. See p. 260.

Plate 45 As a foreground to the surviving fragment of Wakehurst Place, built by Sir Edward Culpeper in 1590, are the mansion pond and terrace lawn laid out by Gerald Loder before the First World War. See p. 261.

Plate 46 Mr Neville's American-styled layout of Peacehaven in 1962. Even after forty years of building, the unfinished appearance of the township is evident, particularly on the landward edge. The little use made of the fine natural coastline and the absence of any landscaping also draw attention to the very unimaginative design. See p. 267.

Plate 47 The Low Weald of Sussex is rich in mellow brickwork brought to a high pitch of perfection in the eighteenth century, hiding old frames or 'brick-nogged' between them. Such cottages as these at Plaistow have been 'discovered' by business people who wish to set up house in a beautiful district. See p. 101.

Plate 48 The Wey and Arun Canal near Pallingham in the Low Weald. The cottages were built for canal-keepers. There is a possibility that the reed-filled canal will be reopened shortly for pleasure purposes. See p. 182.

Plate 49   The Downs near Brighton have fallen foul of ugly wirescapes and rows of monotonous terrace building and bungalows. See p. 271.

The *living landscape* (*1860–1974*)

the Society of Sussex Downsmen, which was founded by Arthur Beckett in 1926 at the height of the crisis. Arthur Beckett and his society made out a case for the orderly development of the coastline which won the support of all thinking people, and took the lead in the sustained fight to conserve the finest stretches of the Sussex coast. To such efforts the preservation of notably beautiful parts of Sussex is due, including the Seven Sisters cliffs, Beachy and Seaford Heads, the hills of Salvington, Highdown, Newtimber, Thundersbarrow, Cissbury Ring and Sullington Warren. All who cherish the Downs and the remaining unspoilt parts of the Sussex coast have cause to remember with gratitude and admiration those who successfully maintained the rural amenities of Sussex in the early days of town and regional planning and before the Great Depression put the speculative builders temporarily out of business.[11]

The inter-war bungalow building is readily identifiable in the landscape. Generally speaking, all the resorts sprawled outwards in the form of ribbon-building, and their fabric unfolds in sequence from the classical terraces at their core, through the villas of the Gothic Revival, to the bungalows built by the mile on their edge. Each extension marks, in the main, the colonisation of the coast by a different social class, using a different mode of travel. The worst examples of ribbon-building are along the A22 road out of Eastbourne and along the coast road between Worthing and New Shoreham. It was predicted in 1867 that Brighton and Worthing esplanades, then being actively and grandly extended, would join at Shoreham. Unhappily, this gap was filled in the inter-war years only by poor quality dwellings, and Lancing, in consequence, is a rather undistinguished bungalow town. Woodingdean, originally a 'shack town', was absorbed by Brighton in 1928 when it was replanned

[11] The Society of Sussex Downsmen, Hove, Annual Reports 1926–40, *The Times*, 15th March and 21st March 1926, 12th February 1936, and *passim*.

as a bungalow settlement with the aim of improving its appearance. One of the more successful creations is Saltdean, a promotion of C. W. Neville, who laid out green-tiled bungalows in tree-lined avenues following the contour. All these bungalow towns suffer from monotony of scale and building material and have extravagantly destroyed large areas of open space and agricultural land.

The most notorious inter-war housing development was Peacehaven, the earliest promotion of C. W. Neville. The obvious disparity between the founder's ideals and their execution into bricks and mortar and the contrast between the euphony of the town's name and the infamy of its fatally marred surroundings, made the howls of execration all the louder. The promise of Peacehaven as a model town went unfulfilled and by 1924 it was plain that it was only a travesty of a Garden City.

> Though the child of Garden Cities,
> When she grows her regal beauty
> Will proclaim her Queen of all . . .

sang the Peacehaven Estate Company in its innocent idealism.[12] There can hardly have been a stronger strain of wishful thinking in modern town building.

Although Letchworth and Hampstead Garden Suburb had set fine precedents for residential layout, Mr Neville's model was the grid-iron plan of the western American township, from which his town-making experience was drawn. No restrictions were placed on the type of dwelling erected nor on the interval between purchase of a house plot and the completion of the building. On the eve of the Depression the town still had a half-built appearance. It was over-stocked with shops straggling along more than a mile of the main coast road. None of the town's streets had been made up. Its promenade, merely an unkempt grass

[12] *Peacehaven Post*, Vol. 1 (1921).

sward above the cliff-top, was fast receding under wave attack towards adjacent buildings; and little in the way of mains drainage had been provided (Plate 46). Since the last war, however, the planning authority have made up the streets, provided normal town amenities and filled up the gaps between the bungalows in southern Peacehaven.

It was too late to stop the haphazard development along the main coast road, an admixture of shops, workshops, factories, bungalows, garages and builders' yards. The northern part, where muddy roads and paths run through widely dispersed bungalows, little wooden dwellings and unsightly sheds and caravans, still bears the look that Peacehaven acquired in the 1920s. A recently proposed plan for a new town centre may mean that after an interval of fifty years the reality of Peacehaven will more closely match the dream of its founders.

The post-war scene

In the post-war era agricultural innovation has been responsible for much change in the countryside. The South Downs have undergone the most radical change. Bulldozers, tractors and combine-harvesters are the new tools which make possible the cultivation of the thin, flinty Chalk soils. Artificial fertilisers have replaced traditional sheep-folding as a means of sustaining arable. Under the impetus of the need for more food during the last war and the shortage of foreign exchange since, the ploughing-up of the Downs has been encouraged by grants and other inducements. In consequence, the layer of short turf, woven into a soft springy fabric by the intertwined roots of as many as twenty species to a square foot, has been converted to arable. Now nearly the entire downland from the Hampshire border to Beachy Head is divided into huge farms worked on a rotation of cereals, beans and ley grasses. The

Southdown flocks, adapted to folding and turf-grazing, have been largely replaced by beef cattle. Prophecies that downland farmers were juggernauting their way to speedy self-destruction by working their own doom with falling yields have proved false. The new aspect of the Downs is here to stay for the foreseeable future. Vistas of vast 'prairie' expanses devoid of enclosures except barbed-wire fences, meet the eye. Agriculture has become an industry requiring industrial-type buildings of a scale and material new to the downland, though the change of land use is not unprecedented, similar patterns having been created by ploughing-up during the Napoleonic Wars. Repton then commented in his *Landscape Gardening* that it was only the capitalist who "can contemplate with delight his hundred acres in a single enclosure", an observation which holds true today.

In the process of converting downs to arable much woodland in the more wooded western Downs has been grubbed during the last twenty years. It is a matter of great regret that hundreds of acres of prehistoric field patterns have been obliterated in preparing the land for tillage; boundary ditches have been filled in and the sites of countless earthworks and other ancient relics of human action in the landscape levelled by bulldozers, as if a few extra acres of barley were the only aim in life. It is sad, too, that Vaughan Cornish's suggestion that "some enactment should ensure the preservation for all time of a selected area of this pastoral country"[13] was not taken up. Nevertheless, the Nature Conservancy has bought land under the National Parks and the Countryside Act of 1948 and has created nature reserves at Lullington Warren and Kingley Vale, for example, where good facilities are provided for the study of flora and fauna in habitats little altered by human action. Not all the changing character of the Downs is attributable to man. The sharp reduction in the rabbit population following the myxamatosis epidemic in the 1950s

[13] V. Cornish, *National Parks and the Heritage of Scenery* (1930), p. 55.

has affected vegetation. The remaining grass grows thicker and coarser, hawthorn and other scrub has advanced and ling, formerly grazed by rabbits, has extinguished much of the purple bell heather.

Although extensive reclamation of the Downs for tillage has reduced their recreational value they can still make a large contribution to the leisure needs of the dense population of south-east England where mobility is rapidly increasing. The Hobhouse Committee reported in 1947 that "there is no other area within easy reach of London which provides such opportunities for the enjoyment of lovely scenery and peaceful walks . . ." This Committee recommended that the South Downs should become one of the National Parks in Britain, but subsequent extensive reclamation of downland grazings made this impossible. The Downs, however, were designated as an Area of Outstanding Natural Beauty and it is hoped that this status will afford some measure of control over their development. A recent successful venture, secured with the co-operation of land-owners, has been the opening of the South Downs Way, a continuous bridlepath and footway mainly along the crest of the chalk escarpment.

Agricultural innovation in the Sussex Weald, following a trend observable throughout its history, has been later and less extensive than elsewhere in Sussex. Yet mechanised arable farming, profitable even on cold, stiff soils and hilly terrain, is altering the wooded pattern of the landscape which gives the Weald its special charm. Bulldozing of living hedges (just at the time when they are being replanted in West Germany), and the grubbing of shaws are giving the countryside a more open appearance. Oak and other beautiful standing trees are not being replaced. Coppice-with-standards, long neglected in the Weald, is now being cleared to make new fields.

The loss of shaws is particularly disturbing since, as previously mentioned, these are amongst the oldest regional characteristics of the Wealden landscape. Growing in them is a wealth of plant life providing food and shelter for a rich variety of wild creatures. Carpeted with sheets of bluebells or burned brown and gold in autumn, a walk amongst them is not quickly forgotten. It would be gratifying if only a portion of the present wooded scene could be preserved before it is too late. One recalls Cornish's statement that "whereas every feature of the wild landscape in England can be matched or excelled in other countries the unspoilt parts of agricultural Britain have a beauty which is unique in the history of civilisation".[14] The landscape of the Sussex Weald is a priceless national heritage which will be visually degraded and its record of historical development on the ground largely destroyed unless some inducement is offered to farmers for retaining something of its present character.

Unfortunately, shaws are no longer economic and William Morris's plea, made nearly a century ago, that no one should be allowed "to cut down for mere profit trees whose loss would spoil a landscape",[15] is still dismissed as a Utopian vision of an ideal England. The discouraging prospect is that shaws, hedgerow and coppice will largely disappear from all but the least drained parts of the Weald in the course of the next ten to twenty years. This constitutes one of the most serious threats than man has presented to the Sussex environment. The survival of these last remaining vestiges of the dwindling wilderness on any substantial scale will depend on whether the future management sufficiently balances the needs of farming and wildlife—two considerations not necessarily incompatible. This has been already recognised on some estates, such as Penhurst, near Battle, where many small parcels of woodland are being traditionally restored, ensuring that shaws will continue as part of the Wealden panorama for years to come.

[14] V. Cornish, *op. cit.*, p. 4.
[15] W. Morris, *On Art and Socialism*, ed. H. Jackson (1947), p. 111.

Whilst the Sussex countryside has undergone these changes, the enlargement of the urban area has gained rapid momentum. The coast again sustains the heaviest destructive pressure and is now one of the most crowded parts of Britain (Plate 49). The magnetic attraction of the district for those intending to retire or commute to London seems irresistible. The symbolic Yorkshire mill-owner who built up a fortune and dreamed of retiring to 'Hoove' is now succeeded by thousands of townspeople from the Midlands and the North who aspire to a home by the sea in their retirement. The drift of the elderly southwards to places like Eastbourne and Worthing has provoked the light-hearted jibe that Sussex has become 'Costa Geriatrica'. To find employment for younger people the resorts are encouraging light industry, and so, tucked away in remote corners, one finds at every seaside place its factory and trading estate. Tongues of urban development thrust out from pre-war nuclei have now created an almost continuous urban corridor along the coastal strip between Newhaven and Bognor. Small towns and villages, once with individual character, are now engulfed in monotonous uniform building in which the old man-made boundaries are meaningless. One of the consequences of the relentless tide of building has been the disappearance of nearly all the glasshouses near Worthing which between 1880 and 1939 made the brand 'Worthing Grown' famous for tomatoes, grapes and flowers. For a time at the turn of this century Worthing was the leading horticultural centre in Europe, and to its vineries and nurseries came men for training from the Lea Valley, the Channel Islands, and also Belgium and Holland, before these developed their own extensive and thriving industry. From Worthing itself glass spread eastwards towards Shoreham and westwards towards Angmering, but little now remains in this district due to the rapid loss of prime horticultural land to building.

One of the most visible signs of pressure on land is in

the changing townscapes of the resorts. Redevelopment of central areas by multi-purpose building has taken place in Brighton and is under way in Worthing. Tall blocks of flats are rising from the wreckage of the Gothic Revival all along the Sussex coast. In addition, the recreational impact has brought an enormous expansion of mooring facilities for small boats. The comprehensive Marina scheme of Brighton, involving shops, flats, restaurants, a casino, and yachting facilities, is one of the biggest of its kind. So much natural beauty of the Sussex coast has already been destroyed that this and similar developments demand careful planning in the future.

In the Weald the most extensive changes have occurred around Crawley and at Gatwick, which has served as London's second airport for more than a decade. Crawley itself was the post-war generation's answer to Peacehaven. As one of the earliest New Towns of Britain it is designed on the neighbourhood principle, a community of some 5000 people, provided with local shops, schools and other basic services. Each neighbourhood is laid out in tree-lined avenues with wide verges and is segregated from the chief shopping centre and industrial quarters intended to make the town self-contained. Steadily increasing air traffic at Gatwick is having a big impact on the surrounding area. Motorways 23 and 25, at present under construction, will converge near the airport and high-rise hotels lie on its perimeter (one of which closed within a year of completion, cumbering the landscape with the rubbish of an unsightly building). The *Strategic plan for the South East* accepted by the Government in 1971 and now the basis of regional planning, provides for industrial and residential development of a corridor across the Weald between Crawley and Hassocks. This proposal follows the suburbanisation of this tract in the wake of the London to Brighton railway and demonstrates how, again and again, the past landscape history of Sussex is influencing its modern development.

Another instance of this is the government's intention to permit further urban development in the Peacehaven and Newhaven area.

So much of the tone of the preceding paragraphs has been of a 'text for sorrow' that it is proper to draw attention to some recent developments inspiring hope. There are ever-increasing signs that both government and the public at large are at last alert to the deteriorating Sussex environment, and wish to manage it in ways which do not compromise its visual character. Embodied in the Countryside Act of 1968 is the statement: "In the exercise of their functions relating to land under any enactment every Minister, Government Department and Public Body shall have regard to the desirability of conserving the natural beauty and amenity of the countryside." These are not empty words, as several recent planning proposals and government decisions relating to Sussex have proved and, as a county which was early concerned over the control of rural development, this positive planning for posterity is heartening. It is also likely that the towns will not be permitted to develop in a manner detrimental to the human habitat. One sign of this is a recent conclusion of the Brighton Urban Structure Plan team that the present urban environment of Brighton, with its fine townscape, between Downs and sea, is one of the best in Britain and that growth on a large scale either by outward expansion into the Downs or by high-density urban renewal would be seriously detrimental.[16] Another is the intention expressed in the *Strategic Plan for the South East* to preserve the character of country towns and attractive villages. The long-term plan for Petworth, envisaging only modest growth and conservation of the tortuous streets in its core, is but one example of recent decisions reflecting concern for the historic beauty of Sussex. A different contribution to the rising threat to amenity is the recent attempt by K. D. Fines

[16] *Brighton Urban Structure Plan: Alternative Strategies* (1972).

to evaluate land objectively in terms of its scenic quality.[17]

In conclusion, a closer look at one locality visually demonstrating both the legacy of the past and contemporary planning problems will serve to heighten the difficulties faced by our present generation in preserving the face of Sussex for the future. The administrative division of Shoreham-by-Sea, containing the three ancient churches and the delightful waterside of the old harbour mentioned previously, has also unspoilt salt marshes above which rise the splendid buildings of Lancing College, a fine example of Victorian Gothic. Shoreham had ospreys nesting in its rural bounds as recently as 1936 but by then S. P. B. Mais, and other writers, were witnessing the 'development' of this lovely landscape. Much of the beauty has now been obliterated by a sprawl of houses over downland, market garden, orchard and even shingle beach. Long, elm-shaded rural lanes are unrecognisable as roaring town streets; electricity power-lines stride relentlessly over the downland skylines; and a hideously ugly iron bridge over the Adur, an epitome of surrounding shabbiness, is choked by dense road traffic. Yet the historic town centre and its riverside setting are still worth preserving, but these are under a new threat, greater than ever before. The ten traffic lanes already converging on the river Adur at Shoreham will soon have to be increased to fourteen and the requisite road bridge and approach roads will need imaginative planning if the old town is not to be torn to pieces as a sacrifice to the motor car. Meanwhile, it is a landscape in distress, its fate still in the balance. During this intense struggle for space William Morris's reminder that "surely there is no square mile of the earth's habitable surface that is not beautiful in its own way if we men only abstain from wilfully destroying that beauty",[18] is more relevant than ever.

[17] K. D. Fines, 'Landscape Evaluation: A Research Project in East Sussex', *Regional Studies*, Vol. 2 (1968), pp. 41–51.

[18] 'Art and the Beauty of the Earth' in William Morris, *On Art and Socialism*, ed. H. Jackson (1947), p. 169.

SELECT BIBLIOGRAPHY

Brookfield, H. C. 'A Regional Study of Urban Development in Coastal Sussex since the Eighteenth Century', unpublished Ph.D. thesis, University of London (1950).

Lowerson, J. *Victorian Sussex* (B.B.C. publication, 1972).

Musgrave, C. *Life in Brighton* (1970).

Pickering, W. F. 'The West Brighton Estate, Hove', unpublished M.A. thesis, University of Sussex (1969).

Porter, W. *The History of Hove* (1897).

Strategic Plan for the South East. H.M.S.O. (1970).

Index

SSEX